Eighteenth Century
German Prose

The German Library: Volume 10
Volkmar Sander, General Editor

EIGHTEENTH CENTURY GERMAN PROSE

Edited by Ellis Shookman
Foreword by Dennis F. Mahoney

CONTINUUM • NEW YORK

PT
1308
. S S
1992

157282
Oct. 1992

1992
The Continuum Publishing Company
370 Lexington Avenue, New York, NY 10017

The German Library
is published in cooperation with Deutsches Haus,
New York University.
This volume has been supported by a grant from the
Marie Baier Foundation.

Printed in the United States of America

Library of Congress Cataloging-in-Publication Data

Eighteenth century German prose / edited by Ellis Shookman ;
foreword by Dennis F. Mahoney.
    p.   cm. — (The German library ; v. 10)
Includes bibliographical references.
ISBN 0-8264-0708-0 — ISBN 0-8264-0709-9 (pbk.)
    1. German prose literature—18th century—Translations into
English.   2. English prose literature—Translations from German.
I. Shookman, Ellis.   II. Title: 18th century German prose.
III. Series.
PT1308.S5   1992
838'.60808—dc20   91-20997
                                                          CIP

Acknowledgments will be found on page 269,
which constitutes an extension of the copyright page.

Contents

Foreword

With the exception of Goethe's *Werther* and possibly his *Wilhelm Meister's Apprenticeship,* German prose of the eighteenth century has not attracted much attention among Anglo-American readers. In part this may have to do with the lack of available translations—which the current volume of The German Library will remedy—but such a lack is more a symptom than a cause. More significant are the effects of the bifurcation between "high art" and "trivial prose" that occurred in German literature and aesthetics thanks to Goethe, Schiller, and the Romantics. These authors, who as a rule were not the most popular prose writers of their day, succeeded in having their own works judged as a canon of perfection by subsequent generations. As a result, German readers and scholars showed scant interest in the antecedents to the Classic/Romantic period of German literature, while Anglophone readers—unaccustomed to the rarefied air of *Wilhelm Meister* and its successors—by and large concentrated whatever attention they paid to German novels on twentieth-century authors such as Hermann Hesse and Thomas Mann.

During the late nineteenth and early twentieth centuries, moreover, German scholars developed the theory that writers in the Age of Goethe had created a uniquely German type of novel, the Bildungsroman (novel of education or development), which combined philosophical depth with the formation and harmonious integration of an individual within society. Although there were scattered attempts to find German Bildungsromane as far back as Wolfram von Eschenbach's medieval epic *Parzival,* the critical consensus arose that such novels did not appear before the first version of

Wieland's *Agathon* (1766–67), and even this work was understood primarily as a prelude to Goethe's *Wilhelm Meister's Apprenticeship* (1795–96), with *Werther* (1774) being regarded as a unique and solitary achievement by the young Goethe.

There has been much controversy in recent years, however, about the suitability of the traditional definition of the Bildungsroman for understanding even the novels of Goethe and the Romantics themselves. For the present context, suffice it to say that research of the past twenty years has demonstrated that during the eighteenth century the great bulk of belletristic prose in Germany did not differ all that greatly from developments in England and France. Indeed, readers of the selections included in this volume are likely to find them far more familiar and approachable than expected. In order to better recognize the reasons for these "family resemblances," it may help to consider the development of German eighteenth-century prose writing within the context of literary, intellectual, and social trends throughout Western Europe.

By the end of the Thirty Years' War in 1648, the German Empire had disintegrated into a loose confederation of over three hundred sovereign states. While the English middle class and the landed gentry succeeded in checking the absolutist tendencies of the king in the course of the seventeenth century, with the French bourgeoisie achieving its political and social emancipation by 1789, in German countries the middle class remained largely dependent on the nobility. Enlightened Absolutism in states such as Prussia and Austria did encourage the development of a bureaucracy and attendent opportunities for educated civil servants; but the direction of state policies remained the privileged sphere of the high nobility. On the other hand the separation of politics from religious and moral principles—a consequence of the religious civil wars of the seventeenth century—led to the creation of a private sphere of morality as the special realm of the middle class. The moral nature of the burgher, in contrast to the "lascivious" way of life of the nobles, became the most characteristic ideological slogan of the eighteenth century throughout the whole of Western Europe.

This new sense of self-worth found expression in the cult of friendship and the practice of letter writing, which spread from England and France to German lands in the course of the eighteenth century and which accounts for the enormous popular success of

Samuel Richardson's epistolary novels. His *Pamela; or, Virtue Rewarded* (1740–41) not only thematizes the virtue of the maidservant who ultimately reforms (and marries) her noble master; it also locates conflict and reconciliation between classes within the family—precisely the sphere in which the new genre was read and discussed. But whereas Sophie La Roche could still give an optimistic conclusion to her *The History of Miss von Sternheim* (1771) by depicting a marriage of its German heroine with an English lord, that part of the novel set in Germany offers far less hopeful prospects. And once writers from the lower social classes such as Karl Philipp Moritz and Ulrich Bräker were emboldened to depict the poverty and helplessness of their origins, an even bleaker picture of social conditions in Germany emerges. No wonder that readers turned to travel literature as a means of escape to more exotic habitats—it was Georg Forster's account of his travels with Captain Cook to the South Seas that made his reputation in German-speaking countries. But when Forster tried to establish the principles of Enlightenment freedom in the short-lived Republic of Mainz (1792–93), his efforts met with abject failure, and he died an exile in revolutionary Paris. His colleague at the court of the archbishop of Mainz, the writer Wilhelm Heinse, found it more prudent to restrict his republican sentiments to his diary and avoid any attempt to found the utopian state depicted in the closing pages of his novel *Ardinghello* (1787).

But while the German territories lagged behind England and France in political and economic terms, by the end of the eighteenth century the publishing industry there was flourishing. In 1740, when German book production first surpassed the levels existing at the outbreak of the Thirty Years' War over a century earlier, theological writings still dominated the market. By 1800, though, the three hundred–odd novels being produced yearly almost equaled the sum total of theological works for clerical, scholarly, and popular use. Parallel to this development, there occurred a change from intensive to extensive reading habits. Whereas traditionally the literate lay populace had repeatedly read and meditated upon the Bible and a few select devotional tracts, by 1770 readers were in the habit of regularly purchasing the latest publications. During the last third of the century, preachers and more conservative Enlightenment figures increasingly decried the "mania for reading" among the general

populace. Such jeremiads notwithstanding, the trend towards bel-
letrism in the book trade proved irreversible, as large numbers of
readers consumed with a passion the most current novels, biogra-
phies, and travel accounts. Karl Philipp Moritz's autobiographical
novel *Anton Reiser* (1785–90) provides a particularly graphic de-
piction of reading imaginative literature as a means of fleeing dreary
and demeaning living conditions.

At the same time, *Anton Reiser* also illustrates the influence of
religious traditions in shaping not only the psyche of its protagonist,
but also the introspective self-analysis already evident in novels of a
Richardsonian vein. Earlier in the eighteenth century German
Pietism had encouraged the development of diaries and religious
autobiographies for the purpose of recording one's progress towards
individual, intimate contact with God. As the search for salvation
became a less pressing concern in the more secularized atmosphere
of the late-eighteenth century, self-analysis—once the means towards
a goal—now became an end in itself. The links with Pietism are
most evident in the writings of Bräker, Moritz, and La Roche; but
Heinse's use of his Italian diaries as the source for scenes from
Ardinghello, as well as the decidedly pantheistic and anti-Christian
spirit of this novel, also suggest the existence of a tradition that
Heinse was attempting to overthrow.

As long as novels like *Ardinghello* were seen only as a step in the
development towards the Bildungsroman of German Classicism and
Romanticism, aspects that did not fit into this development received
scant attention or were criticized as artistic shortcomings. But if one
keeps in mind the residual influence of the novels of the German
Baroque period, with their penchant for learned discourse, then the
works of Heinse and Wieland become more comprehensible. Finally, in the case of Wieland (and later of Jean Paul Richter) the
impact of the comic novel—as produced by authors such as Fielding
and Sterne—should not be overlooked. While Wieland in his *The
History of the Abderites* (1774–81) recounts the foolish behavior of
provincial townspeople in ancient Greece, he expects his readers to
use their "wit," in the eighteenth-century sense of the term, and
reflect upon similar instances of philistinism and religious intolerance in the Germany of their own day. But Democritus, the hero of
this novel, was known in antiquity as "the laughing philosopher,"
and Wieland too is more inclined to react to the backwardness of

eighteenth-century Germany with good-natured humor than with biting scorn or satire. And perhaps contemporary readers will have occasion to discover amusing elements of Abdera in their own hometowns as well.

As the established canon of German literature is reviewed and reevaluated, long-neglected works are beginning to receive the attention they deserve. May this volume of eighteenth-century prose inspire the reader to continue the search for other authors, both male and female, who still await rediscovery.

DENNIS F. MAHONEY

Introduction

The title of this volume—*Eighteenth Century German Prose*—suggests at least two useful ways of framing its contents. First, we need general information about German literary life in the eighteenth century. Second, we need to know what particular kinds of prose were written there and then. Both these needs will be met by this introduction, which also surveys the lives and works of all authors included here, summarizes their writings that I have excerpted, and then gives specific comments on the excerpts themselves. Those texts then appear in order of publication, each followed by a glossary explaining names of fictional characters as well as historical figures, allusions to modern and classical literature and mythology, references to the Bible, geographical locations, words in foreign languages, technical terms, and anything else not clear from its immediate context. Readers who want to know more about the period, its prose, authors, and texts should consult the bibliography, which lists secondary sources in English, complete translations, and handy editions in German. Such readers should also note other, related volumes in The German Library, above all those on Lessing, Goethe, Schiller, Hölderlin, *Sturm und Drang, Eighteenth Century German Criticism,* and *German Poetry from 1750 to 1900* (volumes 12; 18, 19, 20; 15, 16, 17; 22; 14; 11; and 39 respectively).

I wish to thank my colleagues Bruce Duncan and David Sices, both of Dartmouth College, for reading my translations.

1

The eighteenth century was a time of formal and thematic expansion never before seen in German literature. In its early years, German-speaking countries, still reeling from the Thirty Years' War (1618–48), once again began to offer social, economic, political, and cultural life fairly comparable to that of their European neighbors. They still lagged behind the more refined and progressive French and English, however, and much literature written in them merely imitated models supplied by writers from those countries. French fashions were all the rage in the first half of the century, and aesthetic arbiters like Johann Christoph Gottsched (1700–66) accordingly invoked enlightened dictates of reason to teach rules for imitating nature in art and thus for acquiring classicistic good taste. Later, critical emphasis shifted to England and what were regarded as its less stilted, more expressive literary forms, such as plays by Shakespeare and prose by writers like Daniel Defoe, Samuel Richardson, Henry Fielding, and Laurence Sterne. To be sure, this shift was not a neat exchange of paradigms—France for England, ancient for modern, or reason for emotion. The cross-cultural forces underlying it were more complex, as the six selections included in this volume clearly prove. The theoretical debates waged and practical efforts made then nonetheless mark the beginning of modern German literature. For the first time, modern ideas of individuals, society, and their reciprocal links surfaced in German literature. New issues of social life, sexual gender, republican politics, psychology, nature, religion, self-fulfillment, and economic conditions—to name but a few examples—were raised in fictional settings more artful than ever before. Indeed, the twenty years in which the texts included here appeared, between 1770 and 1790, are remarkable in German literary history for at once summing up past traditions and pointing to future experiments. In fact, these seminal decades leading up to the French Revolution witnessed a revolution in German literature as well.

This second revolution took place in literary media, above all in prose fiction. Long considered aesthetically inferior to poetry, prose became more respected in the eighteenth century for a number of philosophical, religious, and social reasons. Such change is especially clear in the case of novels. Critics had dismissed earlier "romances" as improbable, irresponsible, and even immoral flights of fancy. Many later novels were therefore renamed "histories" to suggest that they were reasonable, accurate, and true. Such histories were sanctioned as vessels of virtue and truth, assuming moral and didactic qualities that helped establish the novel as a serious genre. As such, their reception reflected an important turn away from religious belief and toward secular ethics. With its self-scrutiny and soul-searching contrition, for example, the religious sect called Pietism encouraged its faithful to write autobiographies that inspired similar introspection in nonreligious texts. Other kinds of prose described real or imaginary cities, countries, and continents, showing cultures satirically or reverentially and thus shedding light on national limitations. Distinctions between physical and psychological landscapes, though, seem difficult to draw in texts that so closely relate inward to outward travels. Novels enjoyed new prestige for social reasons, too. Traditional poetics relegated classes other than the nobility to comic roles, but the new novels showed virtuous bourgeois characters who could not be dismissed as breaches of aesthetic decorum. The middle classes themselves were also an ever-growing audience and market for prose fiction. They did not always know what to make of it, though, and the status of fiction therefore remained dubious, a fact clear from both the extreme caution often urged when reading it and the more refined aesthetic games that authors of fictional "histories" sometimes played with their made-up "sources." Thanks to such stimulating overlap of philosophical, religious, social, and aesthetic contexts, eighteenth-century German prose seldom became prosaic.

2

Sophie von La Roche was the most famous female writer in late-eighteenth-century Germany. She was born on December 6, 1731, and grew up in Augsburg. After two brief engagements—one to her cousin Wieland—she married a nobleman who held diplomatic and administrative posts in Mainz and Trier. At first taking cues from her father and two fiancés, she educated herself (very few women went to schools or universities then), and her home became a literary salon for writers of various stripes throughout the 1770s. Her religious upbringing had been strictly pietistic, though, and she possessed all the domestic qualities thought proper for women of her rank. These several and often-contradictory influences are apparent in her writing, beginning with *The History of Miss von Sternheim* (1771). This first novel tells a woman's story from a new and distinctly female point of view, and it won La Roche recognition and fame throughout Europe, where it was translated into several languages. It was followed by other, less successful "women's novels"—a condescending term both then and now. She also edited the first moral-literary journal by and for women, *Pomona: For Germany's Daughters* (1783–84). After traveling through France, Holland, and England and writing her autobiography, she died on February 18, 1807. By then her grandchildren Clemens and Bettina Brentano had become part of a new literary generation, the younger Romantics.

The History of Miss von Sternheim is a story of virtue rewarded at the end of a very long and difficult trial. Like Samuel Richardson's similar *Pamela* (1740) and *Clarissa* (1748), it is an epistolary novel, consisting largely of letters that its several characters write to each other. This narrative technique presents events from multiple and often-conflicting points of view. From Miss Sophia Sternheim's former chambermaid and companion, the fictional editor of those letters, the reader learns that her father was an extremely virtuous man who married into an old aristocratic family not long after being ennobled himself. After her parents' sudden deaths, she is sent to an aunt who still resents her mother's marrying beneath her station and therefore scoffs at Sophia and the strict bourgeois notions of virtue that she brings to an aristocratic court. Indeed, to advance her own husband's career, the aunt tries to make Sophia the local prince's mistress, a plot that fails as soon as Sophia discovers it but that drives her into the arms of an evil Englishman, Lord Derby. Sophia also falls prey to her own anglophilia, a result of having English ancestry. Derby deserts her soon after the sham marriage ceremony that he stages to unite them, and she eventually recovers by doing good deeds for the poor (especially women) under the assumed and telling name "Madame Suffering." Her renown for such generous philanthropy enables her to move to England with Lady Summers, who turns out to be related to the woman Derby has since married for real. Lest she expose his seamy past, he has Sophia kidnapped and confined in the Scottish Highlands. She is roughly treated and given up for dead there, but Lords Rich and Seymour, brothers both in love with her, rescue her in the end. She then marries Seymour, whom she has loved all along, and becomes a model wife and mother. Although she earns men's respect and can live without them (one notable passage shows the pros and cons of marriage as seen by an older and wiser widow), Sophia and her author thus stop short of more radical solutions to her wrenching choice.

The excerpt that I have chosen is the journal that Sophia, as Madame Suffering, keeps for herself and her best friend Emilia during her confinement in the Scottish Highlands. Psychologically, this episode is the lowest point of her story, and the desolate landscape parallels her bleak state of mind. Both the setting and the tone are rather melodramatic, but they convey the essence of her remarkable life very effectively. Cut off from her correspondents, she can neither send nor receive the kinds of letters quoted elsewhere in the novel. Her resulting self analysis is all the more revealing, though, for such lack of contact with the outside world. We see wounded pride, despair, and dissatisfaction with her apparent fate at the hands of the villainous Derby. We also see calm resolve, firm belief in God, and trust in the education that she received as a young woman. Indeed, she takes solace in putting virtue into practice so that others may share the advantages she earlier enjoyed. Such faith in active virtue and practical pedagogy is strong, though not without tensions and contradictions. Sophia embraces high-blown moralism, for example, yet pays close attention to minute details of daily life. Her emotions sometimes seem overwrought precisely for being subject to her rigorous standards of virtue, her repeated denigration of her ego often sounds self-centered, and she even takes a certain pride in her lack of vanity. These facts do not detract from the urgency of her plight but rather lend depth to a character that La Roche herself once described as a "little girl on paper." It is similarly ironic that Miss Sophia Sternheim becomes disillusioned with England, the country that supplied her own author's models and themes, but then no calls for women's emancipation are raised in her story either. Instead, the emphasis is on social work and self-cultivation, all in hopes of teaching women how to get along within what now would be called patriarchal society. That *The History of Miss von Sternheim* itself was edited and published by Wieland demonstrates such limits to women's roles in the eighteenth century.

3

Georg Forster led a brief but tremendously adventursome life. Born near what is now the Polish city of Gdansk on November 27, 1754, he grew up without much formal education. Nevertheless, he distinguished himself as an artist, a scholar, and a man of the world, which he got to know firsthand from his substantial travels. His father, a pastor by trade and a naturalist by passion, took him to Russia and then to England, where they both joined Captain James Cook's second voyage to the South Seas from 1772 to 1775. The young Forster went along as assistant to his father, Cook's official naturalist, and the two collaborated on *A Voyage round the World* (1777), a travelogue that Georg wrote in English (and then helped translate into German). He subsequently earned his living as a translator, reviewer, teacher, professor, and librarian. His other writings include a second travelogue—*Views on the Lower Rhine* (1791–94)—and essays on numerous anthropological and political subjects. Politics, in fact, determined the further course of his life. A staunch supporter of the French Revolution, he tried to help start a new German republic in Mainz, and he even went to Paris to ask that the French national assembly annex all occupied German territories west of the Rhine. He was therefore declared an enemy of the Holy Roman Empire, and he died at the age of forty, exiled in Paris, on January 12, 1794. Although he did not write fiction, his work shows that he read it, and he enjoyed considerable literary fame. Coleridge drew on his *Voyage* in the "Rime of the Ancient Mariner," and the Romantic critic Friedrich Schlegel praised his prose as "classic."

His *Voyage round the World* substantiates such claims by going far beyond the usual limits of eighteenth-century travel writing. Composing it, though, was no easy matter. His father had apparently been commissioned to write the official account of Cook's trip, but the man's gruff manners and obstinate temper had so alienated the British Admiralty by the time they got back to England that it broke their agreement, deprived him of the illustrations that he needed to turn a profit, and finally forbade him to publish anything at all. Georg was neither tainted nor bound by these events, however, and rushed to finish his story before Cook's own version came out in print. The result is a running commentary on the expedition, from its starting point in Plymouth to its stops in the South Seas (New Zealand, Tahiti, Samoa and the Easter Islands, New Caledonia, and many others), its approaches to the Antarctic, and its trip back to England. Far from just listing such exotic ports of call, Forster reflected on the cultures that he encountered there, including the European one that had sent him. He did not want to bore readers with nautical details, and his observations take a philosophical turn seldom seen by armchair travelers.

That turn is most evident in the chapter reprinted here, Forster's description of Cook's second visit to Tahiti ("O-Taheitee"). It tells of beautiful landscape, "romantick scenery," and the natural abundance of foreign plant and animal life. More importantly, it tries to explain the friendly natives' appearance, customs, and character. We learn about their language, diet, dwellings, and rivalries, as well as about their religious beliefs, government, and economy. This news is sometimes strange indeed. Long fingernails are a sign of leisure, men and women shun each other at meals, and more than one lonely sailor takes sexual liberties with the willing young women. Although hospitable rather than hostile, the Tahitians steal from the crew without compunction, yet they are also happy to trade fruit for glass beads, nails, and other trinkets. Such odd behavior sometimes leads to confrontation, and Cook can easily frighten them by firing his sailors' muskets or his ship's cannon. Forster himself fears that Europeans' artificial needs and desires (such as the appetite for meat) will corrupt the unspoiled Tahitians, whom he suspects are relieved to find most Britons no more savage than themselves. Such dim views of colonialism are by no means simplistic. Forster knows that commerce civilizes no less than it overrefines, and he hardly idealizes his hosts' primitive virtues. Nonetheless, he clearly shares some of Jean Jacques Rousseau's sympathy for the noble savage, judging Tahiti "one of the happiest spots on earth." Other writers followed Forster's lead in admiring the island. The lyricist Christian Adolf Overbeck (1755–1821) even drew up plans for a group of fellow German poets to emigrate there and live in an ideal republic of letters. Such was the suggestive force of Forster's Tahiti!

4

Christoph Martin Wieland was a man of many talents, which he displayed in a wide range of forms, styles, and media. A poet, essayist, novelist, translator, and publisher, too, he was a witty idealist, humane skeptic, and an ironic cosmopolite. He was born on September 5, 1733, and grew up in the imperial city of Biberach. The eclectic quality of his later writing is foreshadowed by his reading classical literature, learning about the Enlightenment, and devouring *Don Quixote*—all while enrolled in a pietistic school. He spent the 1750s going through a more or less "seraphic" phase of forced religious sentimentality in Switzerland, and after two engagements (one to Sophie La Roche) and a love affair that caused a local scandal, he married and settled down as a senator and town clerk back home in Biberach. There, in the 1760s, he acquired a taste for rationalistic, rococo, and erotic French literature from a count who owned a neighboring castle. In 1766–67, he published what is often hailed as the first *Bildungsroman,* a novel named *Agathon,* which shows a young man finding himself and coming of age in numerous tests of virtue and wisdom with the outside world. He also wrote *Musarion* (1768), a poem in which grace, charm, and moderate sensualism put other philosophies to shame, cynical stoicism and dry idealism in particular. After a brief tenure as professor of philosophy in Erfurt, Wieland was appointed tutor to the young duke Karl August of Weimar, where he remained for the rest of his life. Among his other writings, *Alceste* (1773) is a Singspiel important in the early history of German opera, *Der teutsche Merkur* (1773–1810) was a leading literary journal, *Oberon* (1780) is a verse romance translated by an American president (John Quincy Adams), and *The History of the Abderites* (1781) is social satire that combines clever instruction with civilized delight. Wieland was also a translator, rendering Lucian, Horace, and Shakespeare into remarkably supple German. Indeed, no writer before him made German prose so smooth and lucid.

The History of the Abderites appeared between 1774 and 1780 in *Der teutsche Merkur.* It is set in Abdera, a Thracian city known even among ancient Greeks for its inhabitants' stupidity. Wieland tells his story in five loosely connected episodes, each showing cretinism triumphant. In the first, the philosopher Democritus comes home to Abdera after an absence of many years to find its citizens so obtuse and narrow-minded that they make coarse fun of his reason, knowledge, and tolerance. In the second, they ask Hippocrates to declare him incompetent, but the eminent doctor is quick to see that the Abderites themselves—not Democritus—are sick in the head. In the third, the poet Euripides exposes the Abderites' poor taste in theater by staging a performance of his own *Andromeda,* a play that local actors have just botched with him sitting in the audience. This literary satire is followed by a legal one in the next episode, *The Case of the Ass's Shadow.* In the last, the Abderites are overrun and driven out of town by frogs that they worship as part of their ridiculous religion. The legendary ship of fools thus seems to have landed in Abdera, and Wieland makes us laugh at philistinism and folly. Indeed, he explains that Abderites are everywhere and that their shortcomings still persist. His own contemporaries were overly enamored of ancient Greek culture, for example, an intellectual fashion in vogue since the art historian Johann Joachim Winckelmann (1717–68) had written that ancient artworks showed the Greeks' "noble simplicity and quiet grandeur." The Swiss theologian Johann Caspar Lavater (1741–1801) took such judgments to extremes, arguing that the Greeks must have been far better and more beautiful people than modern Europeans. Wieland deflates such overblown hypotheses with his Abderites, who are neither noble nor quiet and at best grandiose simpletons.

The Case of the Ass's Shadow is a justly famous spoof on litigious society. In ancient Greek, arguing about an ass's shadow means making a mountain out of a molehill. Wieland's fictional plaintiff and defendant do just that, taking the phrase literally when they fight about who owns the shadow cast by a real, live ass that one rents from the other on a hot summer day. The plot thickens as greedy, long-winded lawyers twist facts and bend the law to win their clients' cases and as slow-witted, corrupt judges stall the wheels of justice. Wieland takes satirical aim at religious rabble-rousers and illiterate demagogues, too, laughing at factionalism, petty intrigue, and the general idiocy of small-town life. His skillful treatment of these themes has moved creative figures as diverse as the composer Richard Strauss and the Swiss playwright Friedrich Dürrenmatt to adapt *The Case of the Ass's Shadow*. Wieland does not simply deride the Abderites, however, and his last word on them is good humor rather than sarcasm. Although he would teach his readers to think and act more reasonably, he remains skeptical about the effect of such education and knows that imagination is not only the source of the Abderites' silly errors but also—within more refined limits—a faculty needed to appreciate his own fiction. This aesthetic twist complicates his suggestion that ignorance is bliss indeed and blessed are the dumb.

5

Karl Philipp Moritz's social and psychological insights are unique in eighteenth-century German novels, yet they closely correspond to his own life and times. He was born on September 15, 1756, in Hameln (fabled home of the Pied Piper) and grew up oppressed by religious strife, domestic quarrels, and economic hardship. After false starts as apprentice to a hatmaker, as a student, and an actor, he held several increasingly important teaching posts in and near Berlin for the rest of his life. He spent time in England as well as Italy and described both in trenchant travelogues. He also wrote two novels, *Anton Reiser* (1785–90), a psychological self-analysis, and *Andreas Hartknopf* (1786–90), its similar but more allegorical counterpart. Each is socially critical, but Moritz also published important treatises on aesthetics and ancient mythology in which he shared and honed Goethe's serene classicism. Meanwhile, he edited his own *Magazin zur Erfahrungsseelenkunde* (1783–93), a pioneering work on empirical psychology. Its full title includes the ancient Greek proverb "gnothi sauton" (know thyself) and thus sums up his angle on the Enlightenment, described by its foremost philosopher Immanuel Kant with the related watchword "sapere aude" (dare to think for yourself). Moritz dared to think hard both for and about himself in his broader social and aesthetic context. He died on June 26, 1793.

Anton Reiser tells the sad but fascinating story of Moritz's own childhood, early youth, and adolescence. Its title character's school days, apprenticeship, reliance on stranger's financial aid, sporadic studies, and vain notions of a career in the theater are all largely autobiographical. How Moritz handles such painful subjects is clear from its subtitle, *A Psychological Novel*. Steeped in pietistic concepts of personal worthlessness and sin, Anton develops an inferiority complex that Moritz describes in many terms of the word *self*. Anton's self-denial makes him self-conscious, causes self-doubt and self-hate, leads to a loss of self-confidence, and results in neurotic self-delusion. He compensates for rough treatment and benign neglect alike by drawing attention to himself, torn between the need for recognition by others and the equally strong urge to hide behind his own four walls. His name sheds metaphorical light on such an emotional loner longing to get out and see the world: "Anton" alludes to Saint Anthony, a hermit, and "Reiser" come from the German verb meaning "to travel." Anton's psychological ups and downs soon make him an anxious hypochondriac. Far from merely describing Anton's symptoms, however, Moritz cites religious, social, and economic causes for such melancholy and depression. His narrative voice is sober, rational, and detached, reporting from an analytic, critical, and even ironic distance. Just how Moritz himself finally got there remains a mystery, but his microscopic focus on sights, sounds, smells, words, and the random mental associations that such various stimuli have for Anton is meant to be educational. Although he exposes Pietism, moreover, both the form and the content of Moritz's story distinctly recall it. Indeed, *Anton Reiser* is much like the diaries that many pietists kept to map their route to divine grace. As such, it is a prime example of the eighteenth-century shift from religious to secular reading and writing. It does not depict its author's salvation in the end, however, when Anton shows no promise of becoming a well-adjusted adult. His story has therefore rightly been called an "anti-Bildungsroman."

The excerpt translated here is the first of four books into which *Anton Reiser* is divided. In it, we see the sources of his trouble from the start. His spiritual life is suffocating, claustrophobic, and over-religious, yet he takes solace in numerous long sermons, even if for rhetorical rather than religious reasons and because his notes on them get him better grades than his classmates. His childhood diseases are serious, but they pale beside his mental distress. Moritz shows fears and fantasies, vanity and a sense of shame, and the extremes of self-esteem, self-pity, and self-reproach that Anton feels while lurching between hope and despair at home as well as in school. The destructive games that he plays to vent his aggressions are only one sign of such jumbled emotions. This study in child psychology is also one of child labor. Anton's apprenticeship presents working conditions of social classes lower than those shown in most other eighteenth-century fiction. Like him, Moritz's readers see the narrow horizons of an artisan's workaday world, where social inequities seem mere accidents of birth. Anton briefly escapes these pitiless surroundings by reading fiction and going to the theater, not knowing that they serve him merely as surrogates for real life. He wants to enjoy such pleasures of the imagination, but Moritz sternly rails against its pains. Indeed, the novel lashes out at the suffering caused by overindulging imagination and all less-than-genuine penchants for poetry. Like many a work of fiction that brings its hero down to earth, *Anton Reiser* thus seems a message at odds with its medium. But like the pietistic cast of Moritz's own narration, this suspicion of fiction also makes his case study more urgent.

6

Wilhelm Heinse was a rebel with a cause—the Renaissance. In the same mood for Italy that has inspired so many German authors, he gave verbal accounts of its visual art that make him seem the picture of a Renaissance man himself. He was born near Weimar on February 15, 1746, and studied law and philosophy at Jena and Erfurt, where Wieland was his teacher. He worked as a nobleman's secretary and a private tutor while launching his literary career with translations of French poetry and Petronius's *Satyricon* (noted to be a source for Fellini's film of the same name). He also wrote incisive essays on art that he saw in Düsseldorf, praising Raphael and Rubens in particular. He then spent three years in Italy, from 1780 to 1783, and published translations of works by two of its foremost poets, Tasso and Ariosto. After returning to Germany, he served as reader and electoral librarian to the archbishop of Mainz. His second novel, *Ardinghello* (1787), is set in Italy and contains both high adventure and learned discussions of art and philosophy. Two other novels similarly treat theoretical issues of music and chess. In all these texts as well as in essays on history and politics, Heinse displays the enthusiasm and dynamic temperament praised in the late-eighteenth century as signs of "Storm and Stress." His style of writing forcefully conveys such effusive virtues. He died on June 22, 1803.

Ardinghello opens with its title character (a Florentine painter whose real name is Prospero Frescobaldi) pulling its nearly drowned narrator out of a Venetian canal. Forever bound to him in friendship by this act of heroism, the narrator later receives long letters from Ardinghello that make up most of this largely epistolary novel. It is divided into five parts. In the first, Ardinghello loves a lady of Venice and kills her husband in a vendetta avenging the murder of his own father. The second takes place in Genoa, where his further romantic interests get him mixed up with pirates and Turks. The third is more reflective, containing political views on a Florence still tightly controlled by the Medici. The fourth, sent from Rome, adds further reflections on art, religion, and a pantheistic concept of nature.

Finally, in the fifth, Ardinghello and his friends establish a utopia on two small islands in the Aegean, where freedom means free love as well as political liberty, and where the flesh can be emancipated along with the women. These events start soon after the death of Ardinghello's apparent model, Benvenuto Cellini (1500–1571). Like Goethe's translation of Cellini's famous autobiography, Heinse's novel links antiquity, the Renaissance, and the eighteenth century by showing the kind of violently well-rounded "genius" celebrated by angry young adherents of "Storm and Stress." Like Goethe's "Roman Elegies" (1788), it also shows sensualism from an aesthetic point of view and vice versa. Although such erotic aesthet icism may seem amoral, it is a way of life that the philosopher Friedrich Nietzsche would have found bracingly "dionysian." Like Wieland, Heinse thus dispels Winckelmann's speculation that ancient artworks reflected their sitters' majestic calm. His synaesthetic concept of art, moreover, refutes Gotthold Ephraim Lessing's strict separation of poetry and painting in *Laocoön* (1766). When new, *Ardinghello* was read with great and no doubt prurient interest, though not all Heinse's fellow writers liked mixing orgies and erudition. Johann Gottfried Herder (1744–1803) was riled by such "intellectual debauchery," and one early historian of German literature rejected its plea for what he considered "nudism, promiscuity, and women's suffrage." More recent scholars have hailed its author as a master of German prose.

In the excerpt included here, readers will see some of Ardinghello's superhuman talents as a painter, poet, musician, statesman, lover, and soldier of fortune. It does not contain any long digressions on art and politics like those found in the rest of his story, but the time, place, and tone are all pure Renaissance—at least as Heinse imagined it. On the run after the murder that he commits in part 1, Ardinghello crosses the Apennines and arrives in Genoa. His vivid descriptions of the sea and landscape prove the power of Heinse's style, and his brilliance as a musician not only shows his artistic gifts but also prompts spontaneous feelings of friendship toward kindred souls. His singing Homer just to entertain noble wedding guests sets him apart from the rest of Renaissance society, but his virtuosity is coupled with tough virility when he kills his share of pirates who attack and abduct the bride and her ladies-in-waiting. His strong feelings for both the flirtatious bride herself and one of those beautiful ladies help show why he has at least one woman in every Italian port, though he also seems sincerely touched by the latter's bitter complaint that all men are only out to snare the fair sex. More than just a swashbuckling hotspur, Ardinghello is thus a charismatic and sensual man whose fictional brothers include Prometheus and Faust. Indeed, he is a character who lives life to the hilt and—despite his name, which combines "ardor" and "chilliness"—never blows hot and cold.

7

Ulrich Bräker wrote about his native Switzerland as a self-made man who had very little indeed to lose. He was born on December 22, 1735, and grew up poor in a remote mountain valley. After a youth spent in abject poverty, he was pressed into the service of Frederick the Great during the Seven Years' War but deserted at the battle of Lobositz in October 1756. He walked home, tried to set himself up in the weaving business (still little more than a cottage industry in Switzerland then), and eked out a living during the many hard times that he saw for most of his life. Although almost totally uneducated, he was certainly intellectual, reading on his own and writing on the side about topics as disparate as Shakespeare's plays and the economics of the local textile trade. His major work is the autobiographical *Life Story and Real Adventures of the Poor Man of Toggenburg* (1789). He also wrote diaries, dialogues, and several other short texts. He died on September 11, 1798.

The literary charm of *The Poor Man of Toggenburg* lies in its simple and direct tone of voice. Although he shows some passing acquaintance with more refined writers, Bräker gives straightforward and unadorned accounts of various stretches of time in his past and present life. He introduces his family, boyhood friends, and not-so-good neighbors, including a ghoulish child molester. He recalls his idyllic chores tending sheep in Alpine meadows as well as his initially shy and awkward behavior with women, and he explains how greedy people lured and tricked him into working for a Prussian recruiting officer. He tells how he left but came back home after serving in the Prussian army, built a house, married, and had constant trouble keeping food on the table and his creditors at bay. Like Moritz's Anton Reiser, he escapes such dire circumstances by reading, and he later writes about everything from his faith in divine providence to dissatisfaction with his children. His "life story" thus bears strong resemblance to both pietistic and Rousseauistic confessions, though it differs from them by linking its insights into human nature to the economically hard facts of a truly poor man's life.

The excerpt that I have chosen traces Bräker's story from the time he sets out to fight in the Seven Years' War until he returns to Switzerland after running away from battle. We see him marching to Berlin, which he describes from the lowly perspective of a raw recruit in an army drilled to fear its own officers more than its enemy. Initially, serving Prussia had improved his social mobility and relieved his economic plight, but here he is simply a small and unwitting cog in a military machine. After finally realizing that he is in the army now, and then surviving boot camp, he goes off to war against the enemy, Austria and Saxony. Forced to do such dirty work for a foreign country, he neither sees, understands, nor cares about any of its larger strategic and political implications. He has no taste for glory and just wants to go home, which he quickly does as soon as he gets—or rather seizes—the chance. Bräker relates such serious business in earthy, colorful language and can still laugh at himself, proof of the engaging blend of innocence and irony unique to *The Poor Man of Toggenburg*. In its own humble way, then, his writing confirms the extreme importance of Switzerland in eighteenth-century German literature.

The six texts selected here thus show a cross section of forms and themes that are representative as well as special examples of eighteenth-century German prose. Each author is outstanding in his or her own way, yet their writings give us a good idea of what their contemporaries were reading from Berlin and Weimar to Zurich and the Rhine. Needless to say, a volume like this can only scratch the surface of a literature rich for many other reasons, too. May its readers be moved to find them.

E. S.

Sophie von La Roche

From
THE HISTORY OF
MISS VON STERNHEIM

DRAWN FROM ORIGINAL DOCUMENTS
AND OTHER RELIABLE SOURCES
BY ONE OF HER FRIENDS

Madame Suffering in the Scottish Highlands

Emilia! Dear beloved name! Once you were my comfort and the pillar of my life; now you add to my suffering. The plaintive voice, the letters of your unfortunate friend no longer reach you. All, all is torn from me, and my heart must also bear the burden of feeling bitter grief at the anguish of my friends. Best Lady Summers!—Dearest Emilia! Why must your kind hearts share the torturous lot that destiny has dealt my unfortunate soul?—O God, how hard you punish the single false step that I took from the path of bourgeois virtue!—Can my secret marriage have offended you?— Poor thoughts, where do you stray? No one hears you, no one will read you; these pages will die and decay with me. No one but my persecutor will learn of my death, and he will be glad to know that the evidence of his inhumanity is buried with me. O Fate, you see my submission, you see that I ask nothing of you. You want to crush me slowly. Do so—only save my virtuous friends' hearts from the grief that troubles them on my behalf!

Third Month of My Misery

I have survived another month and have regained my senses only to know the full extent of my woe. Happy days, where are you, when I raised my hands to God in thanks at the first sight of the morning light and was glad to be preserved? Now ever new tears moisten my eye, and I wring my hands anew to mark the first hour of my renewed existence. O my Creator, can it be that you would rather see the bitter tears of my woe than the overflowing ones of childlike gratitude?

* * *

Hopeless, robbed of all prospects of help, I struggle against myself. I reproach myself with my sadness as if it were a crime and follow the urge to write. A sense of a better future stirs within me.—Oh! But did it not speak even louder in my bygone days? Did it not deceive me?—Fate!—Have I abused my happiness?—Did my heart cling to the glitter that surrounded me? Or has my crime been pride in the soul that I received from you? Poor, poor creature, with whom do I dispute? I, animated handful of dust, rise against the power that tests—and sustains—me. Will you, O my soul, will you with murmurs and impatience pour the worst evil into the cup of my suffering? Forgive, O God, forgive me, and let me seek out the blessings with which you have surrounded my sensitive heart even here.

* * *

Come, you faithful memory of my Emilia, come and witness how your friend's heart renews its pledge of virtue, how it returns to the path of its duties, renounces its stubborn sensitivity, and no longer closes its eyes to the signs of a benevolent and everlasting Providence.—It's now nearly three months since a deceitful call in the park at Summerhall brought me not to my tender, friendly Emma, but rather under the sway of one of the cruelest human beings, who made me travel day and night, in order to bring me here. Derby! No one but you was capable of this barbarism! Even as I labored for your pleasure, you spun new webs of grief for me.—You must have very little sense of honor and magnanimity, since you could not imagine that they would remove me from your sight and bid me be silent! What kind of sport do you make with the gloom of a heart whose whole sensitivity you know?—Why, O Providence, why must all the malicious schemes of this corrupt being succeed, and why all the good designs of the soul that you gave me be cast out into these sad mountains?

* * *

How unsteady self-love makes the course of our virtue! Two days ago my heart was full of noble resolve to proceed patiently on the thorny path of my unhappy fate, but my self-love recalls memories that distract my gaze from the present and the future and fix it solely on the unalterable past.—Are ethics, knowledge, and experience thus lost on me? And shall a vile foe have the double power not only to strip me of my outward appearance of happiness, as a ravisher would tear a dress, but also to destroy my convictions, attention to duty, and love of virtue in my soul itself?

* * *

Happy, yes very happiest hour of my life, when I found my whole heart again, when once again awakened in me the blissful sensation that even here the paternal hand of my Creator has provided for the greatest goods of my soul! It is he who rescued my reason from the madness that threatened to overcome me in the first weeks. He gave my coarse hosts humanity and compassion for me. The pure moral feeling of my soul is gradually rising above my melancholy gloom. The serenity of the sky that surrounds this wilderness, though I sigh when I see it, fills my heart with just as much hope and peace as the sky at Sternheim, Vaels, and Summerhall. These towering mountains speak to me of the almighty hand that made them. Everywhere the earth is filled with evidence of his wisdom and goodness, and everywhere I am his creature. He wanted to bury my vanity here, and the last trying hours of my life shall pass solely before his eyes and the witness of my heart! Perhaps they will not last long. Should I not seek to fill them with the virtue that still remains in my power to practice?—Thought of death, how salutary you are when you come to us along with the assurance that our souls are immortal! How keenly you awaken our sense of duty, and how eagerly you make us want to do good! I thank you for overcoming my gloom and for renewing the strength of virtue in my soul! You have made me fervently decide to fill my last days with noble convictions and to see whether I cannot do good even here.

* * *

Yes, I can, I will still do good. O patience, you virtue of the suffering, not of the fortunate, whose wishes are all granted, attend me and teach me calmly to obey the decrees of fate!—One painstakingly gathers the individual roots and herbs that heal our bodily ills. One should be just as concerned with seeking cures for our moral diseases. Like the former, they can often be found just a step away from our abode. But we are used to always seeking the good at a distance and to overlook with disdain what lies near at hand. That is what I did. My wishes and my laments led my sensitivity far from what surrounded me. How late do I recognize what a blessing it was to have brought an entire roll of paper with me, which has served me so well until now whenever I gather my thoughts. Was it not the goodness of Providence that protected me from all harm on my difficult journey here and that preserved all that would be useful to me in my idle hours?

* * *

Emilia, sacred friendship, beloved memory! Your image rises smilingly from the rubble of my happiness. You have cost me tears, many tears.—But come, these pages shall be consecrated to you! From my early youth, my most secret feelings poured into your true, tender heart. Chance can preserve these papers, they can still reach you, and you shall see from them that my heart has never forgotten the virtue of yours and its goodness to me. Perhaps a tear of your faithful love will someday fall on these few remains of your unfortunate Sophia. You will not be able to weep it on my grave; for I shall be the sacrificial victim buried here by Derby's wickedness. And since the thought of death and eternity puts an end to my laments and wishes, let me describe to you the sudden fall that brings me to my early grave. Formerly, I was too shaken whenever I thought of it.

* * *

I arrived here half-dead and for three weeks was in a state of mind that I cannot describe. The letters that I wrote during my recovery show what I was like in the second and third month of my stay. But judge for yourself how shattered my sentiments were, Emilia, from the fact that I could not pray. I did not call for death, but fully feeling the surfeit of misfortune that had befallen me, I would not have avoided a bolt of lightning about to strike me. I spent whole days on my knees, not out of submission, not to beg heaven for mercy. Pride, wounded pride had entered my soul along with the thought of undeserved misery. But, O my Emilia, that thought increased my distress and closed my heart to every active virtue in my circumstances; and only active virtue can trickle the balm of solace into the wounds of the soul. I felt this the first time that I looked kindly on the poor five-year-old girl ordered to watch me, because she was trying to raise my dejected head with her little hands. I did not understand her language, but her tone of voice and the expression on her face were natural and tender and innocent. I clasped her in my arms and shed a flood of tears. They were the first comforting tears I had wept, and the gratitude I felt for this creature's love was mixed with the feeling that God had given this poor child the power to let me taste the sweetness of compassion. From that day on I date the *recovery of my soul*. I now began thankfully gathering up the crumbs of happiness that lay next to me here in the dust. My exhaustion, the pains that the oaten bread caused me, made me think my death was near. I no longer had any witness of my life around me. I wanted to return a tranquil, loving heart to my Creator, and this thought renewed all the strength in the virtuous mainsprings of my soul. I took my little benefactress with me into the small, secluded corner that I occupy in this cottage, I shared my bed with her, and from her I took my first lessons in the pitiful language spoken here. I went with her into my landlords' room. The husband had long worked in the lead mines, but he has become too sickly to do so now, and he and his wife and children raise oats and hemp on a small plot of ground that Lord Hopton gave him near an old ruined castle. To use the oats, they grind them with stones, and they have to clothe themselves with the hemp. They are poor, good-natured people, whose whole wealth consists entirely of the few guineas that they have received for keeping me. They were glad that I had grown calm and came to see them. Each one tried to teach me their language, and in two weeks I had learned enough of it to ask and to answer short questions. These people know how far beyond the house they may let me go, but the husband took me somewhat farther on one of the last days of autumn. Oh, how barren nature is here! One sees that its bowels are leaden. With tears in my eyes I looked at the rugged, meager piece of field where my oaten bread grows and at the sky flowing above me. Memory made me sigh, but a glance at my emaciated guide made me say to myself: I enjoyed my fill of good fortune in my youth, but this good man and his family have been in need and misery as long as they have lived. They are creatures of the same divine author, their bodies lack no sinew, no muscle necessary to satisfy physical needs. In this, there is no difference between us. But what large parts of their souls and powers sleep and remain inactive! How hidden, how incomprehensible are the reasons that allow no difference to arise in our bodily form but leave whole millions of creatures lagging in moral growth and action! How fortunate I am even today, thanks to the lasting cultivation of my mind and my feelings toward God and humanity! True happiness, sole possession that we gather on earth and can take with us, I shall not reject you out of impatience. I shall reward my poor hosts' goodness with friendliness.—I eagerly kept at their language and learned by asking about their occasional harshness to the little girl that she was not their child but Lord Derby's, that the child's mother had died at their cottage, and that Derby no longer gave them anything for her support. At this news I had to go to my corner. I painfully felt my whole misfortune again. The poor mother! She was beautiful, like her child, and young, and good.— My grave will be near hers. O Emilia, Emilia, how can, O how can I endure this trial! The good girl came and took my hand, which was hanging from my humble bed, while my face was turned to the wall. I heard her coming. Her touch, her voice made me shudder, and I tore my hand away from her in disgust. Derby's daughter was odious to me. The poor girl went crying to the foot of my bed and wailed. I felt how wrong it was to make unhappy innocence suffer. I vowed to suppress my disgust and to show love for my murderer's child. How happy I was when I sat up and called her. Leaning on her little bosom, I made a vow to show her kindness. I shall not break it, I paid for it too dearly!

*   *   *

O Derby! How full, how full you make the measure of your severity against me! Today a messenger comes and brings a large bundle of supplies for embroidering. He who sent it mocks me basely. Since time hung heavy on my hands without embroidery at court, he wrote, it might also do so here. He therefore was giving me work for the winter. He would send for it in the spring. It is for a bedroom; the patterns are enclosed.—I want to begin it, yes I will. He will get the finished pieces after my death. He shall see the remains of the barbarism that he has perpetrated against me and remember how happy I was the first time he saw my fingers at work. He will also have to think of how he plunged me into an abyss of misery and there made me perish.

* * *

Nevermore, O Fate! Nevermore will I yield to the murmurs of my self-love! How it distorts our judgment! I complained about what has become my pleasure. My work brightens my dreary winter days. My hosts watch me with coarse delight, and I give their daughter instruction in it. The girl beamed with pride when she had finished sewing the first little leaf. Misfortune and want have often been the mother of invention; so, too, for me. I know that Lord Hopton, who owns the lead mines, has a house a few miles from here and that he sometimes goes there for a few days. On his last visit he brought along a sister whom he dearly loves and who, being a widow, is often with him. Upon this lady I rest hopes that are reviving as my life goes on. I have given my hosts the idea of having their daughter Maria enter this lady's service. I promised to teach her everything that she needs to know. I am already teaching her to speak and write English. She knows how to embroider, and since want drove me to make two caps from the lace of my neckerchief, she has learned that art, too. I give her lessons in the rest as we go along. The girl is so quick to grasp and to judge that it often astounds me. She shall lead the way to my freedom; for by means for her I hope to become known to Lady Douglas. O Fate, leave me this hope!

* * *

I want to tell my Emilia about another bit of my torturous fate. You know how clean I always kept my linen, but here I had not changed at all for I do not know how long. Finally, when I could think clearly, I became dissatisfied with the lack of clothing, and on further reflection I was glad that I had on a very white linen dress at the time of my abduction. I immediately took it off and thanked modish opulence for making its many pleats; for I could conveniently cut three chemises from it and still keep a short dress besides. I made my apron into neckerchiefs and my petticoat into aprons, so that I can change my clothing, which I keep quite clean with a little light lye. I iron it with a warm stone. I have also taught little Lidy to sew, and she makes quite nice stitches in the ground of my embroidery. My hosts clean their dwelling very tidily every day for my sake, and my oatcakes begin to agree with me. Our basic needs are slight, my Emilia. I rise sated from the meager table, and my hosts are astounded to hear me talk of other parts of the world. I still have my parents' portraits. I showed them to these people and told them as much about my education and former way of life as they could grasp and as was good for them. Unaffected, compassionate tears trickled from their eyes when I spoke of the good fortune that I had enjoyed and explained to them the patience that really is in my heart. I seldom speak of you, my dear! I am not strong enough to think too often of losing you, to think of your grief for me. If only my suffering could buy you freedom from yours, and my kind lady from hers, I would endeavor not to say that I suffered any more. But fate knew what would torture me most. It knew that my innocence and my principles would console and calm me. It knew that I would learn to bear poverty and want. It therefore made me feel the sorrow of my friends, a feeling that wounds me incurably, since it would be a crime if I tried to free myself from it.—How happy this feeling used to make me, when I, in possession of my wealth, could satisfy every wish I overheard my friends make and ease every pain I perceived. It has been two years since I splendidly stepped out into the glittering crowd, had prospects of happiness before me, saw myself loved, and could pick and choose.—O my heart, why did you protect yourself so long from this memory? You never again dared think the name *Seymour,* but now you cry when you wonder what he would say.— Oblivion! Oh, remove this burden, never let me remember him. His heart never knew what mine felt for him, and now it is too late!—My paper, alas Emilia, my paper is almost gone. I dare not write much more. The winter is long; I want to keep the rest for the story of my still-faint hopes. O my child! A few sheets of paper were my happiness, which I can no longer enjoy! I will save canvas and sew letters into it.

In April

O Time, most beneficent of all beings, for how much good do I have you to thank! You gradually removed the deep impressions left by my suffering and lost happiness, and you placed them at an obscure distance while spreading a tender serenity upon the objects that surround me. Experience, which you led by the hand, taught me to know active wisdom and patience. Every hour that I became more acquainted with them diminished the bitterness of my grief. You, Time, who heals all wounds to the spirit, will also pour the balm of calmness into my few friends' souls and put them in a position to enjoy the happy prospects of their lot without troubling themselves sourly about me. You have recalled to my soul the comfort of my Creator's goodness, which shelters even the lowliest worm beneath small grains of sand. You let me find that goodness in these barren mountains, renewed in me the use of my skills, and roused and busied virtues slumbering in the lap of luxury. Here where the natural world distributes its few gifts sparingly among its sad inhabitants, here I have spread the moral wealth of virtue and knowledge in the cottage of my hosts, and with them I enjoy and sample its sweetness. Completely stripped of everything that bears the name of fortune, prestige, and power, my life entrusted to the hands of these strangers, I became their moral benefactress by expanding their love of God, enlightening their reason, and calming their hearts, since I showered delight on my poor hosts during their hours of rest with my stories of other parts of the world and the fates of its inhabitants. With love, care, and instruction I have strewn the sad, innocent days of a doubly unfortunate orphan with flowers. Far from the enjoyment of all that people regard as well-being, I enjoy the true gifts of heaven, *the joy of doing good* and *serenity of the spirit,* as fruits of true philanthropy and experienced virtue.—Pure joy, true wealth! You will escort me into eternity, and the first thankful praises sung by my soul will be for possessing you.

At the End of June

Emilia, have you ever been able to put yourself in the position of a person who fears for her life in a fragile skiff on the stormy sea and who looks about tremblingly for some glimmer of hope? Long tossed by the waves, she is seized with despair. At last she spies an island that she hopes to reach. Folding her hands in prayer she cries: "O God, I see land!"—I, my child, feel all this: *I see land*. Lord Hopton is in his house on the hill, and Lady Douglas, his sister, has taken on my hosts' daughter. She went with her brother and a piece of embroidery to offer her services to the lady. Full of wonder at her work and her replies, the lady asked who had taught her, and the good girl's grateful heart told what she knew and felt about me. The noble lady was moved to tears. She vowed to take on the girl at once, saw that the young people were fed, and sent the son home alone with two guineas for his parents and the promise that she would come to them herself before her departure. She sent special greetings to me and blessed me for my efforts with the girl. I have asked her for paper, pens, and ink. I want to take this opportunity to write to my Lady Summers; but I shall leave the letter open for Lady Douglas, to show her my uprighteousness. It would be a crime if I did not use every opportunity to gain my freedom when noble means of doing so present themselves. I will also ask Lord Hopton to show mercy to my poor hosts. The good people cannot contain their joy at seeing their daughter provided for and at the money that they therefore received. They caress and bless me in turn. I shall not leave my orphan behind. Since I have accustomed her to good treatment, the child would be doubly unhappy at the loss, and all my days would be disturbed by memories of her if I returned to happiness and left her prey to outright misery.

* * *

O, my friend! It was ominous that the image of a skiff erring on the tempestuous sea occurred to me in my last letter. I was destined to feel the sharpest pains of the soul and then to die at the first glimpse of hope. The unspeakable wickedness of my persecutor sweeps me along as a foaming wave sweeps skiff and people into the abyss. He retained this power, but I was deprived of all means of help. Soon a lonely grave will put an end to my laments and show my soul the ultimate reasons why I have had to bear this cruel destiny. I am calm, I am content. My last day will be the happiest that I have had in two years. Lady Summers will send my packet of papers to you, my friend, whom I shall love tenderly to the very end, and your heart will take comfort in the thought that all my suffering has vanished in blissful eternity. My last strength is devoted to you. You were witness to my happy years. You shall also know, as far as I am able to say, how my gloomy days came to an end.

I was full of hope and surrounded by cheerful prospects when Derby's most trusted villain arrived to make the odious suggestion that I should betake myself to his lordship in London. He did not love his wife, it was said, had also become sickly himself, and spent most of his time at a country house in Windsor, where my company would be very agreeable to him. He himself wrote in a letter that if I voluntarily came and loved him, he would divorce Lady Ashton and confirm our marriage as the law and my own merit required; but that if in my former folly I rejected this suggestion, I would have to accept whatever fate he thought fit for me.—I had to listen to this, for I refused to read the letter. The worst part of this unbearable insult was that I had to see the cursed wretch who had performed my false marriage. Distressed and embittered in the extreme, I rejected all these unworthy offers, and the barbarian avenged his master after my second formal refusal by violently seizing me by the arm and around the waist and dragging me out of the house, toward the old tower, and pushing me into a door, raging and cursing and saying that I could rot there so that he and his master would finally be rid of me. My struggling and the terrible fear that I might be taken to London by force had exhausted me and deprived me of half my senses. I fell headlong into a vault filled with rubble and mud, injuring my left hand and half my face on the stones, so that I bled profusely from my nose and mouth. I do not know how long I lay there unconscious. When I came to again, I was all enfeebled and filled with pain. The foul, damp air that I breathed soon constricted my chest so much that I believed to be near the last moment of my life. I saw nothing, but I felt with one hand that the ground was steeply sloped, and at the slightest movement I therefore feared falling into a cellar, where I would have given up the ghost in despair. My misery and the sensations of it that I had cannot be described; I lay there the whole night. It rained hard. The water ran in toward me under the door, so that I became completely soaked and numb; and utterly dejected by my misfortune, I wished for death. I seemed racked by inner convulsions. That much I recall. When I came to my senses again I was on my bed, around which my poor, frightened, hosts stood and wailed. My orphan was holding my hand and sobbing anxiously. I felt very ill and asked those people to fetch Lord Hopton's clergyman because I was about to die. I asked them with uplifted hands. The son went forth, and the parents told me that they had not dared help me until Sir John (as they called him) had departed. How terrible the lot of poverty, which seldom has courage enough to oppose the power of wealthy vice!

The rain had delayed the villain, but they say he went to the door of the tower again, opened it and listened, reared his head in annoyance, and left without closing the door or saying anything further to them. They had waited another hour for fear of him and then had come with a light to find me, whom they took for dead and carried out. The clergyman came, and Lady Douglas with him. Both regarded me carefully and compassionately. I extended my hand to the lady, who took it kindly in her own. "Noble lady," I said with tears in my eyes, "God will reward your soul for this philanthropic concern for me. Please believe that I am worthy of it." I noticed that her eyes were fixed on my hand and the portrait of my mother, so I said to her, "It is my mother, a granddaughter of Lord David Watson.—And here," as I raised the other hand, "is my father, a worthy nobleman in Germany. Both have long gone to their eternal reward, and soon, soon I hope to be with them." I said this with my hands folded in prayer. The lady wept and told the clergyman to feel my pulse. He did so and assured her that I was very ill. She looked around with kind devotion and asked if I could not be taken away. "Not without mortal danger," said the clergyman. "Ah, that pains me," replied the dear lady as she squeezed my hand. She went out and the clergyman started to speak with me. I briefly told him that I came from a noble family, had been torn from my homeland by vile deceit and a false marriage, and that mylady Summers, whose protection I had enjoyed, could vouch to them for me. I also told him to take the papers that I had written to her and that lay hidden behind a board. Even without his asking, I added a confession of my principles and bade him enter into correspondence with your husband. Lady Douglas knocked and came to my bed with Maria, my hosts' daughter, who carried a small box. In it she had all kinds of cordials and medicines, which she gave me. Little Lidy came in, too, and fell to her knees at the side of my bed. The lady regarded the girl and me with increasing sadness. Finally, she took her leave, leaving Maria with me, and the clergyman promised to come back in the morning. But he did not come all day. Yet twice someone asked about me. I was better this morning than I had been yesterday. I therefore wrote to you. Now it is almost six o'clock in the evening, and I am growing visibly worse, as my trembling, uneven script will show you. Who knows what will become of me tonight? I thank

God that I am mortal and that my heart could still speak with yours. I am completely composed and near the moment when happiness and misery are indifferent.—

Nine O'clock at Night

For the last time, my Emilia, I have stretched my weak, enfeebled arms out toward where you live. God bless you and reward your virtue and your friendship for me! You will receive a paper that your husband should deliver himself to my uncle, Count R. It concerns my estate.

Everything that I have from the von P. family shall be given to the sons of Count Löbau. Your brother-in-law, the bailiff, has an inventory of it.

Half of what I received from my beloved father shall be dedicated to the education of indigent children. One part of the other half I give to your children and to my friend Rosina. From the other part, my poor hosts here are to be given a thousand thalers, and the unfortunate Lidy as much again, but from the rest a tombstone shall be erected to me, at the foot of my parents' graves, with the simple inscription:

In Memory of Their Not Unworthy Daughter, Sophia von Sternheim

I want to be buried here at the foot of the tree under which I have so often knelt this spring and implored God to give me patience. Here, where my spirit was tormented, my body shall decay. And it is mother earth that will cover me until I shall one day, in transfigured form, join the ranks of the virtuous and once again see you, too, my Emilia. Meanwhile save, O my friend, save my memory from the disgrace of vice! Say that I returned my soul to its Creator full of childlike trust in God and full of love for my fellow creatures, true to virtue, but unhappy, in the clutches of most bitter grief; that I tenderly blessed my friends and sincerely forgave my enemies. Plant, my dear, a cypress near a rock in your garden, and let it be entwined by a solitary tree rose. Consecrate that place to my memory. Go there sometimes. Perhaps I shall be allowed to hover around you and to see the tender tear you shed when you regard the falling rose blossom. You have seen *me, too* bloom and fade. Fate hid from your sight only the last drooping of my head and the last sigh from my bosom.—That is well, my Emilia. You would suffer too much if you could see me.—The bottom of my soul is at peace. I shall gently fall asleep, for destiny has made me tired, very tired. Farewell, best, friendly soul. Let your tears for me be tranquil, like the one that now wells in my dim eyes for you.— —

Translated by Ellis Shookman

Glossary

Derby. Evil, lascivious, and depraved young English lord who pursues Sophia and stages a sham marriage ceremony to wed her in a weak moment, then deserts her in a remote German inn. After returning home, marrying another woman for real, and discovering that one of this new wife's relations has brought Sophia to England, Derby has Sophia abducted and confined in the Scottish Highlands.

Guinea. English gold coin issued from 1663 to 1813 and equivalent to twenty-one shillings; so called because such coins supposedly were made out of gold from Guinea, a region in West Africa.

John. English manservant who works for Lord Derby; disguised as a preacher, he helps Derby trick Sophia by performing their bogus marriage ceremony.

Rosina. Sophia's chambermaid and sister of her best friend Emilia, addressee of most of her letters. Rosina is also the fictional editor—and occasional narrator—of Sophia's story.

Seymour. Young and emotional English lord who suppresses his passion for Sophia, but whom she loves all along and marries in the end.

Sons of Count Löbau. Sophia's cousins, sons of the evil aunt whose schemes drive her into Derby's arms in the first place.

Sternheim. Country estate that is Sophia's ancestral home.

Summers, Lady. Englishwoman who invites Sophia, whom she meets in Germany as the philanthropic Madame Suffering, to accompany her back to England.

Summerhall. Lady Summers's estate in England; site of Sophia's abduction.

Thaler (or Taler). One of several large silver coins issued by various German states from the fifteenth to the nineteenth centuries.

Vaels. Home of Sophia's friend and correspondent Emilia, where Sophia herself—as Madame Suffering—does many good deeds for women, orphans, and the poor.

Von P. Abbreviated name of the aristocratic family of Sophia's mother.

Georg Forster

From
A VOYAGE
ROUND THE WORLD

In His Brittanic
Majesty's Sloop, *Resolution*

Anchorage in O-Aitepeha Harbor, on the lesser Peninsula of O-Taheitee.—Account of our Stay there.— Removal to Matavai Bay.

Devenere locos lætos et amœna vireta
Fortunatorum nemorum, sedesque beatas.
Largior hic campos æther, et lumine vestit
Purpureo.

Virgil

It was one of those beautiful mornings which the poets of all nations have attempted to describe, when we saw the isle of O-Taheitee, within two miles before us. The east wind which had carried us so far was entirely vanished, and a faint breeze only wafted a delicious perfume from the land, and curled the surface of the sea. The mountains, clothed with forests, rose majestic in various spiry forms, on which we already perceived the light of the rising sun: nearer to the eye a lower range of hills, easier of ascent, appeared, wooded like the former, and colored with several pleasing hues of green, soberly mixed with autumnal browns. At their foot lay the plain, crowned with its fertile breadfruit trees, over which rose innumerable palms, the princes of the grove. Here everything seemed as yet asleep, the morning scarce dawned, and a peaceful shade still rested on the landscape. We discerned however a number of houses among the trees, and many canoes hauled up along the sandy beaches. About half a mile from the shore a ledge of rocks level with the water extended parallel to the land, on which the surf broke, leaving a smooth and secure harbor within. The sun beginning to illuminate the plain, its inhabitants arose, and enlivened the scene. Having perceived the large vessels on their coast, several of them hastened to the beach, launched their canoes, and paddled towards us, who were highly delighted in watching all their occupations.

The canoes soon passed through the openings in the reef, and one of them approached within hale. In it were two men almost naked, with a kind of turban on the head, and a sash round their waist. They waved a large green leaf, and accosted us with the repeated exclamation of *tayo!* which even without the help of vocabularies, we could easily translate into the expression of proffered friendship. The canoe now came under our stern, and we let down a present of beads, nails, and medals to the men. In return, they handed up to us a green stem of a plantain, which was their symbol of peace, with a desire that it might be fixed in a conspicuous part of the vessel. It was accordingly stuck up in the main shrouds, upon which our new friends immediately returned towards the land. In a short time we saw great crowds of people on the seashore gazing at us, while numbers in consequence of this treaty of peace, which was now firmly established, launched their canoes, and loaded them with various productions of their country. In less than an hour we were surrounded by a hundred canoes, each of which carried one, two, three, and sometimes four persons, who placed a perfect confidence in us, and had no arms whatsoever. The welcome sound of *tayo* resounded on all sides, and we returned it with a degree of heartfelt pleasure, on this favorable change of our situation. Coconuts, and plantains in great quantity, breadfruit and several other vegetables, besides some fresh fish were offered to us, and eagerly exchanged for transparent beads, and small nails. Pieces of cloth, fishhooks, hatchets of stone, and a number of tools were likewise brought for sale and readily disposed of; and many canoes kept plying between us and the shore, exhibiting a picture of a new kind of fair. I immediately began to trade for natural productions through the cabin windows, and in half an hour had got together two or three species of unknown birds, and a great number of new fishes, whose colors while alive were exquisitely beautiful. I therefore employed the morning in sketching their outlines, and laying on the vivid hues, before they disappeared in the dying objects.

The people around us had mild features, and a pleasing countenance; they were about our size, of a pale mahogany brown, had fine black hair and eyes, and wore a piece of cloth round their middle of their own manufacture, and another wrapped about the head in various picturesque shapes like a turban. Among them were several females, pretty enough to attract the attention of Europeans, who had not seen their own countrywomen for twelve long months past. These wore a piece of cloth with a hole in the middle, through which they had passed the head, so that one part of the garment hung down behind, and the other before, to the knees; a fine white cloth like a muslin was passed over this in various elegant turns round the body, a little below the breast, forming a kind of tunic, of which one turn sometimes fell gracefully across the shoulder. If this dress had not entirely that perfect form, so justly admired in the draperies of the ancient Greek statues, it was however infinitely superior to our expectations, and much more advantageous to the human figure, than any modern fashion we had hitherto seen. Both sexes were adorned, or rather disfigured, by those singular black stains, occasioned by puncturing the skin, and rubbing a black color into the wounds, which are mentioned by former voyagers. They were particularly visible on the loins of the common men, who went almost naked, and exhibited a proof how little the ideas of ornament of different nations agree, and yet how generally they all have adopted such aids to their personal perfection. It was not long before some of these good people came aboard. That peculiar gentleness of disposition, which is their general characteristic, immediately manifested itself in all their looks and actions, and gave full employment to those, who made the human heart their study. They expressed several marks of affection in their countenance, took hold of our hands, leaned on our shoulder, or embraced us. They admired the whiteness of our bodies, and frequently pushed aside our clothes from the breast, as if to convince themselves that we were made like them.

Many of them seeing us desirous of learning their language, by asking the names of various familiar objects, or repeating such as we found in the vocabularies of former voyagers, took great pains to teach us, and were much delighted when we could catch the just pronunciation of a word. For my own part, no language seemed easier to acquire than this; every harsh and sibilant consonant being banished from it, and almost every word ending in a vowel. The only requisite was a nice ear to distinguish the numerous modification of their vowels, which must naturally occur in a language confined to few consonants, and which, once rightly understood, give a great degree of delicacy to conversation. Amongst several other observations, we immediately found that the O or E with which the greatest part of the names and words in Lieutenant Cook's first voyage begin, is nothing else than the article, which many eastern languages affix to the greater part of their substantives. In consequence of this remark, I shall always in the sequel either omit this prefix, or separate it from the word itself by a hyphen: and I cannot help taking notice that M. de Bougainville has been fortunate enough to catch the name of the island without the additional O, and expressed it as well as the nature of the French language will permit, by Taïti, which, with the addition of a slight aspirate, we pronounce Taheîtee, or Tahitee.

Seeing an opening in the reef before us, which was the entrance to the harbor of Whaï-Urua, in the lesser peninsula of O-Taheitee, we sent a boat to sound in it, which found convenient anchorage. The boat afterwards proceeded to the shore, where a crowd of the natives gathered round it, and we heard the squeaking of pigs, which was at this time a more welcome sound to us, than the music of the most brilliant performer. Our people, however, were not so fortunate as to purchase any of them, all their offers being constantly refused, under the pretext that these animals belonged to the *aree*, or king.

A canoe now came alongside, of a somewhat larger size than the rest, and brought a handsome man, above six feet high, and three women, who all came on board. The man, who immediately informed us that his name was O-Taï, seemed to be a person of some consequence in this part of the island, and we supposed he belonged to that class of vassals, or freeholders, who are called Manahounas in the first voyage of Captain Cook. He came on the quarterdeck, to all appearance thinking that a place where our chiefs were stationed best became him. He was remarkably fairer than any of the natives we had yet seen, and resembled in color the West Indian mestizos. His features were really handsome and regular; he had a high forehead, arched eyebrows, large black eyes, sparkling with expression, and a well-proportioned nose; there was something remarkably sweet and engaging about his mouth; the lips were prominent, but not disagreeably large; and his beard was black, and finely frizzled; his hair was of a jetty color, and fell in strong curls down his neck; but seeing that we all had ours queued, he made use of a black silk neckcloth, which Mr. Clerke made him a present of, to imitate our fashion. The body was in general well proportioned, though somewhat too lusty, and his feet were rather too large to harmonize perfectly with the rest. By the help of vocabularies we asked this man several questions. One of the first was whether Tootahàh was well? To this we were answered that he was dead, being killed by the men of Tiarraboo, or the smaller peninsula, and that O-Aheatua was *e-aree,* or the king of the latter; which was confirmed by all the other natives. Of his three female companions, one was his wife, and the other two his sisters: the latter took great pleasure in teaching us to call them by their names, which were both sufficiently harmonious; one was called Maroya, and the other Maroraï. They were still fairer than O-Taï, but their stature was small in comparison to his, being at least nine or ten inches less. The last mentioned was a graceful figure, with the most delicate and beautiful contours, in the hands and all above the zone. Their face was round, and their features far from being so regular as those of the brother; but an ineffable smile sat on their countenances. They seemed never to have been aboard a ship before, so much were they struck with admiration on beholding its variety of objects. They did not content themselves with looking around the deck, but descended into the officers' cabins, whither a gentleman conducted them, and curiously examined every part. Maroraï took a particular fancy to a pair of sheets which she saw spread on one of the beds, and made a number of fruitless attempts to obtain them from her conductor. He proposed a special favor as the condition; she hesitated some time, and at last with seeming reluctance consented; but when the victim was just led to the altar of Hymen, the ship struck violently on the reef, and interrupted the solemnity. The affrighted lover, more sensible of the danger than his fair mistress, flew in haste upon deck, whither all the rest of our people crowded from their several occupations. The tide, during a perfect calm, had driven us by insensible degrees towards the reef of rocks; and actually set us upon it, before we could come into the entrance of the harbor, which was as it were within our reach. Repeated shocks made our situation every moment more terrifying; however, providentially there was no swell which broke with any violence on the rocks, and the seabreeze, which must have brought on absolute destruction to us, did not come in all day. The officers, and all the passengers, exerted themselves indiscriminately on this occasion, hoisted out the launch, and afterwards by heaving upon an anchor, which had been carried out to a little distance, succeeded in bringing the vessel afloat. The natives on board, seeing us work so hard, assisted us in manning the capstan, hauling in ropes, and performing all sorts of labor. If they had had the least spark of a treacherous disposition, they could not have found a better opportunity of distressing us; but they proved themselves good-natured, and friendly in this, as on all other occasions. The heat during this violent exertion of our strength was immense; the thermometer being upwards of ninety degrees in the shade, and the sun blazing in a perfectly clear sky. The *Adventure* was close to us, and escaped sharing the same distresses, by dropping an anchor in time. It was another fortunate circumstance that the reef shelved in this place so as to admit of anchorage, which is indeed rarely the case, the coral rock being perpendicular in most parts. It was about three o'clock when we were afloat again, after working for about an hour and a half. We now took some refreshments in a hurry, and as our situation was still extremely precarious, in case an easterly wind had come on, we manned the boats of both sloops, and were towed off to sea, where we felt a land breeze gently swelling our sails about five o'clock. As soon as we were sure of it, we dispatched the boats to the assistance of the *Adventure;* but she had already slipped her cables, in order to take advantage of the favorable wind, and followed us. We stood off and on all night, and saw the dangerous reefs illuminated by a number of fires, by the light of which the natives were fishing. One of the officers retiring to rest found his bed deprived of the sheets, which in all probability the fair Maroraï had taken care of, when forsaken by her lover; though she must have managed this little concern with considerable ingenuity, as she had appeared on deck before any suspicion had fallen upon her.

The next morning we resumed our course towards the shore, and stood in along the north part of the lesser peninsula. We were in a short time surrounded, as the day before, by the natives, who in a great number of canoes brought us abundance of vegetable, but no animal food, and whose clamors were sometimes loud enough to stun our ears. These canoes very frequently overset, but the natives were not much discomposed by such accidents, as both sexes were expert swimmers, and reestablished themselves in a moment. Seeing that I inquired for plants, and other natural curiosities, they brought off several, though sometimes only the leaves without the flowers, and vice versa; however, among them we saw the common species of black nightshade, and a beautiful *erythrina,* or coral flower; I also collected by these means many shells, corallines, birds, etc.

About eleven o'clock we anchored in a little harbor called O-Aitepeha, on the northeast end of the southern or lesser peninsula of Taheitee, named Tiarraboo. Here the concourse of natives still increased, and we saw their canoes coming towards us from all parts. They were eager to obtain our beads, nails, and knives, for which an immense quantity of their cloth, mats, baskets, and various tools, as well as abundance of coconuts, breadfruit, yams, and bananas were exchanged. Many of them came on deck, and took the opportunity of conveying away a number of trifles; nay, some went so far as privately to throw overboard the coconuts, which we had already purchased, to their comrades, who immediately picked them up, and sold them to our people again. To prevent our being imposed upon for the future in this manner, the thieves were turned out of the vessel, and punished with a whip, which they bore very patiently.

The heat was as great as it had been the day before, the thermometer standing at ninety degrees in the shade, when the sky was covered with clouds; the winds likewise dying away again at noon to a perfect calm. Notwithstanding the waste of fluids which the weather occasioned, we could not say that we found the climate affected us too much, or was very disagreeable. On the contrary, allowing for the violent exercise we had undergone at the striking of the ship, we found ourselves more refreshed by the bare proximity of the shore than we could have expected. The breadfruit and yams proved a luxurious and most welcome substitute for worm-eaten biscuit; while plantains, and a fruit of the shape of an apple, called *e-vee* by the natives, furnished out a delicious dessert. Our only remaining wish, with regard to eatables, was to be able to purchase some hogs and fowls, which might supply the place of salt beef.

In the afternoon the captains, accompanied by several gentlemen, went ashore the first time, in order to visit O-Aheatua, whom all the natives thereabouts acknowledged as *aree,* or king. Numbers of canoes in the meanwhile surrounded us, carrying on a brisk trade with vegetables, but chiefly with great quantities of the cloth made in the island. The decks were likewise crowded with natives, among whom were several women who yielded without difficulty to the ardent solicitations of our sailors. Some of the females who came on board for this purpose seemed not to be above nine or ten years old, and had not the least marks of puberty. So early an acquaintance with the world seems to argue an uncommon degree of voluptuousness, and cannot fail of affecting the nation in general. The effect, which was immediately obvious to me, was the low stature of the common class of people, to which all these prostitutes belonged.

Among this whole order we saw few persons above the middle size, and many below it; an observation which confirms what M. de Buffon has very judiciously said on the subject of early connections of the sexes (see his *Histoire Naturelle*). Their features were very irregular, and in general very ordinary, except the eyes, which were always large and full of vivacity; but a natural smile, and a constant endeavor to please, had so well replaced the want of beauty, that our sailors were perfectly captivated, and carelessly disposed of their shirts and clothes to gratify their mistresses. The simplicity of a dress which exposed to view a well-proportioned bosom and delicate hands might also contribute to fan their amorous fire; and the view of several of these nymphs swimming nimbly all round the sloop, such as nature had formed them, was perhaps more than sufficient entirely to subvert the little reason which a mariner might have left to govern his passions. A trifling circumstance had given cause to their taking the water. One of the officers on the quarterdeck intended to drop a bead into a canoe for a little boy about six years old; by accident it missed the boat and fell into the sea; but the child immediately leaped overboard, and diving after it brought it up again. To reward his performance we dropped some more beads to him, which so tempted a number of men and women, that they amused us with amazing feats of agility in the water, and not only fetched up several beads scattered at once, but likewise large nails, which, on account of their weight, descended quickly to a considerable depth. Some of them continued a long while under water, and the velocity with which we saw them go down, the water being perfectly clear, was very surprising. The frequent ablutions of these people, already mentioned in Captain Cook's former voyage, seem to make swimming familiar to them from their earliest childhood; and indeed their easy position in the water, and the pliancy of their limbs, gave us reason to look on them almost as amphibious creatures. They continued this sport, and their other occupations about us, till sunset, when they all withdrew by degrees to the shore.

In the evening the captains with their company returned on board, without having seen the king, who, perhaps mistrusting their intentions, had sent word that he intended to visit us the next day. They had taken a walk along the shore to the eastward, attended by a great crowd of the natives, who insisted on carrying them on their shoulders over a fine brook. After they had passed it, the natives left them, and they proceeded accompanied by one man, who guided them to an uncultivated projecting point, where different kinds of plants grew in wild luxuriance among several sorts of shrubs. On coming out of the shrubbery they saw a building of stones, in form of the frustrum of a pyramid; the base might measure about twenty yards in front, and the whole consisted of several terraces or steps above each other, which were ruinous and overgrown with grasses and shrubs, especially on the back or inland part. This the native said was a burying place and place of worship, *marai*, and distinguished it by the name of *marai no-Aheatua*, the burying-place of Aheatua, the present king of Tiarraboo. Around it were placed perpendicularly, or nearly so, fifteen slender pieces of wood, some about eighteen feet long, in which six or eight diminutive human figures of a rude unnatural shape were carved, standing above each other, male or female promiscuously, yet so that the uppermost was always a male. All these figures faced the sea, and perfectly resembled some which are carved on the sterns of their canoes, and which they call *e-tee*. Beyond the marai they saw a kind of thatch erected on four posts, before which a lattice of sticks was placed in the ground, hung with bananas and coconuts *no t' Eatua*, "for the Divinity." They sat down to rest themselves under the shade of this roof, and their guide, seeing them a good deal exhausted, took several of the bananas and offered them with the assurance that they were *mâa maitai*, "good eating." They accepted them after this recommendation, and finding them really as delicious as they had been described, made no scruple to feast with the gods. As the evening was now advancing, they returned to the seashore, well pleased with their reception among these good-natured people, and brought on board a few plants, which we soon recognized as the productions common to tropical countries.

We contemplated the scenery before us early the next morning, when its beauties were most engaging. The harbor in which we lay was very small, and would not have admitted many more vessels besides our own. The water in it was as smooth as the finest mirror, and the sea broke with a snowy foam around us upon the outer reef. The plain at the foot of the hills was very narrow in this place, but always conveyed the pleasing ideas of fertility, plenty, and happiness. Just over against us it ran up between the hills into a long narrow valley, rich in plantations, interspersed with the houses of the natives. The slopes of the hills, covered with woods, crossed each other on both sides, variously tinted according to their distances; and beyond them, over the cleft of the valley, we saw the interior mountains shattered into various peaks and spires, among which was one remarkable pinnacle, whose summit was frightfully bent to one side, and seemed to threaten its downfall every moment. The serenity of the sky, the genial warmth of the air, and the beauty of the landscape, united to exhilarate our spirits.

The launches of both ships were sent to *o Whai-urua,* to fetch the anchors which we had left there when we struck on the reef. A party of marines and seamen were ordered onshore at the same time, to carry on a trade for provisions, and to fill our empty casks with fresh water. For this purpose they occupied the remains of an abandoned shed or cottage on the beach, which at once gave them shelter from the sun, and secured them against the thievish disposition of the people. Before Captain Cook went ashore he received a visit from a man of some note, called o-Poòe, who brought his two sons on board. They presented the captain with some of their cloth and some little trifles, and in return they received knives, nails, beads, and a shirt, in which having dressed themselves, they accompanied us to the shore.

Our first care was to leave the dry sandy beach, which could afford us no discoveries in our science, and to examine the plantations, which from the ships had an enchanting appearance, notwithstanding the brownish cast which the time of the year had given. We found them indeed to answer the expectations we had formed of a country described as an elysium by M. de Bougainville. We entered a grove of bread trees, on most of which we saw no fruit at this season of winter, and followed a neat but narrow path, which led to different habitations, half-hid under various bushes. Tall cocopalms nodded to each other, and rose over the rest of the trees; the bananas displayed their beautiful large leaves, and now and then one of them still appeared loaded with its clustering fruit. A sort of shady trees, covered with a dark green foliage, bore golden apples, which resembled the anana in juiciness and flavor. Betwixt these the intermediate space was filled with young mulberry trees *(morus papyrifera,)* of which the bark is employed by the natives in the manufacture of their cloth; with several species of arum or eddies, with yams, sugarcanes, and other useful plants.

We found the cottages of the natives scattered at short distances, in the shade of fruit trees, and surrounded by various odoriferous shrubs, such as the gardenia, guettarda, and calophyllum. The neat simplicity of their structure gave us no less pleasure than the artless beauty of the grove which encompassed them. The pandang or palm-nut tree had given its long prickly leaves to thatch the roofs of the buildings, and these were supported by a few pillars made of the bread tree, which is thus useful in more respects than one. As a roof is sufficient to shelter the natives from rains and nightly dews, and as the climate of this island is perhaps one of the happiest in the world, the houses seldom have any walls, but are open on all sides. We saw, however, a few dwellings constructed for greater privacy, which were entirely enclosed in walls of reeds, connected together by transverse pieces of wood, so as to give us the idea of large bird cages. In these there was commonly a hole left for the entrance, which could be closed up with a board. Before every hut, on the green turf or on dry grass, we observed groups of inhabitants lying down or sitting in the eastern style, and passing their happy hours away in conversation or repose. Some of them got up at our approach, and joined the crowd that followed us; but great numbers, especially those of a mature age, remained in their attitude, and only pronounced a kind *tayo* as we passed by them. Our attendant crowd seeing us gather plants, were very ready to pluck and offer the same sorts to us, which they found attracted our notice. Indeed a variety of wild species sprang up amidst the plantations, in that beautiful disorder of nature, which is so truly admirable when checked by the hand of industry, and infinitely surpasses the trimness of regular gardens. Among them we found several species of grasses, which though thinner than in our northern countries, yet by growing always in the shade, looked fresh and formed a soft bed of verdure. The soil was by their means kept sufficiently moist to give nourishment to the trees, and both were in a thriving state, owing to the reciprocal assistance which they gave each other. Various little birds dwelled in the shade of the breadfruit and other trees, and had a very agreeable note, though common report among Europeans has denied the powers of harmony (I know not on what grounds) to the birds of warm climates. The heads of the tallest coco trees were the usual residence of a kind of very small parroquets of a beautiful sapphirine blue, while another sort of a greenish color, with a few red spots, were more common among the bananas, and appeared frequently tame in the houses of the natives, who seemed to value them for their red feathers. A king's fisher, of a dark green, with a collar of the same hue round his white throat, a large cuckoo, and several sorts of pigeons or doves, were frequently seen hopping from branch to branch, and a bluish heron gravely stalked along the seaside, picking up shellfish and worms. A fine brook, rolling over a bed of pebbles, came down a narrow valley, and supplied our waterers at its discharge into the sea. We followed its stream for a little while till we were met by a great crowd of natives at the heels of three men, dressed in various pieces of their red and yellow cloth, and provided with elegant turbans of the same. Each of them had a long stick or wand in his hand, and one of them was accompanied by a woman, whom upon inquiry we found to be his wife. We demanded what their appearance meant, and were answered they were the Te-apoonee; but when they observed we did not understand enough of their language to comprehend this term, they added that they were Tata-no-t'Eatooa, men belonging to the divinity, and to the maraï, or burying place; I suppose we might call them priests. We stopped with them some time, but as we did not see that any religious or other ceremony was performed, we returned to the beach. About noon Captain Cook reembarked with us, and with the two sons of O-Poòe without having seen Aheatua, who for reasons unknown to us, still refused to admit us to his presence.

The two young fellows sat down to dinner with us, and partook of the vegetables, but did not touch our salt provisions. After dinner, one of them took an opportunity of stealing a knife and a pewter spoon, not contented with a number of presents which he had received from the captain, without having made any return on his part, and which ought to have prevented him from infringing the laws of hospitality. The theft being discovered, he was kicked from the deck, jumped overboard, and swam to the next canoe, where he seated himself, perhaps in defiance of our power. Captain Cook fired a musket over his head, upon which he took to the water again, and overset the canoe. A second musket was leveled at him, but he dived when he saw the flash, and did the same when the *third* was discharged. Captain Cook now manned his boat, and went to take the canoe, under which the man took shelter; but he soon abandoned it, and swam to a double canoe near the first, which was accordingly pursued. This canoe however got ashore through the surf, and the natives on the beach took up stones, which they leveled at our boat's crew, who thought it advisable to retreat. However, a four pounder directed towards the shore frightened the inhabitants sufficiently so that our people could seize two large double canoes, and bring them alongside of the ship.

We left the ship after this disturbance in order to take an afternoon's walk ashore near the watering place, and to restore the confidence of the people, who had entirely forsaken us on account of our open hostilities. We pursued a different path from that which we had taken in the morning, and found great quantities of bananas, yams, eddies, etc., planted round every cottage, inhabited by friendly good-natured people, who seemed however a little more shy or reserved than usual, on account of what had happened. At last we arrived at a large house, neatly constructed of reeds, which we were told belonged to Aheatua, who was in another district at present. Here we saw a hog, and a couple of fowls, the first which the natives exposed to our sight, having hitherto been very careful to conceal them, and always refusing to part with them, under the pretext that they were the property of the aree or king. They made use of the same excuse at present, though we offered a hatchet, which in their eyes was the most valuable merchandise we had. After a short stay, we returned the same way we came, and brought a small collection of new plants on board. About sunset a boat was sent off, out of the harbor, to bury in the sea one Isaac Taylor, a marine, who died this morning of a complication of disorders. Ever since we had left England, this man had been feverish, consumptive, and asthmatic; his complaints always kept increasing, and at last turned to a dropsy, which carried him off. All our people on board were now well, except one, whose remarkable scorbutic habit of body always laid him up as soon as we came out to sea, where prophylactics and wort could but just keep him alive. However this man, as well as the *Adventure*'s crew, who were much affected with the scurvy when they came in here, recovered amazingly by walking onshore, and eating quantities of fresh fruit.

Early the next morning some of the natives came off to us in a small canoe, and begged for the restitution of those larger ones which had been taken from them on the day before. Captain Cook, who perceived the trade to have slackened in consequence of that seizure, none of the inhabitants coming to the ship, and few to the watering place, returned the canoes, as the best means to reconcile us to the confidence of the natives; and though the effects of his indulgence were not instantaneous, yet in a day or two our trade was perfectly reestablished.

After this peaceful prelude we went on shore, in pursuit of botanical discoveries. A smart shower of rain which had fallen overnight had cooled the air considerably, and made our walk extremely pleasant, before the sun could become troublesome. The whole country had profited by this rain, for every plant and tree seemed revived by it, and the groves exhaled a sweet refreshing smell. Whether it was owing to the early hour of our excursion, or to the beauty of the morning, our ear was saluted by the song of many small birds, which enlivened this delightful country. We had not walked far, when we heard a loud noise in the wood, which resembled the strokes of a carpenter's hammer. We followed the sound, and at last came to a small shed, where five or six women were sitting on both sides of a long square piece of timber, and beat the fibrous bark of the mulberry tree here, in order to manufacture it into cloth. The instrument they used for this purpose was a square wooden club, with longitudinal and parallel furrows, which run smaller and closer together on the different sides. They ceased a little while to give us time to examine the bark, the mallet, and the timber on which they performed their operations. They also showed us a kind of glutinous water in a coconut shell, which was made use of from time to time, to make the pieces of bark cohere together. This glue, which, as we understood, was made of the *hibiscus esculentus,* is indispensably necessary in the manufacture of those immense pieces of cloth, sometimes two or three yards wide, and fifty yards long, which are composed of little bits of bark, taken from trees never so thick as the wrist. We carefully examined their plantations of mulberry trees, but never found a single old one among them; as soon as they are of two years growth they are cut down, and new ones spring up from the root, for fortunately this tree is one of the most prolific in nature, and if suffered to grow till it flowered and could bear fruits, might perhaps totally overrun the country. The bark must always be taken from young trees; and these are carefully drawn into long stems, without any branches, except just at the top, so that the bark is as entire as possible. The method of preparing it before it comes under the mallet, we were not yet acquainted with at this time. The women employed in this manner were dressed in old and dirty rags of their cloth, and had very hard and callous hands. We proceeded a little farther up in a narrow valley, where a well-looking man invited us to sit down in the shade before his house. There was a little area paved with broadish stones, on which he spread banana leaves for us, and brought out a little stool made of the bread-tree wood, cut out of one piece, on which he desired one of us to sit down, whom he took to be the principal person. Seeing us all seated he ran into his house, and brought out a quantity of breadfruit baked, which he laid before us on fresh banana leaves. To this he added a matted basket full of the vee, or Taheitee apples, a fruit of the *spondias* genus, which resembles the anana, or pineapple, in the taste, and entreated us to partake of these refreshments. We breakfasted with a hearty appetite, sharpened by the exercise we had taken, the fine air of the morning, and the excellence of the provisions. We found the Taheitee method of dressing breadfruit and other victuals, with heated stones under ground, infinitely superior to our usual way of boiling them; in the former all the juices remained, and were concentrated by the heat; but in the latter, the fruit imbibed many watery particles, and lost a great deal of its fine flavor and mealiness. To conclude this treat our host brought us five fresh coconuts, which he opened by pulling the fibers off with his teeth. The cool limpid liquor contained in them he poured into a clean cup, made of a ripe coconut shell, and offered that to each of us in our turns. The people in this country had on all occasions been good-natured and friendly, and for beads sometimes sold us coconuts and fruit, if we called for them; but we had not yet seen an instance of hospitality exercised in so complete a manner during our short stay. We therefore thought it our duty to recompense our friend as much as lay in our power, and presented him with a number of transparent beads and iron nails, with which he was highly satisfied and contented.

We continued our walk into the country from this seat of patriarchal hospitality, notwithstanding the uneasiness which many of the natives expressed, among the crowd that followed us. When they saw us persist in our expedition, the greatest part of them dispersed to their different habitations, and only a few of them attended us, who made it their business to act as our guides. We came to the foot of the first hills, where we left the huts and plantations of the natives behind us, and ascended on a beaten path, passing through an uncultivated shrubbery mixed with several tall timber trees. Here we searched the most intricate parts, and found several plants and birds hitherto unknown to natural historians. With these little acquisitions we returned towards the sea, at which our friends the natives expressed their satisfaction. We found a vast concourse of inhabitants on the beach at our trading place, and saw that our people had bought a great quantity of large eddies and other roots, but few breadfruits, which were now very scarce, only a few trees bearing them so late in the season, while most of the others were already shooting forth the embryo of a new crop. The excessive heat of the sun now tempted us to bathe in a branch of the adjacent river, which formed a deep pond of some extent; and being refreshed with this bath we returned on board to dinner. In the afternoon we had heavy rains, attended with wind, during which the *Adventure* drove from her moorings, but was brought up again by a timely maneuver. This bad weather confined us on board, where we arranged the plants and animals which we had hitherto collected, and made drawings of such as were not known before. Our three days' excursions had supplied us only with a small number of species, which in an island so flourishing as Taheitee, gave a convincing proof of its high cultivation; for a few individual plants occupied that space, which in a country entirely left to itself, would have teemed with several hundred different kinds in wild disorder. The small size of the island, together with its vast distance from either the eastern or western continent, did not admit of a great variety of animals. We saw no other species of quadrupeds than hogs, and dogs which were domestic, and incredible numbers of rats, which the natives suffered to run about as pleasure, without ever trying to destroy them. We found however a tolerable number of birds, and when the natives gave themselves the trouble to fish, we commonly purchased a considerable variety of species, as this class of creatures can easily roam from one part of the ocean to the other, and particularly in the torrid zone, where certain sorts are general all round the world.

If the scarcity of spontaneous plants was unfavorable to the botanist, still it had the most salutary effects with regard to the whole company on board both our vessels, since their place was occupied by great quantities of wholesome vegetables. We daily bought an abundance of yams, eddies, and Taheitee apples; together with some bananas and breadfruit, which, on account of the season, were grown very scarce. The wholesome regimen which we had by this means been able to keep, had visibly, and I might almost say miraculously, operated to restore to their health all those who were ill of the scurvy at our arrival; and the only inconvenience we felt from it was a kind of flux, owing to the sudden change of diet, with which a few of the people were afflicted. Not content with this fortunate supply, we could not help casting longing eyes towards the hogs which we saw in great numbers on all our excursions into the country, though the natives were always careful to hide them in low sties, covered over with boards, forming a kind of platform, on which they sat or lay down. We tried all possible means to engage the people to sell some of them to us, and offered hatchets, shirts, and other goods of value to the Taheitians, but still without success, their constant answer being that these animals were the king's (*aree*'s) property. Instead of acquiescing in this refusal, and acknowledging the kind disposition of the natives, who furnished us at least with the means of recovering our strength, and restoring our sick, a proposal was made to the captains, by some persons in the ships, to sweep away by force a sufficient number of hogs for our use, and afterwards to return such a quantity of our goods in exchange to the natives, as we should think adequate to the spoil we had taken. This proposal, which nothing but the most most tyrannical principles, and the meanest selfishness could have dictated, was received with the contempt and indignation which it justly deserved.

Our acquisitions in natural history being hitherto so inconsiderable, we had leisure every day to ramble in the country in search of others, as well as to pick up various circumstances which might serve to throw a light on the character, manners, and present state of the inhabitants.

On the twentieth towards noon, I directed my walk, in company with several officers, to the eastern side of the harbor. We soon came to a rivulet, which was wide and deep enough to admit a canoe upon it, by means of which we ferried over to the opposite shore, where we perceived a house of some extent, among the bushes. Before it we saw a quantity of the finer sorts of Taheitee cloth spread out on the grass, which the natives told us, had been washed in the river; and close to the house, suspended on a pole, we observed a target of a semicircular form, made of wickerwork, and plaited strings (of the coconut fibres,) covered with the glossy bluish-green feathers of a kind of pigeon, and ornamented with many shark's teeth, displayed in three concentric semicircles; I inquired whether it was to be purchased, but was answered in the negative, and concluded that it was only exposed to the air, in the same manner as we are used to do from time to time, with things which we preserve in close boxes. A middle-aged man, who lay stretched at his case in the hut, invited us to sit down by him, and curiously examined my dress; he had long nails on his fingers, upon which he valued himself not a little, and which I found were a mark of distinction, since only such persons as had no occasion to work could suffer them to grow to that length. The Chinese have the same custom, and pride themselves as much in it; but whether the Taheitians derive it from them, or whether chance has led them both to the same idea, without any communication with each other, is possibly beyond the art of Needham and Des Guignes to determine. In different corners of the hut we saw some women and some men, separately eating their dinner of breadfruit and bananas, and both parties, as we approached them, desired us to partake of their provisions. The singular custom, which forces the sexes to shun each others' company at their meals, is already mentioned by former voyagers, who have been equally unsuccessful with ourselves in discovering its cause.

We left this hut, and strolled through an odoriferous shrubbery to another, where we found O-Taï, his wife, and children, and his sisters Maroya and Maroraï. The officer who had lost his bed sheets was with us, but thought it to no purpose to inquire for them, and rather tried to ingratiate himself with the fair one. Beads, nails, and various trifles were presented to her, which she readily accepted, but remained inexorable to the passionate solicitations of her lover. As she had in all probability obtained the possession of the sheets, which she coveted, and for which alone she could have submitted to prostitution, it seems nothing could afterwards tempt her to admit the transient embraces of a stranger. This is the most likely construction we could put upon her conduct, and it became more probable to us, when we considered that she belonged to a family of some note, and that, during Captain Cook's long stay on the island in the *Endeavour*, there had been few, if any, instances that women among the better sort of people had demeaned themselves so far.

After a short stay with them, I returned to our trading place, but finding all our boats gone off, ventured to embark in a single canoe, without an outrigger, and was safely brought on board the *Resolution* for a single bead, which was all I had left after this excursion.

At daybreak the next morning we went ashore again, on another walk to the eastward. We observed the plain to widen, as we advanced beyond the east point of Aitepèha harbor, and of course growing richer in breadfuit and coconut trees, bananas, and other vegetable productions, on most of which we saw the buds of a future crop. The houses of the natives were likewise found to be more numerous, and many seemed to us neater and newer than those near our anchoring place. In one of them, which was of the closer sort, walled in with reeds, we saw a great many bundles of cloth, and cases for targets suspended from the roof, all which, as well as the house itself, we were informed belonged to Aheatua. We walked about two miles in the most delightful groves or plantations of fruit trees, where the natives were just returning to their various employments. Among them we easily noticed the manufacturers of cloth, by the hollow sound of the mallet. However, it must not be supposed that the necessities of these people urgently required their constant application to work; for our appearance soon gathered a crowd of them about us, who followed us all day as far as we went, and sometimes even neglected their meals on our account. It was not without some interested motives that they attended upon us. Their general behavior toward us was good-natured, friendly, and I may say officious; but they watched every opportunity of conveying away some trifles with amazing dexterity, and many among them, whenever we returned the kind looks they gave us, or smiled upon them, thought that a proper time to take advantage of our good disposition, and immediately with a begging tone said, *tayo, pòë,* "friend, a bead!" which, whether we complied with or refused, did not alter their good temper. When these petitions became too frequent, we used to mock them, be repeating their words in the same tone, which always produced a general peal of good-humored laughter amongst them. Their conversation was commonly loud, and it seemed that our appearance was their principal topic; every newcomer was immediately made acquainted by the others with our names, which they reduced to a few vowels and softer consonants, and was entertained with a repetition of what we had said or done that morning. His first request was generally to hear a musket fired off, which we complied with on condition that he should show us a bird as a mark. However, we were frequently at a loss how to behave, when he pointed out a bird at four or five hundred yards distance, as they had no idea that the effects of our firearms were limited to a certain space. As it was not prudent to let them into this mystery, we always pretended that we could not see the bird, till we came near enough to shoot it. The first explosion frightened them considerably, and on some produced such violent consternation that they dropped down on the ground, or ran back about twenty yards from us, where they remained till we quieted their fears by professions of friendship, or till their more courageous brethren had picked up the bird which we had killed. But they soon became more familiar, and though they always expressed some sudden emotion, yet they conquered by degrees the appearance of fear.

Notwithstanding the friendly reception which we met with on all sides, the natives were very anxious to keep their hogs out of sight, and whenever we inquired for them seemed uneasy, and either told us they had none, or assured us they belonged to Aheatua their king. As we perceived their reluctance to part with these animals, we thought it best to take no further notice of them, and though we saw great numbers of them confined in pigsties almost in every hut, we pretended not to know that there were any, or not to care for them; this proceeding we always found had the good effect of increasing the confidence of the people towards us.

Having advanced a mile or two, we sat down on a few large stones, which formed a kind of paved area before one of the cottages, and desired the inhabitants to bring us some breadfruit and coconuts, in exchange for beads. They very readily supplied us with a quantity of each, on which we breakfasted. The crowd who followed us sat down at a distance from us, at our desire, in order that they might have no opportunity of snatching up any of our arms, or other apparatus, which we were obliged to lay out of our hands, while we made our meal. To add to our good cheer, we were presented with a coconut shell full of a kind of diminutive fresh fish, which the natives are used to eat raw, without any other sauce than salt water. We tasted them, and found them far from disagreeable;

however, as we were not used to eat them without being dressed, we distributed them, with the remains of the fruit, to our favorites among the crowd.

Thus refreshed, we continued our walk, but turned towards the hills, notwithstanding the importunities of the natives, who urged us to continue on the plain, which we easily perceived arose merely from their dislike of fatigue. We were not to be diverted from our purpose; but leaving behind us almost the whole crowd, we entered, with a few guides, a chasm between the two hills. There we found several wild plants which were new to us, and saw a number of little swallows flying over a fine brook, which rolled impetuously along. We walked up along its banks to a perpendicular rock, fringed with various tufted shrubberies, from whence it fell in a crystalline column, and was collected at the bottom into a smooth limpid pond, surrounded with many species of odoriferous flowers. This spot, where we had a prospect of the plain below us, and of the sea beyond it, was one of the most beautiful I had ever seen, and could not fail of bringing to remembrance the most fanciful descriptions of poets, which it eclipsed in beauty. In the shade of trees, whose branches hung over the water, we enjoyed a pleasant gale, which softened the heat of the day, and amidst the solemn uniform noise of the waterfall, which was but seldom interrupted by the whistling of birds, we sat down to describe our new acquisitions before they withered. Our Taheitian companions seeing us employed, likewise rested among the bushes, viewing us attentively and in profound silence. We could have been well pleased to have passed the whole day in this retirement; however, after finishing our notes, and feasting our eyes once more with the romantic scenery, we returned to the plain. Here we observed a great crowd of the natives coming toward us, and at their near approach perceived two of our shipmates, Mr. Hodges and Mr. Grindall, whom they surrounded and attended on their walk. We soon joined them, and resolved to continue our excursion together. A youth, of a very promising countenance, who had distinguished himself by showing a particular attachment for these gentlemen, was entrusted with Mr. Hodges's portfolio, where he preserved the sketches and designs, which he had frequent opportunities of making on his walk. No favor, or mark of affection could I believe have given this youth so much real pleasure, as the confidence they had placed in him, upon which he seemed to value himself among his countrymen. Perhaps this circumstance, joined to the peaceable appearance of our gentlemen, who walked without arms of any kind, had a general effect upon all the people that surrounded us, as their familiarity and affection seemed much increased. We entered a spacious hut together, where we saw a large family assembled. An old man, with a placid countenance, lay on a clean mat, and rested his head on a little stool, which served as a pillow. His head, which was truly venerable, was well furnished with fine locks of a silvery gray, and a thick beard as white as snow descended to his breast. His eyes were lively, and health sat on his full cheeks. His wrinkles, which characterize age with us, were few and not deep, for cares, trouble, and disappointment, which untimely furrow our brows, cannot be supposed to exist in this happy nation. Several little ones, whom we took to be his grandchildren, and who, according to the custom of the country, were perfectly naked, played with their aged ancestor, which his actions and looks convinced us that the simple way of living to which he had been used had not yet blunted his senses. Several well-made men and artless nymphs, in whom youth supplied the want of beauty, surrounded the old man, and as we came in seemed to be in conversation after a frugal meal. They desired us to sit down on the mats among them, and we did not give them time to repeat their invitation. Their curiosity, which had perhaps never before been gratified with the sight of strangers, now prompted them to examine our dress and our arms, without bestowing their attention longer than a moment on any single object. They admired our color, pressed our hands, seemed to wonder that we had no punctures on them, nor long nails on our fingers, and eagerly inquired for our names, which when known, they were happy to repeat. These names, as they pronounced them, were not so like the originals that an etymologist could easily have deduced them, but in return they were more harmonious, and easily pronounced. Forster was changed into *Mantara,* Hodges into *Oreo,* Grindall into *Terino,* Sparrman into *Pamanee,* and George into *Teoree.* The hospitality which we had found under every roof was not wanting here, and we were offered some coconuts and *e-vees* to quench our thirst after the last walk. One of the young men had a flute made of a bamboo, which had but three holes; he blew it with his nostrils, whilst another accompanied him with the voice. The whole music, both vocal and instrumental, consisted of three or four notes, which were between half and quarter notes, being neither whole tones nor semitones. The effect of these notes, without variety or order, was only a kind of drowsy hum, which could not indeed hurt the ear by its discordant sounds, but made no pleasing impression on our minds. It is surprising that the taste for music should be so general all over the world, when the ideas of harmony among different nations are so distinct! Charmed with the picture of real happiness, which was thus exhibited before us, Mr. Hodges filled his portfolio with several sketches, which will convey to future times the beauties of a scene, of which words give but a faint idea. While he was drawing, all the natives looked on with great attention, and were highly pleased to find out the resemblance between his performances and different persons among them. Our acquaintance with their language, which we were at great pains to improve, was as yet very imperfect, and deprived us of the pleasure which we might have received from a conversation with these good people. A few separate words, and an interlude of dumb mimicry, was all that we had to supply the place of a coherent speech. However, even this was sufficient to amuse the natives, and our docility and endeavors to please seemed to be at least as agreeable to them, as their social temper and willingness to give instruction appeared to us. The old man, without changing his attitude, and continuing to recline his head on the stool, asked us several little questions, such as the captain's name, the name of the country we came from, how long we should stay, whether we had our wives on board, etc. It seemed that he was already apprised of all these things by common report, but wished to have them confirmed from our own mouths. We satisfied his curiosity as well as we could on these points, and after distributing little presents of beads, medals, and other trifles to his family, we set forward once more on our excursion. The many pauses which we made at the hospitable huts of the natives always refreshed us so much that we felt no manner of inconvenience, and could with ease have walked round the whole island in the same manner. The plain at the foot of the mountains offered no impediment to our progress; on the contrary, its paths were well beaten, and its whole surface perfectly level, and covered in many places with a fine growth of grasses. Not a single noxious animal appeared to deter us, and not even a gnat or mosquito hummed unpleasantly about us, or made us apprehensive of its bite. The breadfruit groves, with their abundant foliage, intercepted the rays of the meridian sun, whose action was greatly mitigated by a fresh sea breeze. The inhabitants however, who were used to pass the middle of the day in repose, dropped off one by one in the bushes, so that only a few remained with us. After we had walked about two miles farther to the southeastward, we came to the seashore at a place where it formed a little inlet. Here, surrounded on all sides with plantations, we met with a glade or lawn, in the midst of which we saw a maraï (burying place) built up of three ranges of stones, like steps, each about three feet and a half in height, and covered with grasses, ferns, and small shrubs. Towards the country, at some distance from the building, there was an oblong enclosure round it made of stone, about three feet high, within which two or three solitary cocopalms and some young casuarinas, with their weeping branches, gave an air of solemnity and pleasing melancholy to the scene. At a little distance from the maraï, surrounded by a thick shrubbery, we saw an inconsiderable hut or shed, (tupapow,) where, on a kind of stage about breast high, a corpse was placed, covered with a white piece of cloth, which hung down in various folds. Young cocotrees and bananas were springing up, and dragon trees blossoming around it. Near this we saw another hut, where a quantity of eatables lay for the divinity, (eatua,) and a pole was stuck in the ground, on which we saw a dead bird wrapped in a piece of a mat. In this last hut, which stood on a small eminence, we observed a woman sitting in a pensive attitude, who got up at our approach and would not suffer us to come near her. We offered her a small present, but she refused to touch it. We understood from the natives who were with us that she belonged to the maraï, and that the dead corpse was also a woman's, whose obsequies the first perhaps was performing.

After Mr. Hodges had made several drawings we returned from this place, which had really something grand in its appearance, and seemed calculated to favor religious meditation. In our return we kept along the seashore, till we came to a spacious house, very pleasantly situated amidst a grove of low coco palms loaded with fruit. Two or three fried little fishes, which one of the natives sold us for a few beads, were here shared among us, to stay our appetite, grown very keen again since our breakfast. Several of our company likewise bathed in the sea, as a further refreshment in this warm climate, and having afterwards bought some pieces of cloth, (*ahow*'s) of the country fabric, dressed in them, after the Taheitee fashion, to the infinite pleasure of the natives. Our walk continued along the shore beyond another maraï, much like the first, to a neat house, where a very fat man, who seemed to be a chief of the district, was lolling on his wooden pillow. Before him two servants were preparing his dessert by beating up with water some breadfruit and bananas in a large wooden bowl, and mixing with it a quantity of the fermented sour paste of breadfruit (called *maheî*.) The consistence of this mixture was such that it could properly be called a drink, and the instrument with which they made it, was a pestle of a black polished stone, which appeared to be a kind of basalt. While this was doing, a woman who sat down near him crammed down his throat by handfuls the remains of a large baked fish, and several breadfruits, which he swallowed with a voracious appetite. His countenance was the picture of phlegmatic insensibility, and seemed to witness that all his thoughts centered in the care of his paunch. He scarce deigned to look at us, and a few monosyllables which he uttered were only directed to remind his feeders of their duty, when we attracted their attention. The great degree of satisfaction which we had enjoyed on our different walks in this island, and particularly the pleasure of this day's excursion, was diminished by the appearance and behavior of the chief, and the reflections which naturally arose from thence. We had flattered ourselves with the pleasing fancy of having found at least one little spot of the world, where a whole nation, without being lawless barbarians, aimed at a certain frugal equality in their way of living, and whose hours of enjoyment were justly proportioned to those of labor and rest. Our disappointment was therefore very great, when we saw a luxurious individual spending his life in the most sluggish inactivity, and without one benefit to society, like the privileged parasites of more civilized climates, fattening on the superfluous produce of the soil, of which he robbed the laboring multitude. His indolence, in some degree, resembled that which is frequent in India and the adjacent kingdoms of the East, and deserved every mark of indignation which Sir John Mandeville expressed in his Asiatic travels. That worthy knight, who, topful of chivalry, and the valorous spirit of his time, devoted his life to constant activity, was highly incensed at the sight of a monster of laziness, who passed his days "withouten doynge of ony dedes of armes," and lived "everemore thus in ese, as a swyn that is fedde in sty, for to ben made fatte."

On leaving this Taheitian drone we separated, and I accompanied Messrs. Hodges and Grindall, whose good-natured friend, the carrier of the portfolio, had earnestly invited us to his habitation. We arrived there toward five in the evening, and found it a small but cleanly cottage, before which a great abundance of fresh leaves were spread on a stony place, and a prodigious quantity of the best coconuts and well-roasted breadfruit were laid out in fine order. He immediately ran to two elderly persons, who were busy in frightening the rats from this plentiful store of provisions, and introduced them to us as his parents. They expressed great joy on seeing the friends of their son, and entreated us to sit down to the meal which lay before us. We were at first struck with astonishment on finding it entirely prepared at our arrival, but we soon recollected that our friend had sent off one of his comrades several hours beforehand, very probably with directions to provide for our entertainment. As this was the first regular meal to which we sat down this day, it will easily be conceived that we fell to with a good appetite, and gave infinite satisfaction to the good-natured old people and the generous-minded youth, who all seemed to think themselves happy in the honor which we did to their excellent cheer. With such a venerable pair ministering to us, if I may be allowed to indulge in a poetical idea, we ran some risk of forgetting that we were men, and might have believed ourselves feasted by the hospitable Baucis and Philemon, if our inability to reward them had not reminded us of mortality. However, all the beads and nails which we could muster amongst us were offered to them, rather as a mark that we preserved a grateful sense of their good heart, than as any retribution. The youth went on with us to the beach opposite to our vessels, and brought on board a great quantity of provisions, which we had left unconsumed at our dinner. He was there presented with a hatchet, a shirt, and various articles of less value by his friends, and returned that very evening on shore to his parents, being probably enriched beyond his warmest expectation.

The usual trade had been carried on about the ships, and on the beach opposite to them, during our absence, without any material incident, except Captain Cook's meeting with *Tuahow*, the same native who had accompanied him a considerable way when he made the circuit of Taheitee in a boat, in the course of his first voyage. We found him and two of his countrymen on board at our return, they having resolved to take up their night's lodging with us, which, though usual at Matavaï Bay during the *Endeavour*'s voyage, none had hitherto ventured upon in this place. Tuahow being already familiarized with our way of living, and acquainted with the various objects which commonly struck his countrymen with wonder, eagerly entered into discourse with us, as he found us attentive to his questions. He inquired after *Tabane,* Mr. Banks; *Tolano,* Dr. Solander; *Tupaya,* (Tupia) and several persons in the *Endeavour* whose names he recollected. He rejoiced to hear that Mr. Banks and Dr. Solander were well, and having often renewed his question, always received the same answer to it; upon which he asked whether they would not come back to Taheitee, accompanying it with a look which strongly expressed the wish of seeing them again. When he heard of Tupaya's death, he was desirous of being informed whether it had been violent or natural, and was well pleased to hear from such circumstances as we could by broken words and signs communicate to him, that sickness had put a period to his life. In return, we questioned him concerning the death of *Tootahàh,* who had appeared as the acting chief of the island in Captain Cook's former voyage. We plainly understood that a great naval fight had happened between that chief and old *Aheatua,* the father of the present king of Tiarraboo, in which neither party had gained a decisive advantage; but that Tootahàh afterwards marching his army across the isthmus, which separates the two peninsulas, had been defeated in an obstinate engagement, in which himself, Tuboraï-Tamaide, and many other persons of distinction on his side were slain. A peace was soon after concluded with *O-Too* the king of O-Taheitee, who, after Tootahàh's decease, had assumed the power of the sovereignty, of which before he had only enjoyed the title. Old Aheatua, according to Tuahow's account, died but a few months after this peace, and his son, of the same name, who, according to the custom of this country, had already, during his father's lifetime, borne the title of *te-aree* (the king,) and received the honors annexed to that dignity, now likewise succeeded to its more essential part, the management of affairs.

This subject being exhausted, we took out the map of O-Taheitee, (engraved for captain Cook's former voyage) and laid it before Tuahow, without telling him what it was. He was however too good a pilot not to find it out presently; and overjoyed to see a representation of his own country, immediately with his finger pointed out the situation of all the whennuas, or districts, upon it, naming them at the same time in their order, as we saw them written on the chart. When he came to O-Whai-urua, the next district with a harbor, to the south of our present anchoring place, he pulled us by the arm to look on attentively, and related that there had been a ship (paheï) which he called paheï no Peppe, and which had lain there five days; that the people in her had received ten hogs from the natives, and that one of the crew ran away from the ship, and now lived upon the island. From this account we concluded that the Spaniards had sent another vessel to examine O-Taheitee, probably first discovered by their navigators, and which of late years had been so frequently visited by the English, as might justly rouse their attention, on account of the proximity of their own extensive possessions in South America. Strange as it may seem, the name of Peppe confirmed us in our conjectures, notwithstanding its vast difference from España, from whence we supposed it originated; because we were by this time well acquainted with the custom of mutilating all foreign names, which the Taheitians possess, even in a higher degree than the French and English. We put several questions relative to this ship to Tuahow, but could never obtain any farther intelligence from him, except that the man who had left it always accompanied Aheatua, and had given him the advice not to furnish us with any hogs. Whatever self-interested or bigoted motives that man may have had to give Aheatua such an advice, yet it seems to have been in reality the most friendly and valuable which he could have offered to his protector. The way to keep the riches of his subjects, among which are their hogs in the country, and to prevent new wants from prevailing among a happy people, was to get rid of us as soon as he could, by denying us the refreshments of which we stood most in need. It were indeed sincerely to be wished that the intercourse which has lately subsisted between Europeans and the natives of the South Sea islands may be broken off in time, before the corruption of manners which unhappily characterizes civilized regions may reach that innocent race of men, who live here fortunate in their ignorance and simplicity. But it is a melancholy truth that the dictates of philanthropy do not harmonize with the political systems of Europe!

Several of our people having taken a walk on shore, the next day returned on board with the news that they had met with Aheatua, who was at last come to this district in order to give us an audience. They had been admitted into his presence without any ceremony, and his majesty, in the midst of all his court, had given up one-half of his stool *(pappa),* to Mr. Smith, one of our mates, who was of the party. He had at the same time graciously assured him that he wished to speak to Captain Cook, and had as many hogs to give him as *he* had hatchets to pay for them, which was by far the most agreeable news we had heard for some time. They also reported that they had seen a man resembling a European in color and feature, but that upon speaking to him, he had retired into the crowd. Whether this was really a European, or whether the story which Tuahow had told us the evening before had wrought upon the fancy of our men we cannot determine; so much however is certain, that none of us ever saw him afterwards.

In consequence of Aheatua's declaration, the captains, with several officers, Dr. Sparrman, my father, and myself, went on shore early on the twenty-third. We proceeded about a mile along the river from which we filled our casks, being conducted by Opao, one of the natives, who had lodged on board. A great crowd coming down towards us, those who surrounded us pulled off their upper garments, so as to uncover their shoulders, which is a mark of respect due to the king. We presently joined the crowd, in the midst of whom Aheatua sat down on a large stool, cut out of solid wood, which one of his people had hitherto carried. He immediately recollected Captain Cook, and made room for him on his stool, while Captain Furneaux, and the rest of us, chose large stones for our seats. An immense number of natives thronged about us on all sides, and included us in a very narrow circle, increasing the heat to such a degree that the king's attendants were frequently obliged to keep them back, by beating them.

O-*Aheatua,* the king of O-Taheitee-eetee, (Little Taheitee) which is otherwise called Tiarraboo, was a youth of seventeen or eighteen years of age, well made, about five feet six inches high, and likely to grow taller. His countenance was mild, but unmeaning; and rather expressed some signs of fear and distrust at our first meeting, which suited ill with the ideas of majesty, and yet are often the characteristics of lawless power. His color was of the fairest of his people, and his lank hair of a light brown, turning into reddish at the tips, or being what is commonly called sandy. He wore at present no other dress than a white sash, *(marro)* round the waist to the knees, made of the best kind of cloth, and his head as well as all the rest of his body was uncovered. On both sides of him sat several chiefs and nobles, distinguishable by their superior stature, which is the natural effect of the immense quantity of food which they consume. One of them was punctured in a surprising manner, which we had never seen before, large black blotches of various shapes, almost covering his arms, legs, and sides. This man, whose name was E-Tee, was also remarkable for his enormous corpulence, and for the deference which the *aree* (king) paid to him, consulting him almost upon every occasion. The king, during the time he sat on the stool, which was his throne, preserved a grave or rather stiff deportment, scarce to be expected at his years, though it seemed to be studied and assumed, only to make our meeting more solemn. This may be looked upon as a kind of recommendation by some men, but it is unhappily a mask of hypocrisy, which we should hardly have expected at Tahiti. After the first salutation, Captain Cook presented Aheatua with a piece of red baize, a bed sheet, a broad ax, a knife, nails, looking glasses, and beads; and my father gave him similar presents, among which was an aigrette, or tuft of feathers fixed on a wire and dyed of a bright crimson; upon this his majesty set a particular value, and at the sight of it the whole crowd gave a general shout of admiration, expressed by the word *awhay!* The king now inquired for Mr. Banks, which only Tuahow had done before him, and then asked how long we intended to stay, expressing at the same time that he wished we might remain five months. Captain Cook's answer was that as he did not receive sufficient supplies of provisions, he must sail immediately. The king confined his first request to one month, and at last to five days, but Captain Cook persisted in his resolution; Aheatua then promised to send us hogs the next day, but as this had been repeatedly said without any consequence, we took no notice of it now; for even in a state so little refined as Tiarraboo, we found that the real benevolence of the middle class, which manifested itself towards us in hospitality and a number of good and noble actions, gave us no right to trust the specious politeness of the court and courtiers, who fed our hopes with empty promises.

During this conference the crowd, amounting at least to five hundred persons, was so excessively noisy, that it was impossible at times to distinguish a word; and on those occasions some of the king's attendants with a Stentor's voice called out *mamoò!* (be silent!) and enforced his command by dealing out hearty blows with a long stick. The aree, seeing that Captain Cook was not to be persuaded to prolong his stay in this harbor, got up, and walked down along the river with us, while his attendants carried his wooden stool, and the kingly presents which he had received. On this walk he laid aside the gravity, which was not natural to him, and talked with great affability to our common people. He desired me to tell him the names of all the persons from on board both sloops, who were present, to which he added the question, whether they had their wives on board. Being answered in the negative, his majesty in a fit of good humor desired them to look for partners among the daughters of the land, which they understood it was meant at present, in the light of a mere compliment. He sat down soon after close to a house of reeds, into which we all retired, when the sun appeared through the clouds. Here he called for some coconuts, and began to tell the story of the *Paheï no Peppe,* or Spanish ship, of which Tuahow had given us the first intimation. According to the king's account it seemed clear that the ship had been at Whaï-Urua five months before us, and had lain there ten days. He added that the captain had hanged four of his people, and that the fifth had escaped the same punishment by running away. This European, whom they named O-Pahoòtu, we inquired after to no purpose, for a long while; till his majesty's attendants seeing us very eager to become acquainted with him, assured us he was dead. We have since heard that about the time mentioned by the natives, Don Domingo Buenechea, sent out from the port of Callao in Peru, had visited O-Taheitee, but what the particulars of that voyage are has never transpired. While we remained in the house E-Tee, the fat chief, who seemed to be the principal counselor of the king, very seriously asked us whether we had a God *(Eatuâ)* in our country, and whether we prayed to him *(epoore?)* When we told him that we acknowledged a Divinity, who had made everything, and was invisible, and that we also were accustomed to address our petitions to him, he seemed to be highly pleased, and repeated our words with notes of his own to several persons who sat round him. To us he seemed to signify that the ideas of his countrymen corresponded with ours in this respect. Everything concurs indeed to convince us that this simple and only just conception of the Deity has been familiar to mankind in all ages and in all countries, and that only by the excessive cunning of a few individuals, those complex systems of absurd idolatry have been invented, which disgrace the history of almost every people. The love of empire, or the pursuit after voluptuousness and indolence, seem to have inspired the numerous branches of heathen priests with the idea of keeping the minds of the people in awe, by awakening their superstition. The natural love of the miraculous has made it easy for them not only to put their projects in execution, but likewise to weave their prejudices so firmly into the web of human knowledge, that to this moment the greater part of mankind pay them homage, and blindly suffer themselves to be cheated in the grossest manner.

While E-Tee was conversing on religious matters, King Aheatua was playing with Captain Cook's watch. After curiously examining the motion of so many wheels, that seemed to move as it were spontaneously, and showing his astonishment at the noise it made, which he could not express otherwise than by saying it "spoke" *(parou,)* he returned it, and asked what it was good for. With a great deal of difficulty we made him conceive that it measured the day, similar to the sun, by whose altitude in the heavens he and his people are used to divide their time. After this explanation, he called it a little sun, to show us that he perfectly understood our meaning. We were just getting up to return towards the beach, when a man arrived who brought a hog along with him, which the king presented to the captain, at the same time promising to give him another. With this small beginning we rested satisfied, and taking our leave, without any troublesome ceremony, only pronouncing a hearty *tayo* (friend), which had more meaning in it than many a studied speech, we returned on board.

In the afternoon the captains went onshore with us again to the king, whom we found where we had left him in the morning. He took that opportunity of requesting the captains again to prolong their stay at least a few days; but he received the same answer as before, and was plainy told that his refusing to provide us with livestock was the reason of their intended departure. Upon this he immediately sent for two hogs, and presented one to each of the captains, for which he received some ironwares in return. A Highlander, who was one of our marines, was ordered to play the bagpipe, and its uncouth music, though almost insufferable to our ears, delighted the king and his subjects to a degree which we could hardly have imagined possible. The distrust which we perceived in his looks at our first interview was now worn off; and if we had stayed long enough, an unreserved confidence might have taken its place, to which his youth and good nature seemed to make him inclinable. The studied gravity which he had then affected was likewise laid aside at present, and some of his actions rather partook of puerility, among which I cannot help mentioning his amusement of chopping little sticks and cutting down plantations of bananas with one of our hatchets. But, instead of cultivating any farther acquaintance with him, we took our last leave towards the close of the evening, and returned to the sloops, which unmoored before night.

The inhabitants, seeing us prepare for sailing the next morning, came off in a vast number of small canoes, loaded with coconuts and other vegetable provisions, which they sold excessively cheap, rather than miss the last opportunity of obtaining European goods. The taste for baubles, which unaccountably prevails all over the world in different degrees, was so extravagant here, that a single bead was eagerly purchased with a dozen of the finest coconuts, and sometimes preferred even to a nail, though the last might be of some use, and the bead could serve merely as an insignificant ornament. We observed that the trade was carried on much fairer this time than at our arrival, the natives being perhaps apprehensive that any little fraud might break off a commerce, in which they now appeared deeply interested. They accompanied us for this purpose till we were a mile or two without the reefs, and then returned to the beach, where we had left Lieutenant Pickersgill with a boat, in order to take advantage of their present disposition.

We were now able to breathe a little, after the continual hurry which had been the necessary consequence of the multiplicity of new objects around us, and of the short space of time which we had to observe them. This interval of repose was the more acceptable, as it gave us leisure to indulge the reflections which had crowded upon us during our stay. The result of these was a conviction, that this island is indeed one of the happiest spots on the globe. The rocks of New Zealand appeared at first in a favorable light to our eyes, long tired with the constant view of sea, and ice, and sky; but time served to undeceive us, and gave us daily cause of dislike, till we formed a just conception of that rude chaotic country. But O-Taheitee, which had presented a pleasing prospect at a distance, and displayed its beauty as we approached, became more enchanting to us at every excursion which we made on its plains. Our long run out of sight of land might have been supposed at first to have had the same effect as at New Zealand; but our stay confirmed instead of destroying the emotions which we had felt at the first sight; even though we had no room to be so well pleased with the refreshments we had obtained, which were not by far so plentiful as the fish and wildfowl of New Zealand, and still obliged us to have recourse to salt provisions. The season of the year, which answered to our month of February, had naturally brought on a scarcity of fruits; for though it does not manifest itself here by refrigerating the air, as in countries remote from the tropics, yet it is the season when all vegetation recovers the juices which have formed the late crop, and prepares them for a new one. At this time several trees entirely shed their leaves, several plants died away to the very root, and the remaining ones looked parched on account of the want of rain, which commonly takes place then, because the sun is in the opposite hemisphere. The whole plain therefore was arrayed in a sober brownish and sometimes sallow color. Only the lofty mountains preserved richer tints in their forests, which are supplied with more moisture from the clouds that hang on their summits almost every day. From thence, among other things, the natives brought great quantities of wild plantanes (*vehee*), and that perfumed wood (*e-ahai*), with which they give their coconut oil (*monòë*) a very fragrant smell. The shattered state in which we saw the tops of these mountains seemed to have been the work of an earthquake; and the lavas, of which many of the mountains consist, and of which the natives make several tools, convinced us of the existence of former volcanoes on this island. The rich soil of the plains, which is a vegetable mold, mixed with volcanic decays, and a black irony sand, which is often found at the foot of the hills, are further proofs of this assertion. The exterior ranges of hills are sometimes entirely barren, and contain a great quantity of yellowish clay, mixed with iron ochre; but others are covered with mold, and wooded like the higher mountains. Pieces of quartz are sometimes met with here, but we never saw indications of precious minerals or metals of any kind, iron excepted, and of that there were but small remains in the lavas which we picked up; but the mountains may perhaps contain some iron ore rich enough for fusion. As to the piece of saltpeter, as big as an egg, which Captain Wallis mentions as a product of Tahitee, with all respect for his nautical abilities, I beg leave to doubt of its existence, since native saltpeter has never yet been found in solid lumps, as appears from Cronstedt's Mineralogy.

The view of O-Taheitee, along which we now sailed to the northward, suggested these cursory observations on its fossil productions, while our eyes remained eagerly fixed on the spot which had afforded us such a fund of real amusement and instruction. Our reflections were only interrupted by the summons to dine on fresh pork, which was instantly obeyed with an alacrity that sufficiently proved our long abstinence. We were agreeably surprised to find this pork entirely free from the luscious richness which makes it resist the stomach so soon in Europe; the fat was to be compared to marrow, and the lean had almost the tender taste of veal. The vegetable diet which the hogs are used to at O-Taheitee seems to be the principal cause of this difference, and may have had some influence even on the natural instincts of these animals. They were of that small breed which is commonly called the Chinese, and had not those pendulous ears, which, according to the ingenious count de Buffon, are the characters of slavery in animals. They were likewise much cleanlier than our European hogs, and did not seem to have that singular custom of wallowing in the mire. It is certain that these animals are a part of the real riches of the Taheitians, and we saw great numbers of them at Aitepeha, though the natives took great pains to conceal them. But they are so far from being their principal dependence, that I believe their total extirpation would be no great loss, especially as they are now entirely the property of the chiefs. They kill their hogs very seldom, perhaps only on certain solemn occasions; but at those times the chiefs eat pork with the same unbounded greediness with which certain sets of men are reproached at the turtle feasts in England; while the common sort rarely if ever taste a little bit, which is always held as a great dainty among them. Notwithstanding this, all the trouble of breeding, bringing up, and fattening the hogs is allotted to the lowest class of people.

We were becalmed in the evening, and during a great part of the night, but had a southeast wind the next morning, so that we stood in shore again, in sight of the northernmost part of O-Taheitee, and of the adjacent isle of Eimeo. The mountains here formed larger masses, which had a more grand effect than at Aitepeha. The slopes of the lower hills were likewise more considerable, though almost entirely destitute of trees or verdure; and the ambient border of level land was much more extensive hereabouts, and seemed in some places to be above a mile broad. Towards ten o'clock we had the pleasure to see several canoes coming off from the shore towards us. Their long narrow sails, consisting of several mats sowed together, their streamers of feathers, and the heap of coconuts and bananas on board, had all together a picturesque appearance. For a few beads and nails they disposed of their cargoes, and returned on shore to take in another. About noon our boat arrived with Lieutenant Pickersgill, who had been very successful in trading at Aitepeha, having purchased nine hogs and a quantity of fruit. His majesty, Aheatua, had been present at the trading place the whole time, and after seating himself near the heap of ironwares, which our people had brought on shore, desired to market for them, and was extremely equitable in giving hatchets of different kinds for hogs of proportionate sizes. In the intervals however, he amused himself as he had done the evening before, with chopping small sticks, with which our sailors were much entertained, and after their manner made many shrewd observations on triflers. Mr. Pickersgill, having expended his stock in trade, put off from Aitepeha in the afternoon, and came the same evening to Hiddea, the district of O-Rettee (Ereti) where M. de Bougainville lay at an anchor in 1768. Here he was hospitably entertained by the worthy old chief, who is so justly celebrated by that gallant French navigator; and the next morning his brother Tarooree embarked with our officer, in order to visit the ships which they saw in the offing. When he came on board we found he had a kind of impediment in his organs of speech, by which means he substituted a *K* wherever the language required a *T;* a fault which we afterwards observed in several other individuals. He favored us with his company at dinner, as well as another native named O-Wahow, who was the first that had come aboard from this part of the island, and to whom my father had immediately presented a few beads and a small nail, merely to try his disposition. In return he produced a fishhook neatly made of mother of pearl, which he gave to his new friend. A larger nail was the reward of this good-natured action; and on the receipt of this he sent his boy to the shore in his canoe. Towards four o'clock the canoe returned, and brought on board this man's brother, and a present of a number of coconuts, several bunches of bananas, and a clothing mat. There was something so generous in O-Wahow's way of acting, above all the little ideas of bartering, that we could not fail to express the highest regard for him. A much more considerable present was returned to him, rather to confirm him in his noble sentiments, than as a compensation for his gift. With that he retired in the evening, promising to return to us again, and expressing such extravagant emotions of joy as are commonly the effects of unexpected good fortune.

In the meanwhile we gradually approached the shore, a faint breeze helping us on, and the evening sun illuminating the landscape with the richest golden tints. We now discerned that long projecting point, which from the observation made upon it had been named Point Venus, and easily agreed that this was by far the most beautiful part of the island. The district of Mataväi, which now opened to our view, exhibited a plain of such an extent as we had not expected, and the valley which we traced running up between the mountains was itself a very spacious grove, compared to the little narrow glens in Tiarraboo. We hauled round the point about three o'clock, and saw it crowded with a prodigious number of people, who gazed at us with fixed attention; but as soon as we came to an anchor, in the fine bay which it shelters, the greater part of them ran very precipitately round the whole beach, and across One-tree-hill to O-Parre, the next district to the westward. Among the whole crowd, we saw only a single man whose shoulders were covered with a garment, and he, according to our friend O-Wahow's testimony, was O-Too, the king of O-Taheitee-Nue (the Greater Taheitee). His person was tall, and very advantageously proportioned, but he ran very nimbly along with his subjects, which the natives on board attributed to his apprehensions on our account.

Though it was near sunset when we came to an anchor, yet our decks were in a short time crowded with natives of all ranks, who recognized their old friends in many of our officers and sailors, with a degree of reciprocal joy which cannot easily be described. Among them was the old, venerable O-Whaw, whose peaceable character and good offices to our people are taken notice of in the account of Lieutenant Cook's first voyage, particularly upon the occasion when one of the natives was murdered. He immediately recollected Mr. Pickersgill, and calling him by his Taheitean name, Petrodero, enumerated on his fingers that this was the third visit he made to the island, that gentleman having been here both in the *Dolphin* and the *Endeavour*. A chief, named Maratata, paid Captain Cook a visit with his lady, (Tedua)-Erararee, who was a very good-looking young woman, and both received a number of presents, though it appeared that these were their sole motives for coming on board. A very tall, fat man, the father-in-law of Maratata, accompanied them, and was equally fortunate in collecting presents amongst us, which he took no other method to obtain, than downright begging. They all exchanged names with us in sign of friendship, everyone choosing a particular friend, to whom he was attached; customs which we had never observed in our former anchoring place, where the natives were infinitely more reserved, and in some degree diffident of our intentions. Towards seven o'clock they left the ship, not without promising to return the next morning, which, from the good reception they had met with, did not seem to admit of a doubt.

All night the moon shone clear in a cloudless sky, and silvered over the polished surface of the sea, while the landscape lay before us like the gay production of a fertile and elegant fancy. A perfect silence reigned in the air, which was agreeably interrupted by the voices of several natives that had remained on board, and enjoyed the beauty of the night with their friends, whom they had known in a former voyage. They were seated at the sides of the vessel, and discoursed on several topics, making their words more intelligible by different signs. We listened to them, and found that they chiefly put questions concerning what had happened to our people since their last separation, and gave accounts in their turn of the tragical fate of Tootahah, and his friends. Gibson, the marine, who was so much delighted with this island in Captain Cook's former voyage that he made an attempt to stay behind, was now chiefly engaged in this conversation, as he understood more of the language than the rest of the crew, and was on that account greatly valued by the natives. The confidence which these people placed in us, and their familiar, unreserved behavior, gave us infinite satisfaction, as it contrasted so well with the conduct of the people of Aitepeha. We now saw the character of the natives in a more favorable light than ever, and were convinced that the remembrance of injuries, and the spirit of revenge, did not enter into the composition of the good and simple Taheitians. It must surely be a comfortable reflection to every sensible mind, that philanthropy seems to be natural to mankind, and that the savage ideas of distrust, malevolence, and revenge, are only the consequences of a gradual depravation of manners. There are few instances where people, who are not absolutely sunk to a state of barbarism, have acted contrary to this general peaceable principle. The discoveries of Columbus, Cortez, and Pizarro in America, and those of Mendanna, Quiros, Schouten, Tasman, and Wallis in the South Sea, agree in this particular. It is highly probable that the attack which the Taheitians made upon the *Dolphin* took its origin from some outrage unknowingly committed by the Europeans; and supposing it did not, if self-preservation be one of the first laws of nature, surely from all appearances these people had a right to look on our men as a set of invaders, and what is more than all, to be apprehensive that even their liberty was at stake. When, after a fatal display of superior European force, they were convinced that nothing farther than a short stay for refreshment was intended, that the strangers who came among them were not entirely destitute of humane and equitable sentiments; in short, when they found that Britons were not more savage than themselves, they were ready to open their arms to them, they forgot that they had had a difference, and bid them partake of each kindly production of their isle. They all exerted themselves in acts of hospitality and testimonies of friendship from the lowest subject to the queen, that every one of their guests might have reason to say, he regretted his departure from this friendly shore:

> Invitus, regina, tuo de litore cessi!
> Virgil.

Glossary

Adventure. See **Cook.**

Anana. Pineapple.

Arum. A genus of herbs in Europe an Asia; a plant of the Araceae family; a starch obtained from cuckoopint root.

Banks, Sir Joseph (1743–1820). British naturalist who accompanied Captain Cook on the latter's first voyage around the world.

Basalt. Dark gray to black igneous rock.

Baucis and Philemon. In Greek mythology, a poor elderly couple that showed warm hospitality to the gods Zeus and Mercury, who were disguised as humans but revealed their divine identity by never letting the two old people's pitcher run out of wine. Zeus rewarded their generosity by turning their humble house into a temple and by changing them into two intertwined trees at the moment of the death that they wanted to share no less than their long life together.

Black nightshade. A cosmopolitan weed with poisonous foliage, white flowers, and edible black berries.

Bougainville, Louis-Antoine de (1729–1811). French navigator; made a voyage around the world in 1767–69, visiting Tahiti and other islands in the Pacific. He described that trip in his *Description d'un voyage autour du monde* (1771–72), which helped popularize Rousseau's theories on the morality of human beings in their natural state, uncorrupted by civilization.

Buenechea, Don Domingo de (d. 1775). Spanish explorer and navigator.

Buffon, Georges-Louis Leclerc, comte de (1707–88). French naturalist and author of the monumental *Histoire naturelle* (1749–1804), a popular and brilliantly written compendium of data on natural history interspersed with his own speculations and theories.

Casuarina. A genus of trees, shrubs, and woody plants.

Clerke, Charles (1743–79). Lieutenant aboard the *Resolution.*

Cook, James (1728–79). English explorer and navigator who sailed the *Endeavour* to Tahiti in 1768 during an expedition to chart the transit of Venus. He visited the South Pacific again from 1772–75 aboard the *Resolution* and *Adventure*. A third trip there began in 1776. The journals that he kept during the first trip were published in 1773 by the English author John Hawkesworth (1719–73).

Corallines. A genus of red algae that sometimes forms colored deposits like coral and that contributes to reef formation; any animal that resembles a coral.

Cortez, Hernando, or Cortés, Hernán (1485–1547). Spanish conquistador, conqueror of Mexico, defeated Montezuma and the Aztecs.

Cronstedt, Axel Fredrik, Baron (1722–65). Swedish mineralogist and chemist who wrote *An Essay towards a System of Mineralogy* (1758).

Des Guignes, Joseph (1721–1800). French orientalist.

"Devenere locos laetos . . ." See Virgil.

Dolphin. Ship belonging to expedition led by Samuel Wallis. See **Tahiti.**

Dropsy. Edema, an abnormal swelling or distention in the connective tissue of the body, usually associated with defective circulation.

Eddy. Eddyroot, taro; an edible tuber that is a food staple in the tropics.

Elysium. According the the Greeks and Romans, the dwelling place of happy souls after death.

Endeavour. See **Cook.**

Flux. An excessive and abnormal discharge from the bowels; diarrhea, dysentery.

Frustum. Part of a solid (as a cone or pyramid) intersected between two planes that are either parallel or sometimes inclined to each other.

Furneaux, Tobias (1735–81). Captain of the *Adventure.*

Grindall, Richard (1750–1820). Sailor on the *Resolution,* later vice admiral.

Hibiscus esculentus. A kind of hibiscus—a genus of herbs, shrubs, and small trees—related to hollyhock.

Hodges, William (1744–97). English landscape painter.

Hymen. Greek god of marriage.

"Invitus, regina. . . ." See **Virgil.**

Mandeville, Sir John. Fourteenth-century English author of *The Travels of Sir John Mandeville,* a travel romance completed by 1356, enormously popular, and translated into most European languages. The book claims to be an authentic account of his own travels through the Near and Far East but is actually compiled from the writings of other explorers, such as Marco Polo.

Mendanna. See Quiros.

Mestizo. Mixed blood; person of mixed European and non-Caucasian stock; one of European and American Indian ancestry.

Needham, John Turberville (1713–81). English naturalist.

Pandang. Pandanus, a genus of tropical trees having slender stems like those of palms.

Pickersgill, Richard (1749–79). Third lieutenant and lieutenant-at-arms aboard the *Resolution.*

Pizarro, Francisco (c. 1476–1541). Spanish conquistador, conqueror of Peru and the Incas.

Point Venus. Point on Tahiti from which Captain (then Lieutenant) Cook charted the transit of Venus on his first voyage to the South Seas.

Quirós (or Queirós), Pedro Fernandes de (c. 1560–1614). Portuguese navigator and discoverer who twice sailed to the Pacific, the first time (1595) on the expedition of Alvaro de Mendaña de Neira.

Resolution. See Cook.

Schouten, Willem Cornelis (1567/80?–1625). Dutch navigator who in 1616 found a new route to the Pacific, around Cape Horn rather than via the Strait of Magellan.

Scorbutic. Of, relating to, or diseased with scurvy.

Solander, Daniel Charles (1736–82). Swedish naturalist who accompanied Captain Cook aboard the *Endeavour.*

Sparrman, Anders (1748–1820). Swedish naturalist.

Spondias. A genus of tropical trees.

Stand off, on. To hold a course at sea, sail in a specified direction.

Stentor. Greek hero in the Trojan War, famed for his powerful voice.

Tahiti. The classic "island paradise" of the South Seas, settled by Polynesians in the fourteenth century and discovered by English navigator Samuel Wallis in 1767, before the first of James Cook's three visits (1769, 1773, and 1777).

Tasman, Abel Janszoon (1603?–59). Dutch navigator who made several voyages in the Pacific and Indian Oceans from about 1632–53, discovering Tasmania and New Zealand.

Tootahàh (d. 1773). Ruler on Paea, the larger peninsula of Tahiti.

Tuboraï-Tamaide (d. 1773). Ruler on Paea, the larger peninsula of Tahiti.

Tupaya (d. 1770). Native of Tahiti whom Captain Cook had taken on board and to England during his first voyage.

Virgil (Publius Vergilius Maro) (70–19 B.C.). Roman poet patronized by Maecenas and Augustus. His *Eclogues* and *Georgics* idealize and interpret rural life. In addition to such pastoral poetry, he also wrote the *Aeneid,* an epic narrating the adventures of Aeneas and the founding of the Roman nation. Forster introduces and conludes his text on Tahiti with quotations from the *Aeneid.* **"Devenere locos laetos . . ."** means "They came to a land of joy, the green pleasances and happy seats of the Blissful Groves. Here an ampler ether clothes the meads with roseate light" (VI, 638–41). **"Invitus, regina . . ."** means "Unwillingly, O queen, I parted from thy shores" (VI, 460). (Tr. H. Rushton Fairclough.)

Wallis, Samuel. See Tahiti.

Wort. Herbaceous plant or root.

Zone. Girdle, belt, band.

Christoph Martin Wieland

THE CASE OF
THE ASS'S SHADOW

From THE HISTORY OF THE ABDERITES

Chapter 1

Cause of the Lawsuit and Facti species.

S carcely had the good Abderites recovered a little from the fantastic theatrical fever with which the honest and kindly Euripides' "Cupid, prince of gods and men" had afflicted them; scarcely were the citizens speaking prose with each other again in the streets; scarcely had the druggists started to sell their hellebore and the smiths to make their rapiers and carving knives again; scarcely had the Abderite women chastely and diligently gone back to their weaving; scarcely had the men flung away their tiresome shepherds' reeds and applied themselves again to their various professional occupations with their usual common sense—when the Fates secretly drew out of the thinnest, most insipid, and least tenable threads ever spun by gods or men such a confused web of adventures, haggling, embitterment, insurrection, cabals, factions, and other rubbish that all Abdera eventually got tangled up in it. And since this unholy fabric caught fire thanks to the thoughtless heat generated by aiders and abettors, that famous republic nearly would have perished, perhaps completely, if fate had decreed that it could be destroyed for a lesser reason than frogs and rats.

The whole thing (like all great historic events) started on a very insignificant occasion. A certain dentist named Struthion, born and bred in Megara, had settled down in Abdera many years before. And since he was the only member of his profession in all the land, his practice extended over a considerable part of southern Thrace. His usual mode of bringing that region under tribute was to attend the fairs and markets of every small town and hamlet within a circuit of more than thirty miles, where he sold at a handsome profit not only tooth powder and tinctures but also various nostrums for ailments of the spleen and womb, asthma, rheumatism, etc. For this purpose he had in his stable a very corpulent ass, which was laden on such occasions with both the dentist's own short, thick person and a large bundle full of medicines and provisions.

Now it once came to pass that this ass cast a foal just as Struthion was supposed to visit the annual fair at Gerania and thus was in no condition to make the journey with him. Struthion therefore rented himself another ass as far as the town where he wanted to spend the first night, and its owner accompanied him on foot, to tend the beast of burden and to ride it back home again. Their route ran through a vast heath. It was the middle of summer, and the heat of the day was very strong. The dentist, who began to find it unbearable, looked around thirstily for a shady spot where he could dismount for a minute and get some fresh air. But far and wide there was neither tree nor shrub to be seen, nor any other object that cast a shadow. Finally, when he could think of no other way to ease his pain, he stopped, dismounted, and sat down in the ass's shadow.

"Hey, what do you think you're doing, sir?" the ass driver asked. "What's this supposed to mean?"

"I'm sitting down in the shade for a little while," Struthion answered, "for the sun is beating down intolerably on my head."

"Not so fast, my good sir," replied the other. "That's not what we agreed! I rented you the ass, but no one said anything about its shadow."

"You're joking, good friend," the dentist laughed. "It goes without saying that the shadow comes with the ass."

"Pooh, by Jason! That doesn't go without saying at all," the driver cried quite defiantly. "The ass is one thing, its shadow is another. You rented the ass from me for a certain sum of money. If you also wanted to rent the shadow, too, you should have said so. In a word, sir, get up and go on with your trip or pay me a fair price for the ass's shadow!"

"What?" screamed the dentist. "I paid for the ass, and now I'm supposed to pay for its shadow, too? Call me a silly ass myself if I do anything of the kind! The ass belongs to no one but me this whole livelong day, and I'll sit in its shadow as often as I like and stay sitting there as long as I like, you can depend on that!"

"Are you serious?" asked the other with all the sangfroid of an Abderite ass driver.

"Dead serious," Struthion answered.

"In that case, sir, we'll just have to turn around and go right back to Abdera and the authorities," said the driver. "There we'll soon see which of us is right. As surely as Priapus shows mercy to me and my ass, I'd like to see who can wrest its shadow from me against my will!"

The dentist was sorely tempted to reprimand the driver by giving him a good cuff. He was already clenching his fist, already he raised his stubby arm. But as he took closer stock of his opponent, he thought it better to let that raised arm slowly fall again and to try milder remonstrances once more. But that was a waste of breath. The uncouth fellow insisted that he should be paid for his ass's shadow, and since Struthion just as stubbornly refused to pay, there remained no other way than to return to Abdera and lay the matter before the city magistrate.

Chapter 2

Hearing before the Magistrate Philippides.

Philippides, the city magistrate before whom all disputes of this kind had to be brought in the first instance, was a man of many good qualities—a man who was honorable, level-headed, and diligent in his duties; who listened to everyone very patiently, gave people friendly advice, and had the general reputation of being incorruptible. Moreover, he was a good musician, dabbled in natural history, had written several plays that had been very well received, as was customary in the city, and was almost certain to be chosen nomophylax as soon as that post became vacant.

Along with all these accomplishments, the good Philippides had only a single small fault, which was that whenever two parties appeared before him, the one who spoke last always seemed to be right. The Abderites were not so stupid that they did not notice this, but they believed that a man who possessed so many good qualities could certainly be forgiven a single fault. "Yes," they said, "if Philippides did not have this fault, he would be the best city magistrate that Abdera has ever seen!"

Meanwhile, the fact that this honest man always thought both parties seemed right naturally had the happy result that he considered nothing more important than amicably resolving the suits that were brought before him. And thus the good Philippides' idiocy would have been a real blessing for Abdera, if the watchfulness of the sycophants, who were ill-served by his peaceable nature, had not almost always found means of spoiling its effect.

Struthion the dentist and Anthrax the ass driver, then, came running to this worthy magistrate as if on fire, and both loudly shouted their accusations at once. He heard them with his usual forbearance, and when they had finally finished—or tired of shouting—he shrugged his shoulders and thought the dispute one of the most intricate of all that he had ever heard. "So which of you two," he asked, "is actually the plaintiff?"

"I," answered Struthion, "accuse this ass driver of breaking our contract."

"And I," said Anthrax, "accuse this dentist of trying to get away without paying for something I hadn't rented him."

"Then we have two plaintiffs," said the magistrate, "but where is the defendant? An odd dispute indeed! Tell me what's the matter again and don't leave out any details, but one at a time, for it's impossible to make head or tail of it if both of you shout at once."

"Your Honor," said the dentist, "I rented the use of the ass from him for a day. It's true, we didn't mention the ass's shadow, but then who ever heard of inserting a separate clause for renting a shadow? By Hercules! This isn't the first ass ever rented in Abdera!"

"The gentleman is right about that," said the judge.

"The ass and its shadow go together," Struthion added, "and why shouldn't whoever rents the ass itself also have full enjoyment of its shadow?"

"The shadow is an *accessorium,* that's clear," replied the judge.

"Your lordship," shouted Anthrax, "I'm just a simple man, and I don't know anything about your *axes* and *oriums.* But my own four senses tell me that I'm not obliged to let my ass stand out in the sun for nothing, so that another man can sit down in its shadow. I rented the gentleman the ass, and he paid me half in advance, that I admit. But the ass is one thing, its shadow is another."

"Also true!" murmured the judge.

"If he wants the shadow he'll have to pay half as much for it as for the ass itself, for I only want what's fair, and I ask that you help me get my due."

"The best thing for you two to do about this," said Philippides, "is to settle your differences peacefully. You, honest Anthrax, let the ass's shadow—since it's only a shadow, after all—be included in the rent. And you, Mr. Struthion, give him half a drachma for it. That way both sides can be satisfied."

"I'm not giving him a nickel," screamed the dentist. "I demand justice!"

"And I," screamed his opponent, "insist on justice, too. If the ass is mine, so is its shadow, and I can do whatever I want with my own property. And since that man won't listen to what's only fair and right, I now demand twice as much, and I'd like to see if justice can still be had here in Abdera!"

The judge was greatly perplexed. "Well, where is the ass?" he finally asked, since he was scared and could think of no other way to gain a little time.

"It's standing down on the street outside the door, your lordship!"

"Lead it into the courtyard!" said Philippides.

The ass's owner gladly obeyed, for he thought that the judge's wanting to see the leading figure in this farce was a good sign. The ass was led in. Too bad that it could not speak its own mind on the matter! It just stood there quite calmly, then pricked up its ears, stared first at the two gentlemen, then straight at its master, screwed up its mouth, let its ears droop again, and did not say a word.

"Now see for yourself, Your Honor," cried Anthrax, "whether the shadow of so handsome and stately an animal isn't worth a couple of drachmas among friends, especially on a day as hot as today."

Philippides tried being kind again, and the two parties were already starting to compromise when Physignatus and Polyphonus, two of the most renowned sycophants in Abdera, unfortunately happened to come along. After having heard what was going on, they at once gave matters a different twist.

"Mr. Struthion has justice squarely on his side," said Physignatus, who knew the dentist to be a wealthy, irritable, and obstinate man. The other sycophant, though a little annoyed that his learned colleague had thus beaten him to the draw, cast a sidelong glance at the ass, which seemed a fine, well-fed animal, and urgently took the ass driver's side right away. Neither party would now hear any more talk of compromise, and the honest Philippides saw himself forced to schedule a trial. Both then went home, each with his sycophant. The ass and its shadow, however, the object of the lawsuit, were led off to Abdera's city stable until the matter was settled.

Chapter 3
How Both Parties Seek Support in High Places.

According to the Abderites' municipal laws, all the common people's disputes involving questions of mine and thine were resolved by a court of twenty jurymen, who assembled three times a week in the portico of the temple of Nemesis. With due respect for the sycophants' daily bread, everything that came before this court was put in writing. And since the wheels of justice in Abdera went around in circles and moved at a snail's pace—especially since the sycophants were not obliged to stop until they had nothing more to say—the paperwork commonly took as long as the means of the opposing parties seemed likely to last. But this time many special circumstances combined to move things along more quickly, and the case of the ass's shadow was so far advanced in less than four months that the final verdict was fully expected on the next judgment day.

A lawsuit about an ass's shadow would doubtless cause a sensation anywhere in the world. Just imagine, then, what it was bound to do in Abdera!

Scarcely had rumor of it spread when all other objects of social amusement suddenly lost their charm and everyone talked of the suit with just as much bias as if they themselves stood to gain or lose a great deal. Some declared themselves for the dentist, others for the ass driver. Even the ass itself had its supporters, who thought that the animal was surely entitled to petition the court *interveniendo,* since it was obviously most aggrieved by the unreasonable demand to let the dentist sit in its shadow while it had to stand in the burning sun. In a word, this ass had cast its shadow over all Abdera, and the case was spurred on by liveliness, zeal, and interest that hardly could have been greater if the woe or weal of the entire city had been at stake.

Although these proceedings will hardly surprise anyone who has come to know the Abderites from the foregoing, faithful account of their history, some readers think that they really understand a story only when the workings of its gears and springs and the entire range of its causes and effects are revealed to them. We believe that we shall do such readers no small favor by telling them more fully how it happened that this dispute—which originally concerned people of almost no importance and an object of very little worth—could become important enough to draw the whole republic into its wake.

The entire citizenry of Abdera was divided into guilds (as citizens of most cities in the world always are), and Struthion the dentist, owing to an old observance, belonged to the shoemakers' guild. The reason for this was extremely farfetched, as the Abderites' reasons always tended to be. In the early days of the republic, namely, this guild had included only shoemakers and cobblers. Later all kinds of patchers and menders were added, eventually including surgeons as cobblers of human beings. Finally, *ob paritatem rationis,* dentists also became part of the shoemakers' guild. Except for the surgeons (with whom he was always on bad terms) Struthion accordingly had on his side the whole laudable guild of shoemakers, who (one will recall) made up a considerable part of Abdera's citizens. The dentist thus naturally turned first to his superior, the guildmaster Pfriem. And this man, whose patriotic zeal for the republic's freedoms everyone knows, at once declared with his usual hot temper that he would rather stab himself with his own shoemaker's awl than let the rights and privileges of Abdera be so grossly infringed in the life of anyone belonging to his own guild.

"Fairness," he said, "is the highest good. And what can be fairer than that whoever plants a tree, even if only for the sake of its fruit, should also enjoy its shade, too? And why should that which holds for a tree not hold for an ass as well? Hang it all, what would become of our freedom if a guildsman of Abdera were not even allowed to sit down in an ass's shadow? As if an ass's shadow were any more respectable than the shadow of the town hall or of Jason's temple, where anyone at all can stand, sit, or lie. Shade is shade, whether it comes from a tree or from a monument, from an ass or from His Excellency the Archon himself. In short, Mr. Struthion, you can rely on me," exclaimed Master Pfriem. "That ruffian will not only let you have the shadow but also sadistfy your demand for the ass itself. If not, there would be neither freedom nor property left in Abdera, and it will never come to that—by all the elements!—as long as my name is Guildmaster Pfriem!"

While the dentist thus secured the favor of so powerful a man, the ass driver Anthrax did not fail to court a protector who could at least hold his own against Master Pfriem. Anthrax was not actually a citizen of Abdera, but only a freedman who lived within the circuit of Jason's temple. As its protégé, he was subject to the immediate jurisdiction of the archpriest of Jason, a hero known to be divinely revered in Abdera. Naturally, then, his first thought was how to get that archpriest, Agathyrsus, to take his case seriously. But the archpriest of Jason was a very important person in Abdera, and an ass driver could hardly hope to gain admission to a man of such high rank without going through special channels.

After many consultations with his closest friends, Anthrax finally chose the following course. His wife, named Krobyle, was acquainted with a milliner whose brother was the favored lover of the chambermaid of a certain Milesian dancer who (people said) was in the archpriest's good graces. Not that he—as so often happens—but rather because priests of Jason were not allowed to marry. . . . In short, the world being as suspicious as it is, people admittedly said all manner of things. But the truth of the matter is that the archpriest Agathyrsus was a great admirer of solo pantomime dances. And since, so as not to offend, he could not let the dancer come to him by day, he had no choice but to have her led to his study by night, taking all the necessary precautions while letting her in through a small door in his garden. Now as certain people once saw a thickly veiled person go back out through this door at dawn, rumors flew that it had been the dancer and that the archpriest had taken a very special liking to her, she who indeed could have excited a little something more in anyone other than an archpriest. Be that as it may, suffice it to say that the ass driver spoke with his wife, Mrs. Krobyle with the milliner, the milliner with her brother, and the brother with the chambermaid. And since the chambermaid held sway over the dancer, who was assumed to hold sway over the archpriest, who himself held sway over the magnates of Abdera—

and their wives—Anthrax did not doubt for a minute that he had placed his case in the best hands in the world.

Unfortunately, it turned out that the chambermaid had taken a vow to peddle her influence only if paid, just as Anthrax wanted money for his ass's shadow. She had a kind of price list, according to which the slightest favor asked of her required a token of gratitude amounting to four drachmas. And in this case she was all the less likely to take off even half a drachma, since she had to do great violence to her modesty to recommend a cause in which the leading figure was an ass. In short, this Iris held out for four drachmas, which was exactly twice as much as poor Anthrax stood to win, even if his suit went as well as possible. He thus saw himself right back where he started. For how could a lowly ass driver with no support more solid than the simple justice of his cause possibly hope to prevail against an opponent who had a whole guild behind him and who went around boasting that victory was already within his grasp?

Finally, honest Anthrax thought of a way to win the archpriest over to his side without the intervention of the dancer or her chambermaid. The best thing about it was that he did not have to look far to find it. Without beating around the bush: he had a daughter named Gorgo, who in hopes of somehow finding work in the theater had learned to sing and to play the zither tolerably well. The girl was certainly no beauty, but a slender figure, a pair of big black eyes, and the fresh flower of youth more than made up (Anthrax thought) for what her face lacked. Indeed, when she scrubbed herself, braided her pitch black hair, and put on her Sunday best with a bouquet of flowers at her bosom, she did look a little like Anacreon's wild Thracian maiden. Now when more careful inquiries revealed that the archpriest Agathyrsus was also fond of zither playing and little songs, a great many of which young Gorgo did not sing badly, Anthrax and Krobyle had high hopes of reaching their goal most directly by means of their daughter's talent and good figure.

Anthrax therefore turned to the archbishop's valet, and Krobyle meanwhile taught the girl how to behave so that she might displace the dancer and remain undisputed mistress of the garden door.

Everything went according to plan. The valet, who often was hard pressed by his master's penchant for novelty and variety, seized this favorable opportunity with both hands, and the young Gorgo played her role masterfully for a beginner. Agathyrsus found in her a certain mixture of innocence and willfulness and a kind of wild grace, which charmed him because it was new to him. In short, she had barely sung in his study two or three times when Anthrax learned from a reliable source that Agathyrsus had recommended his just cause to several judges and had rather clearly let it be known that he was not inclined to surrender even the least of Jason's supplicants to the chicanery of the sychophant Physignatus and the factionalism of Guildmaster Pfriem.

Chapter 4

Judicial Proceedings. Petition of the Assessor Miltias. His Verdict and What Ensued.

Meanwhile judgment day had come, when this strange suit would be decided in a court of law. The sycophants had rested their cases, and the records had been submitted to an assessor named Miltias, whose impartiality the dentist's detractors seriously questioned. It could not be denied that he was on intimate terms with the sycophant Physignatus. Besides, it was openly said that Lady Struthion, who was thought one of the prettiest women in her class, had personally recommended her husband's just cause to him several times. But these objections had no legal basis, and it was simply this Miltias's scheduled turn to serve as judge, so the order of business remained unchanged.

Miltias set forth the history of the lawsuit so impartially and gave reasons for and against his decision in such great detail that his audience could not tell for a long time which way he would finally go. He did not deny that much could be said for each side. "On the one hand," he said, "nothing could seem clearer than that whoever rented the ass, the principal corpus, also tacitly included its shadow, the *accessorium;* or (even if one will not admit such an implicit contract) that the shadow automatically goes with the body and that whoever secures enjoyment of the ass therefore also has use of its shadow without further reparation; the more so, as not the least damage is thereby done to the essence and the substance of the ass itself. On the other hand, it seems no less obvious that though the shadow is to be regarded as neither a material nor an immaterial part of the ass, one cannot thus assume that the lessee of the latter also tacitly wanted to lease the former. All the same, since said shadow absolutely cannot exist for itself, without said ass, and since an ass's shadow is really nothing other than a shadow-ass, the owner of the corporeal ass might well be considered the owner of its shadow, too, and therefore cannot be expected to let the lessee of the former have the latter for free. Besides, even if one admits that the shadow is an accessory of the aforementioned ass, no right to it thereby accrues to the lessee, as he has secured through the lease not every use of the ass, but only that use without which the purpose of the lease cannot be fulfilled—that is, his projected trip. But since no existing law in Abdera clearly and distinctly applies to this case, and since a verdict must therefore be rendered solely on the merits of the matter itself, everything comes down to a point that both sycophants have neglected or at least touched on only in passing, namely, to the question whether that which one calls a shadow counts as public property, to which everyone has a right, or as private property, to which individual persons have and can acquire exclusive rights. Now since conventions and customs of the human race, as true oracles of nature herself, rightly assume the force of positive law—which is lacking in this case—and since, according to these universal customs, shadows of things (including things that belong not only to individual persons but also to whole communities and even to the immortal gods themselves) have always and everywhere been accessible to everyone, no matter who, without any hindrance or charge, it therefore follows *ex consensu et consuetudine generis humani* that such shadows should be considered public property—like light, wind, weather, running water, day and night, moonlight, twilight, and all such things—the enjoyment of which is open to all and to which—insofar as said enjoyment might, under certain circumstances, entail something exclusive—whoever first acquires them has a momentaneous right of possession. This principle" (which the shrewd Miltias supported with a host of arguments that we shall spare our readers) "this basic principle can only lead to the conclusion that the shadows of all the asses in Thrace, including the one that is the immediate cause of the lawsuit at hand, can no more be part of an individual person's property than the shadow of Mount Athos or of Abdera's bell tower. Accordingly, the aforementioned shadow can neither be bequeathed nor bought, nor given as a gift *inter vivos* or *mortis causa,* nor rented, nor in any other way made the object of a civil contract. For these and other reasons cited in the case of the ass driver Anthrax, plaintiff, on the one side, versus the dentist Struthion, defendant, on the other, *pcto.* the ass's shadow used and enjoyed by the defendant to the alleged detriment and disadvantage of the plaintiff, the court hereby finds, *salvis tamen melioribus,* that the defendant was fully entitled to use said shadow and that the plaintiff, objections notwithstanding, should not only be denied his improper request but also be sentenced to pay all losses and damages incurred by the defendant, as the court sees fit to assess. By right and just title, etc., etc."

We leave it to our gentle and legally experienced readers to make whatever further observations they like about this (only partially excerpted) opinion of the shrewd Miltias. And since we do not presume to pass judgment on this matter but are instead determined to act only as an impartial historian, we shall simply report that it had been customary since time immemorial in the courts of Abdera for such a speaker's judicial opinion—no matter how it stood—to be ratified either unanimously or at least with a great majority of votes. At any rate, nothing contrary to this practice had been seen for over a hundred years. Indeed, things were arranged so that they could hardly turn out otherwise. For during an assessor's petition, which commonly lasted very long, his learned colleagues seldom paid any attention to his *rationes dubitandi et decidendi.* Most of them stood up, stared out the window, or left to breakfast on cake or small sausages in an antechamber, or to pay a quick visit to a lady-friend. And the few who remained seated and appeared to take an interest in the case spent their time whispering with their neighbors or even fell asleep while listening. In short, there reigned a kind of tacit compromise with the speaker, and it was only for form's sake that all took their seats again a few minutes before he actually came to his closing argument, in order to help ratify his written verdict with all due solemnity.

That was the way it had always been done, even in rather important disputes. But the case of the ass's shadow had the unprecedented honor of making the entire court stay put (except for three to four assessors who had already promised the dentist their votes and who did not want to forfeit their right to sleep while in session), and everyone listened attentively, as befitted such a curious case. And when their votes were counted, it turned out that the verdict was ratified only by a majority of twelve to eight.

As soon as this was announced, Polyphonus, the plaintiff's sycophant, did not fail to raise his voice and appeal the verdict to the Great Council of Abdera as being unjust, biased, and irreparably null and void. Now since the suit was brought about an object that the plaintiff himself had not valued at over two drachmas, and since this amount—even when all legitimate costs and damages were included—was still far short of the *summa appellabilis,* a great tumult arose in the courtroom. The minority declared that what mattered was not the amount of money, but a general legal principle about the right to property, which was not regulated by any law in Abdera and which—given the nature of the suit—therefore had to be brought before the legislators themselves, who alone could decide doubtful cases of this kind.

We cannot explain how Miltias, despite all his sympathy for the defendant, had not foreseen that the patrons of the other party would use this pretext to bring the case before the Great Council. He was simply an Abderite and, in keeping with the established and universal custom of his compatriots, he tended to see all issues one-sidedly, and even then only superficially. Perhaps the fact that he had spent part of the previous night at a large banquet and then, when he came home, had to grant Lady Struthion a rather long audience and had thus presumably not slept enough, serves as a further excuse. At any rate, after much shouting back and forth, Philippides finally said that special circumstances forced him to bring the plaintiff's request for an appeal before the Senate.

With this, he rose, the court dispersed rather tumultuously, and both parties rushed to confer with their friends, patrons, and sycophants about what to do next.

Chapter 5

Sentiments in the Senate. The Fair Gorgo's Virtue and Its Effects.
The Priest Strobylus Appears, and the Matter Becomes More Serious.

The case of the ass's shadow, which had at first merely amused the Abderites by its absurdity, now began to become a matter in which the rights, the imagined honor, and all manner of passions and interests of various and, in part, eminent members of the republic were involved.

Guildmaster Pfriem had gotten it into his head that his fellow guildsman had to win at all costs, and since he turned up almost every evening in places where the common people gathered, he had already won nearly half of them over to his side, and his following grew larger every day.

By contrast, the archpriest had not until now considered the dispute important enough to use all his influence on behalf of his protégé. But things between him and the fair Gorgo had become more serious as she—instead of proving entirely as docile as he had hoped to find her—put up resistance that one would not have expected, given her origins and upbringing. Indeed, she expressed reservations about exposing her virtue yet again to the dangers of a visit through the little garden door. It was therefore quite natural that Agathyrsus no longer delayed in acquiring a more compelling right to this daughter's gratitude with his zeal in support of her father's cause.

The new commotion raised in the city by appealing the case of the ass's shadow to the Great Council gave him the opportunity to speak with several of the most distinguished councillors involved in it. "However ridiculous this business may be in itself," he said, "we simply cannot let a poor man living under Jason's protection be oppressed by so obvious a cabal. What matters here is not the immediate cause, which can often be very slight, even for the most important events, but rather the spirit in which one conducts such affairs and the intentions hidden up one's sleeve or at least in petto. The sycophant Physignatus, who really bears the blame for this whole scandal, must be punished for his insolence, and the domineering and foolish demagogue Pfriem must be reined in before he succeeds in entirely overthrowing the aristocracy."

To tell the truth, there were initially several councillors who saw the case more or less for what it was, and they held it very much against Philippides that he had not had the presence of mind to suffocate such an absurd quarrel right at its birth. But their sentiments gradually shifted, and the vertigo that had already stood part of the citizenry on its head finally seized the greater part of the councillors as well. Some began to consider the case more important because a man like the archpriest Agathyrsus seemed to take such a serious interest in it. Others were upset by the danger that Guildmaster Pfriem's actions could pose for the aristocracy. Some sided with the ass driver simply to be contrary, others from a genuine feeling that he was being wronged, and still others supported the dentist because certain persons with whom they would never be of one mind had declared themselves for his opponent.

But in spite of everything—and as much as the Abderites were, well, Abderites—this minor dispute would never have caused such active ferment in their republic if the evil genius of that commonwealth had not also inspired the priest Strobylus to get mixed up in it for no better reason than his restless spirit and his hatred of the archpriest Agathyrsus.

In order to make this more intelligible to our gentle reader, we shall have to explain things *ab ovo* (as that old poet did in his *Iliad*), especially since certain passages in our story about the episode with Euripides and certain expressions that the priest Strobylus used against Democritus will thus appear in the proper light.

Chapter 6

Relationship between the Temples of Latona and Jason. Contrast in the Characters of the High Priest Strobylus and the Archpriest Agathyrsus. Strobylus Declares Himself Opposed to the Latter and Is Supported by Salabanda, Who Begins to Play an Important Role in the Case.

The Abderites had worshiped Latona (as Strobylus told Euripides) ever since their Lycian colony had been transplanted to Thrace, and the extreme architectural simplity of her little temple could be seen as sufficient proof of this tradition. The endowed income of its priests was just as modest, moreover, as that temple itself was plain. But necessity is the mother of invention, and these gentlemen had long since found ways to make the Abderites' superstition compensate somewhat for the scantiness of their regular income. And since even that failed to suffice, they had finally succeeded in getting the

Senate (which would hear nothing of raising their pay) to set aside certain sums for maintaining Latona's holy frog pond, and the economical and fair-minded frogs left most of the money for their keepers.

Things were very different in the temple of Jason, that famous leader of the Argonauts, whom the Abderites had raised to divine status and publicly worshiped. We can give no other reason for this honor than that several of the oldest and richest families in Abdera traced their lineage back to that hero. According to tradition, one of his grandsons had settled in that city and become the common ancestor of several families, some of which were still in full bloom at the time of our present story. To honor the memory of this hero, from whom they descended, they had at first followed ancient custom and endowed only a small private chapel. In the course of time, it had become a kind of public temple, which the piety of Jason's descendants gradually supplied with many possessions and revenues. Finally, when commerce and good fortune had made Abdera one of the richest cities in Thrace, the Jasonites decided to build their revered ancestor a temple so beautiful that it would do the republic and themselves proud for all posterity. The new temple of Jason was a glorious work and—together with its outbuildings, gardens, and dwellings for the priests, officials, dependents, etc.—constituted one whole quarter of the city. Its archpriest always had to come from the oldest line of Jasonites, and he not only had a very considerable income but also exercised jurisdiction over the people and property belonging to the temple. It is therefore easy to see how the chief priest of Latona could not look at all these advantages indifferently and that envy existed between these two prelates that they passed on to their heirs and that was visible in their behavior on every occasion.

The chief priest of Latona was admittedly regarded as the head of the whole Abderite priesthood. But the archpriest of Jason and his subordinates constituted a special college that enjoyed the protection of the city of Abdera but was still fully independent from it. And though festivals at Latona's temple were the actual high holidays of the republic, its moderate revenues did not permit much extravagance, so it was the feast of Jason that was celebrated with uncommon splendor and great solemnity. Although not quite as distinguished in the eyes of the people, it was at least the one that they looked forward to most. And all the reverence that they felt for the long tradition of serving Latona, and the firm belief of the rabble in her high priest and his holy frogs could not prevent them from paying greater respect to the finer figure cut by the archpriest of Jason. And even though the common people were generally more inclined to favor the priest of Latona, this advantage was outweighed by the archpriest's close connections to the aristocratic houses, which gave him so much influence that an ambitious man in his position would have had no trouble becoming a minor tyrant in Abdera.

In addition to so many causes of the long-standing jealousy and disinclination that divided these two princes of the Abderite clergy, Strobylus and Agathyrsus disliked each other personally, which was a natural fruit of the contrast between their mentalities.

Agathyrsus, more a man of the world than a priest, indeed had little more of the latter than the vestments. The love of pleasure was his ruling passion. And though he did not lack pride, no one whose ambition lets another passion rule alongside it can be called ambitious. He loved the arts and intimate traffic with virtuosi of all kinds, and he had the reputation of being one of those priests who barely believe in their own gods. At least it cannot be denied that he often joked rather freely about the frogs of Latona, and there was even someone who would swear having heard him say that all the goddess's frogs had long ago been changed into awful poets and Abderite singers. That he lived on fairly good terms with Democritus was also not likely to confirm his orthodoxy. In short, Agathyrsus was a man of good cheer, a clear head, and a rather liberal way of life, popular with the Abderite nobility, more popular still with the fair sex, and popular even with the lowest classes of people, thanks to his generosity and his Jasonesque figure.

Even at her most whimsical moment, nature could not have produced a more complete antipode to all that Agathyrsus stood for than the priest Strobylus. This man (like many of his kind) had discovered that a furrowed brow and stiff bearing are infallible means of being considered a wise and blameless man by the great mass of people. Since he naturally looked rather like a sourpuss, it had not been hard for him to get used to seeming grave, which proves no more about most people than the slowness of their wit and the coarseness of their manners. With no sense of the beautiful and sublime, he was a born despiser of all arts and sciences that took this sense for granted, and his hatred of philosophy was simply a mask for the natural loathing felt by an idiot for everyone more reasonable and learned than himself. His judgment was skewed and one-sided, his opinions stubborn, his style of argument vehement and rude, and whenever he felt insulted—either in his own person or in that of Latona's frogs—he was utterly vindictive. Nonetheless, he became pliant to the point of baseness as soon as he could not achieve something important to him without the help of a person whom he hated. What is more, he had the somewhat deserved reputation of being amenable to anything in the world, given the proper dose of darics and philips, which was not entirely inconsistent with his outward character.

From such opposite dispositions and from so many opportunities for envy and jealousy on the part of the priest Strobylus, a mutual hatred necessarily arose in the two men. It was barely constrained by the demands of their class and position, and differed only in that Agathyrsus despised the high priest too greatly to hate him much, while Strobylus envied the former too much to despise him as greatly as he would have liked.

In addition to all this, Agathyrsus, by virtue of his birth and social condition, was for the aristocracy, while Strobylus, notwithstanding his family ties to several councillors, was a declared friend of democracy. Next to Guildmaster Pfriem, he was the man whose personal character, dignity, enthusiastic vehemence, and own popular kind of eloquence had the greatest influence on the mob.

One can easily foresee that the case of the ass's shadow or shadow-ass simply had to take a serious turn as soon a couple of men like these two high priests of Abdera got involved in it.

As long as the trial had been conducted before the city magistrates, Strobylus had taken no other part in it than occasionally declaring that he would have acted just as Struthion had, if he had been in the dentist's place. But no sooner had he learned from Lady Salabanda, his niece, that Agathyrsus had taken on the case of his protégé who had lost in the lower court, than he suddenly felt called to put himself at the head of the opposite party and to support the guildmaster's intrigues with all the esteem in which the councillors as well as the people held him.

Salabanda was too used to having her hand in all Abderite

disputes to be among the last to take sides in this one. Apart from being related to Strobylus, she had another, special reason to make common cause with him—a reason no less weighty for being kept in petto. We have mentioned on another occasion that this lady, be it from purely political motives or perhaps also with a little coquetry—and who knows whether what French high society currently likes to call "a lady's heart" was not mixed in with it, too—at any rate, it was a fact that she always had a number of humble slaves on hand, among whom (people said) at least one or another surely knew why he served her. The privy chronicle of Abdera said that the archpriest Agathyrsus had for some time had the honor of being one of the latter. Indeed, numerous circumstances suggested that this rumor was more than pure speculation. This much is certain: they had long been the most intimate of friends when the Milesian dancer came to Abdera and quickly attracted so much attention from the fickle Jasonite that Salabanda finally could not doubt that she herself had been sacrificed.

Agathyrsus still came to her house on the footing of an old acquaintance, and the lady was too politic to let the slightest change show in her behavior toward him, but revenge was seething in her heart. She did not miss a trick that could draw the archpriest ever deeper into the case and set him more aflame. In secret, though, she so closely watched all his comings and goings and all the doors—front and back, big and little—leading to his study that she very soon found out about his affair with young Gorgo. She could then put Strobylus in a position to shed ugly light on Agathyrsus's zeal for the ass driver's cause, just as she herself secretly tried to make it seem ridiculous.

As little as it took for Agathyrsus to sacrifice political ambitions and advantages in the interest of his pleasures, there were times when the slightest resistance in a matter that did not really concern him at all still piqued his pride. Whenever this happened, his vivacity usually carried him away infinitely farther than he would have gone if he had deigned to reflect on things more cooly. His original reason for meddling with this distasteful business was no longer valid, for despite the instructions of her mother Krobyle, the fair Gorgo had either too little skill or too little endurance to defend herself as staunchly as initially planned against such a dangerous and experienced besieger. But now he was involved in the case for better or worse, his honor was at stake, and he received daily and hourly reports of how the unseemly guildmaster and Strobylus the priest set out against him with their followers, how they threatened him, how arrogantly they hoped to have their way, and other such things—and this was more than enough to make him resolve to use all his power to cast down opponents whom he so wholly despised and to punish them for daring to rise against him. Despite Lady Salabanda's intrigues (which were not spun finely enough to remain hidden from him for long), most of the Senate was on his side. And though his opponents stopped at nothing to turn the people against him, he still had a following of hardy, sturdy fellows, especially in the guilds of tanners, butchers, and bakers. These men were as hotheaded as they were strong-armed, ready in an instant to shout or shove for him and his faction, whichever was necessary.

Chapter 7

All Abdera Splits into Two Factions. The Case Comes before the Council.

Things stood in this state of ferment when all of a sudden the names "Asses" and "Shadows" were heard in Abdera and soon commonly used to designate the two factions.

There is no reliable information about the original source of these surnames. Since factions simply cannot last long without names, though, Struthion's followers among the mob had presumably started calling themselves Shadows because they fought for his right to the ass's shadow, while calling their opponents Asses out of mockery and contempt for trying to equate the shadow with the ass itself. And since the archpriest's followers could do nothing to stop being called by this name, they had gradually grown accustomed to using it themselves (as often happens), even though they did so at first only in jest. They turned the tables, however, by linking everything scornful with the shadow and everything honorable with the ass. "If it has to be one or the other," they said, "every honest man would rather be a real, live ass with all its trimmings than just an ass's shadow."

However it may have happened, suffice it to say that Abdera was divided into these two factions within a few days. And as soon as they had names, the zeal of both sides increased so fast and fiercely that no one at all was allowed to remain neutral. The first question that common people put to each other when they met on the street or at the tavern was always "Are you a Shadow or an Ass?" And if a Shadow was unlucky enough to be the only one of his kind among a number of Asses in such a place, he could do nothing—unless he saved his skin by running away—but either become apostate on the spot or roughly get thrown out the door.

One needs no help from us to imagine how much and how great a disturbance resulted from this situation. The bitterness soon went so far that a Shadow would rather have starved until he really did give up the ghost than buy a single loaf of bread from a baker allied with the opposing faction.

The womenfolk took sides, too, as one might easily suppose, and they did so with a vengeance. In fact, the first blood shed in this singular civil war came from the fingernails of two women hucksters who fell upon each other's physiognomies in the marketplace. It was, however, remarked that by far the greater part of female Abderites openly sided with the archpriest. And where a Shadow was the man of the house, his wife was bound to be an Ass, and generally as hot-tempered and unruly an Ass as can be imagined. Among the many unholy and in part ridiculous consequences of this partisan spirit that had seized the Abderite women, not the least was that many love affairs were abruptly broken off because the stubborn Seladon preferred to abandon his amorous claims rather than his faction. Likewise, many a man who had courted some beauty's favor in vain for years, and who could not have overcome her antipathy by any of the usual means that an unhappy lover tries, suddenly found that he needed no other title to happiness than to persuade his lady that he was an Ass.

Meanwhile, the preliminary question of whether or not to grant the plaintiff's appeal to the Great Council came before the Senate. It was the first time that this worthy assembly addressed the question of the ass, but it quickly became clear that all its members had already taken sides. The archon Onolaus was the only one who seemed worried about putting a tolerable face on the matter. All noticed that he spoke much more softly than usual and uttered these strange and ominous words at the close of his speech: "I fear that the ass's shadow which is now so hotly contested will obscure the glory of Abdera for centuries to come." His opinion was that one would do best to reject the plaintiff's appeal as inadmissible, to affirm the decision made by the municipal court (expect for the matter of fees, which could be waived and cancel each other out), and to swear both parties to eternal silence. But he nonetheless added that if the majority found the laws of Abdera insufficient to settle such a petty dispute, he would have to let the Great Council pass judgment on it. Still, he would recommend searching the archives first, to see if any such unusual cases had come up in olden times and, if so, how they had been handled.

The archon's moderation—which impartial posterity will unanimously judge to his credit, as proof of his true statesmanship—was interpreted as weakness and phlegmatic indifference at the time, when all eyes were blinded by factionalism. Several senators siding with the archpriest announced loud and long that they could not call anything petty that concerned the Abderites' sovereign rights. Where there was no law, there could be no trial, they argued, and the first time that judges were allowed to decide a case simply according to their own notions of right and wrong would spell the end of freedom in Abdera. Even if the quarrel concerned something still less significant, the question would not be how much or how little it was worth, but which of the parties was right. And in the case at hand, since no existing law stated whether or not an ass's shadow was tacitly included in the rent, it would be outright tyranny for either the lower court or the Senate itself to grant the lessee something to which the lessor had at least an equal right. Or rather a far better right, since it in no way necessarily followed from the nature of their contract that the latter's intention had been to rent the ass's shadow. One of these zealous gentlemen went so far as to say, "I've always been an ardent patriot, but I'd rather see Abdera go up in smoke than admit that one of my fellow citizens can willfully presume to deny another even the shadow of a nutshell."

At this, Guildmaster Pfriem completely lost his patience. The fire with which anyone so openly threatened the entire city, he said, ought to be lit with whoever dared speak so boldly. "I never went to college," he added, "but by all the gods, no one can sell me mouse shit just by calling it pepper! You'd have to be out of your mind to want to make a normal person believe that you need a special law when the question is whether someone who has paid good money to sit down on an ass can sit on its shadow, too. It's just silly and disgraceful that so many smart and serious men rack their brains about this business, which any child would have figured out on the spot. Who ever heard of shadows being the kind of thing that people rent?"

"Mr. Guildmaster," interjected the councillor Buphranor, "you're putting your foot in your mouth when you say that. For if the ass's shadow *could* not be rented, it's clear that it *was* not rented. For *a non posse ad non esse valet consequentia*. Thus, according to your own logic, the dentist cannot claim a right to the ass's shadow, and the verdict as such is null and void."

The guildmaster was stunned, and as no objection to this subtle argument occurred to him right away, he started shouting all the louder and called on heaven and earth to witness his oath that he would sooner pluck out his gray beard hair by hair than let anyone make an ass of him in his old age. The gentlemen on his side supported him with all their might, but they were outvoted, and all that they could obtain in the end, with help from the soft-spoken archon and councillor, was that the matter would temporarily remain *in statu quo* until the archives had been searched for a precedent that might resolve this dispute without any further complications.

Chapter 8

The Well-ordered Chancery of Abdera. Precedents That Have No Bearing. The People Want to Storm Town Hall but Are Assuaged by Agathyrsus. The Senate Decides to Turn the Case Over to the Great Council.

The chancery of Abdera—as long as we have the opportunity to say a few words about it—was about as well arranged and ably run as one might expect in such a wise republic. Yet it had two faults in common with many other chanceries, faults that the Abderites had complained about almost daily for centuries, without the idea ever occurring to anyone that it might just be possible to right what was wrong one way or another.

One of these shortcomings was that documents and files were stored in several very stuffy and damp vaults, where they grew moldy and dusty for lack of air, were moth-eaten and worm-eaten, and bit by bit became completely useless. The other was that no matter how hard one looked there, nothing could be found. Whenever this happened, some patriotic councillor tended to remark, usually with the approval of the entire Senate, "It's simply because no order is maintained in the chancery." Indeed, it was hard to imagine a hypothesis that could explain this phenomenon more easily and comprehensibly. Therefore, almost every time the Council decided to have the archives searched, everyone already knew in advance that it was a safe bet nothing would turn up. For this same reason, moreover, the usual announcement at the next session of the Council—"Despite diligent searches, nothing can be found in the chancerey"—was greeted with the coldest indifference as something that one had expected and that went without saying.

Now this was once again the case when the chancery had been charged with looking in the back files to see whether a precedent might be found that could light the way for the Senate's wisdom in resolving the highly burdensome business of the ass's shadow. Nothing had been found, though several gentlemen had been positively certain in the previous session that countless similar cases had to exist.

Nevertheless, an eager councillor from the Asses' faction had dredged up two old lawsuits that had once caused quite a stir in Abdera and that seemed to bear some resemblance to the present one.

The one concerned a quarrel about property rights to a mound lying between two landowner's plots in the municipal pasture. This little knoll measured roughly five or six steps in circumference and may have arisen in the course of time from the confluence of several molehills. A thousand minor details had by and by so vehemently embittered the two families involved in the quarrel that each was determined to lose house and home rather than its right to this molehill. This all the more confused the Abderite judicial system because the evidence on both sides depended on a monstrous combination of infinitely small, dubious, and obscure circumstances.

And twenty-five years later, the case was not only not one step closer to being resolved but, on the contrary, just twenty-five times more tangled up than when it began. It probably never would have come to an end, moreover, if both parties had not finally found themselves forced to make over their plots surrounding the *objectum litis*— together with all appurtenances, rights, and claims, including the disputed right to the molehill itself—to their sycophants as payment for court costs and legal fees. At this stage, indeed on the very same day, the sycophants amicably agreed to consecrate this little hill to the great Themis, to plant a fig tree on it, and to have a monument to that goddess, made of fir wood and painted to look like stone, erected under the tree at public expense. It was also ordered, and underwritten by the Abderite Senate, that the owners of the two plots should be bound to maintain both the monument and the fig tree in common forevermore. And both—the tree in very good condition, but the monument very decayed and worm-eaten—were still standing at the time of the present story as an eternal remembrance of this curious suit.

The other case seemed to be even more closely related to the one at hand. An Abderite named Pamphus owned an estate, the chief amenity of which was that its southwest side had a commanding view of a lovely valley that ran between two wooded mountains, grew ever narrower in the distance, and finally faded into the Aegean Sea. Pamphus often liked to say that he would not part with this view for a hundred Attic talents, and he had good reason to value it so highly, since the property itself was so insignificant that no one who was interested only in turning a profit would have paid even five talents for it. His neighbor on his southwest side, a rather well-to-do Abderite farmer, unfortunately felt moved to build a barn blocking so much of good Pamphus's view that the value of his little country estate would fall by eighty talents, according to his own estimate. Pamphus tried every possible tactic, carrots as well as sticks, to keep his neighbor from building such a fatal barn. But the farmer insisted on his right to improve his ancestral property whenever and however he pleased.

They therefore went to court. Pamphus could not prove that the disputed view was a substantial appurtenance of his property, or that his neighbor's barn would deprive him of light and air, or that his grandfather—who had originally purchased the estate for his family—had paid a single drachma more than it was worth all by itself at the going rate then, or that his neighbor the farmer was obliged by any servitude to halt construction. But his sycophant maintained that the decisive factors lay far deeper and had to be drawn straight from the original source of the right to property. "Were air not a transparent substance," said the sycophant, "then Elysium and Olympus themselves might lie across from my client's estate, and he would never see any more of them than if a wall stood directly in front of his windows and reached right up to the sky. The transparent nature and quality of air is thus the first and true cause of the lovely prospect that graces my client's estate. But now this free and transparent air, as everyone knows, is the kind of property to which all originally have the same right. And precisely for this reason, every share of it not already claimed by someone is to be regared as a *res nullius,* as a thing that does not yet belong to anyone and that therefore becomes the property of whoever first takes possession of it. My client's ancestors have held, possessed, and enjoyed the view now in dispute free and clear ever since time immemorial. They have therefore ocularly occupied the share of air belonging to it, which both by dint of this occupation and by their possessing it uninterruptedly for so long has become an inherent part of the aforementioned estate. And not the least thing can be removed from that estate without upsetting the basic principles of all civil law and order."

The Senate of Abdera had found this logic quite troubling. Its pros and cons were debated at great length and with great subtlety, and since Pamphus was shortly thereafter elected to the Council, the case seemed to become even more complicated and his motives ever more dubious as time went on. The farmer died without living to see the end of the matter, and his heirs, who finally realized that simple countryfolk like themselves could never win against so great a man as a Councillor of Abdera, finally let their sychophant persuade them to settle, pay all the court costs, and abstain from building the disputed barn, the more so as they did not have any more money for it and as the lawsuit had so eaten away at their estate that they did not need a new barn to hold what little they had left to plant.

Now it was pretty clear that these two precedents shed precious little light on how to decide the case at hand, especially since there had been no definitive ruling in either and both had been amicably settled out of court. But the councillor who produced them seemed bent on showing the Senate that no one had ever thought of petitioning the Great Council to hear these two cases—which he thought very like that of the ass's shadow, with regard to both the importance of the disputed object and the subtlety of legal reasoning—and that they had been conducted for many years before the Small Council of Abdera, without anyone ever doubting that it was fully justified to find in such matters.

All the Asses supported this argument of their fellow factionary, and their zeal was all the greater since they had the majority of votes in hand if the case could still be settled in court. But this only made the Shadows oppose them even more stubbornly.

The whole morning was taken up with quarreling and quibbling, and (as often happened with them) the gentlemen would have left their business unfinished when they finally adjourned for lunch, had the matter not been settled at last by a great throng of citizens from the Shadows' faction, who had gathered in front of the town hall at the behest of Guildmaster Pfriem and were reinforced by a crowd of the great unwashed that happened to come along. The archpriest's faction later charged the guildmaster with deliberately stepping up to the window and giving the people signs inciting them to revolt. But the opposing faction flatly denied this accusation and argued that the unseemly din that several Asses suddenly raised had given the citizens gathered below the idea that violence was being done to their representatives. This mistake, they claimed, caused all the commotion.

Be that as it may, a roaring cry was suddenly raised to the chamber windows: "Liberty! Liberty! Long live Guildmaster Pfriem! Down with the Asses! Down with the Jasonites!"

The archon went to the window and bade the crowd be still. But their roar grew louder, and some of the most impudent threatened to burn down the town hall on the spot unless the gentlemen dispersed without delay and submitted the matter to the Great Council and the people. A few rogues and fisherwomen actually broke into the neighboring houses, tore hot brands from the hearths, and came back with them to show the gracious gentlemen that their threats should be taken seriously.

Meanwhile, the crowd drawn by all this commotion cried for a number of Asses, who wanted to come to the rescue of their gentlemen allies with clubs, tongs, hammers, cleavers, pitchforks, and whatever else they could get their hands on. And though they were greatly outnumbered, their courage and the contempt they felt for the whole lot of the Shadows inspired them to return verbal insults with such hard pushing and shoving that noses were bloodied and all were soon locked in hand-to-hand combat.

In this state of affairs, all that could be done back in the council chamber was to resolve unanimously that the council could agree just this once, *citra praejudicium,* and solely for the sake of peace and for the common good, that the suit about the ass's shadow should be brought before the Great Council and decided there.

Meanwhile, the good councillors were squirming so uncomfortably that as soon as they had agreed on this resolution (albeit in a very tumultuous way) they implored Guildmaster Pfriem to go down and calm the angry crowd. The guildmaster, who was only too glad to see the proud patricians so humiliatingly brought to heel, did not hesitate to give them this demonstration of his goodwill and his prestige with the people. But the tumult was already so great that his voice, though one of the most stentorian in all Abdera, was heard no better than the cry of a cadet in the crow's nest of a ship battered by a thunderous storm and roaring, crashing waves. He even came close to losing his own life among the rabble, which was incensed when it saw him (no one recognized him at first). Luckily, the archpriest Agathyrsus—who thought this sudden tumult the ideal time to outflank the opposite faction—happened along just then, carrying his gilded sheepskin in front of him on a pole and followed by all his priesthood. He put an end to the uproar by assuring the rabble that it would receive satisfaction and that he himself would be the first to move that the matter should be settled by the Great Council.

This public assurance by the prelate, his condescension and affability, and the reverence that the Abderite people were used to feeling for the gilded sheepskin had such a salutary effect that all soon calmed down again and the whole marketplace rang with a loud "Long live Agathyrsus!" The wounded very quietly crept home to have their heads bandaged, and the remaining throng streamed along behind the archpriest. The guildmaster, though, had to watch a large part of his otherwise faithful Shadows, infected by the rest of the enthusiastic masses, magnify his opponent's triumph. At that giddy moment, moreover, they easily could have been made to take all the wild malice that they had just been ready to vent on their presumed enemies, the Asses, and let it out instead on their own friends, the Shadows.

Chapter 9

Policy of Both Factions. The Archpriest Exploits His Newly Won Advantage. The Shadows Withdraw. The Trial Date Is Set.

This unexpected advantage that the archpriest had gained over the Shadows affronted them all the more grievously since it not only spoiled the joy and honor of the victory that they had won in the Senate, but also markedly weakened their faction itself. For it made them realize how little they could rely on the support of the fickle mob, which is blown back and forth by every shift in the wind and seldom knows itself what it really wants, much less what those whom it lets sway it have in mind.

Agathyrsus, who was now the avowed head of the Asses, had learned from his emissaries that nothing had done the opposing faction as much good among the common people as the resistance that the ass driver's protectors had initially put up when the case was to be referred to the Great Council.

This council consisted of four hundred men regarded as representatives of the entire Abderite citizenry, and half of them really were mere small merchants and artisans, so every common man felt personally insulted by the thought that anyone might try to limit its privileges. And they were therefore readier than ever to believe Guildmaster Pfriem's pretense that it was all a plot to overthrow their democratic constitution.

Whatever seemed democratic about the Abderite form of government, though, was simply obfuscation and political hocus-pocus. For the Small Council, two-thirds of which were drawn from patrician families, basically did whatever it wanted. And the cases in which the Four Hundred had to be convened were so narrowly circumscribed by the Abderite constitution that the decision when and how often to do so lay almost entirely with the Small Council anyway. Even then, the Four Hundred did no more than very faithfully rubber-stamp what the Small Council had already re- solved. And this was usually all that one expected of these worthy people, who (it was rightly assumed) were too occupied with their own affairs to rack their brains about legislative and administrative matters. But precisely because this privilege of the Abderite com- moners meant so little, they were all the more jealous of it, and it was even more necessary not to let them see the leash on which they were lead when they thought they were walking all on their own.

So it was a stroke of genius on the part of Agathyrsus that he all of a sudden, and at a moment when the effect would be quick and decisive, declared himself to be at the service of the people in a matter that they valued so highly. Without risking anything, he thereby nearly ruined the plans of his opponents, who now had all the more reason to think of new ways and means to regain the advantage from the archpriest and his followers and to obliterate the favorable impression that he had made on the common people.

The heads of the Shadows gathered that same evening at the house of Lady Salabanda and resolved that instead of urging the archon to set an early date for convening the Four Hundred, they should try (if need be) to postpone it, to give the people time to cool down again. Meanwhile, they would surreptitiously and very calmly try to con- vince the townspeople how foolish it would be to let the archpriest and his fellow Asses take credit for something that was hardly an act of goodwill, but merely the result of his own weakness. If it had been in the Asses' power to snatch the mattter away from the Great Council, the Shadows said, they would have done so without much caring whether the people liked it or not. And this sudden departure from their well-known behavior seemed so obvious a trick to split the popular opposition that one should not be deceived by it. On the contrary, one had all the more reason to be on guard, since the idea apparently was to lull the people to sleep with sweet nothings and imperceptibly make it the instrument of its own oppression.

The high priest Strobylus, who was present at this consultation, approved of all that could be done to diminish his rival's popular reputation and to make his intentions seem suspect. "But I very much doubt," he added, "that we shall reap the desired results. I am preparing another and stronger solution, though, which will work all the better for taking him completely by surprise. The time has not yet come for me to explain myself more clearly. Just leave it all to me! Let him flatter himself a little longer with the hope of dragging me, Strobylus, along behind him in triumph. You can be sure I'll throw a wrench into his plans. Meanwhile, if we are honest with each other (as I hope), and if we are serious about defeating our enemies, we must be tight-lipped about this secret plan and its details, which I'll let you know in due time. Agathyrsus must think he's safe. He has to believe that we are on our last legs and that our only hope lies in being confident of having a majority in the Great Council."

Everyone agreed that Strobylus had the right idea, and they adjourned their meeting, quite curious indeed to see what kind of plan he had up his sleeve for Agathyrsus. They were also quite convinced, though, that if it meant toppling the latter, things could not be left to anyone more adroit than Strobylus the priest.

In the meantime, Agathyrsus did not fail to squeeze every possible advantage out of the small victory that he had won over his opponent thanks to his own singular presence of mind at such an opportune moment. He ordered bread and wine handed out among the crowd of common folk who had followed him back to the vestibule of his palace, then he earnestly admonished them all to stay calm. Back home among their friends and neighbors, they overflowed with praise for his person, his kindly manner, and his generosity. But though he knew the republican spirit too well to discount the rabble's favor, he also knew full well that winning it had not yet done him much good. The important thing was to make absolutely sure that the greater part of the Four Hundred were behind him, partly because everything now depended on them, partly because—once he had won them over—he could entertain them more royally than the people at large. He already had a considerable following among them, but except for a number of declared and zealous Shadows, with whom he would have nothing to do, there remained very many—most of them quite wealthy and respected citizens—who had either not yet taken sides at all or who leaned toward the Shadows only because the heads of the opposing faction had been described to them as domineering, violent people who had engineered this whole laughable *Onoskiamachia* simply to cause confusion in the city and to use such deliberate unrest as a pretext and a tool for their own ambitious designs.

Now winning these people over to his side seemed as easy to Agathyrsus as it was decisive for the triumph of his faction. He invited them all to be his guests at dinner that very evening. Most came, and the archpriest, who had a great talent for giving his politics a veneer of openness and honesty, made no secret of having invited them—such upright and sensible men—to help dispel the prejudices against him that (as he heard) the town had been led to believe. "That anyone," he said, "would try to make a man of my station the head of a faction in a dispute between an ass driver and a dentist, a dispute about nothing more than an ass's shadow, seems too ludicrous for me ever to think of refuting such a silly charge. All the same, poor Anthrax is dependent on Jason's temple, so I cannot refuse to assist the man to the extent that justice requires. Without the well-known and irascible vehemence of Guildmaster Pfriem, who has rather untimely declared himself the dentist's friend—not because the latter is right, but only because he belongs to Pfriem's guild—such an insignificant thing could never have become so complex. But once a fire has been lit, there are always people who stand to gain by fueling and tending it. For my part, I have always made it a rule never to meddle in matters that do not concern me. My nonetheless allowing himself to quell the dangerous tumult that the guildmaster's followers caused in front of the town hall this morning was simply the act of a good citizen and patriot. No fair-minded man will misinterpret my intervention and kind coaxing as improper arrogance, I hope, especially since it always better befits the character of a priest to make peace and prevent disorder than to pour oil on the fire, like some people whom I do not need to name. Besides, I do not deny that I have always wanted the case of the ass's shadow to come before the Great Council, the sooner the better, now that it has been botched by the lower court and become a dispute that all Abdera, as it were, feels compelled to take an interest in. Not only so that poor Anthrax can seek proper redress (which he will doubtless receive from that superior court), but also so that some suitable law will finally put an end to the sycophants' unbridled mischief and so that some means can be found to prevent such shameful disputes—which hardly do credit to Abdera—from ever recurring in the future."

Agathyrsus uttered this all so calmly and reasonably that his guests could not help being amazed at the unfairness of those who had tried to make such a right-thinking gentleman seem the prime mover of all the unrest. They now all thought themselves completely convinced of the opposite, and in a few hours he succeeded in turning these worthy people into Asses just as good as any in all Abdera—and they did not even notice, since they still believed themselves to be entirely impartial. Of course, the excellent wines that he trickled into them at dinner had extinguished every shadow of a doubt and made every soul open and receptive to all the impressions that he wanted to give them.

One can easily imagine that this step by Agathyrsus made the opposing faction more than a little uneasy. Among the townspeople who had been indifferent up to then, it caused a revolution that soon became very apparent. All the batteries brought to bear with redoubled zeal against it not only had no effect, but actually had exactly the opposite effect of making the Shadows' evil intentions seem all the more obvious, compared to the prelate's moderation and patriotic cast of mind. Those Shadows would have been completely at a loss for a way to give their almost totally stalled faction some momentum again, if Strobylus the priest had not kept up their spirits and assured them that, as soon as the trial date was set, he would teach that junior Jason (as he liked to call Agathyrsus) a lesson that all the latter's slyness would never prepare him for and that would immediately make the whole matter seem quite different indeed.

The Shadows now seemed to keep so quiet that Agathyrsus and his followers could very plausibly attribute their apparent despair to the little hope that they had left after he had obtained his twofold advantage over them. They therefore redoubled their own efforts to have the archon Onolaus (whose son was a very close friend of the archpriest and one of the most hotheaded Asses) set an early date to convene the Great Council.

Whoever is accustomed to judge the wisdom of a plan or of a practical measure by its results might find a lack of foresight and prudence in the archpriest's complacence at his opponents' sudden inactivity. Indeed, we cannot wholly acquit him of this fault. It certainly would have been more cautious of him to attribute this inactivity to some important scheme that they were quietly hatching, rather than to dashed hopes. But it was one of this Jasonite's faults to overrate his own strength and to scorn his opponents more than sagacity allowed. He almost always acted like a man who does not think it worth the trouble to calculate the damage that his enemies can do him because he is fully convinced that he will never lack means to ward off their worst attacks. But in this situation, a thousand others put in his place and given such favorable auspices would presumably have thought the same thing and have believed that they were acting wisely by exploiting their new friends' goodwill before it cooled down again and by leaving their enemies no time to recover.

That the result did not meet his expectations was due to a trick by Strobylus that Agathyrsus could not foresee for all his cleverness. That trick may have been in keeping with the high priest's basic character, but it was such that one had to see it oneself to believe he could do it.

Chapter 10

What Kind of Mine Strobylus Springs on His Colleague Agathyrsus. Convocation of the Decemviri. The Archpriest Is Summoned to Appear before Them but Finds Ways of Advantageously Extricating Himself from the Matter.

The day before the Great Council was to decide the case about the ass's shadow, which had plunged the hapless city of Abdera into such far-reaching chaos for several weeks, the high priest Strobylus, two other priests of Latona, and several private citizens came rushing to see the archon Onolaus early in the morning. All distraught, they wanted to tell His Grace about a miraculous sign that (as they had every reason to fear) threatened the republic with some great disaster.

For two nights running, it seemed, several people belonging to the temple of Latona had thought that they heard the frogs in the sacred pool make very odd and distressing sounds. Although these people had not dared approach close enough to distinguish them clearly, those sounds were not the frogs' usual "Wrek-kek-kek-koax-koax"—which they had in common not only with all other mortal frogs but also with those in the Stygian marshes (as is clear from

Aristophanes). When this news had been brought to his attention the previous evening, the high priest found it important enough for him and all his subordinate priests to spend the whole night beside the sacred pool. All was perfectly quiet there until about midnight, when a muffled and inauspicious sound arose from the pool. As they approached closer, everyone could clearly distinguish the sounds "Woe! Woe! Pheu! Pheu! Eleleleleleu!" This lamentation lasted no less than a whole hour and was heard not only by the priests but also by all whom Strobylus had brought along to witness such a unique and highly troublesome miracle. There could be no doubt, he said, that the goddess meant to warn her beloved Abdera of some great and imminent danger by means of this strange and menacing portent, or perhaps to call upon it to investigate and punish some as yet undiscovered crime that could draw the wrath of the gods down upon the city. By virtue of his office and in the name of Latona, Strobylus therefore entreated His Grace to convene the worthy collegium of the Decemviri without delay, so that this matter could be weighed in a way befitting its importance and so that the further measures required by such an incident could be taken.

The archon, who had the reputation of leaning rather strongly toward the freethinking of Democritus when it came to the sacred frogs, shook his head at this story and kept the priests waiting quite a while for an answer. But the gravity with which these gentlemen reported the matter and the odd impression that it already seemed to have made on the common people present made it easy for him to foresee that the whole city would soon be full of this alleged miracle and seized with panic toward which he could not remain indifferent. He therefore had no choice but to give the order, right away and in the presence of the priests, that the Decemviri should assemble in the temple of Latona within the hour due to an extraordinary incident.

Meanwhile, Strobylus had seen to it that rumor of a fearful miracle witnessed for the last three nights in Latona's sacred grove had already spread throughout the city. This embittered friends of the archpriest Agathyrsus, who were not so simpleminded as to be fooled by such hocus-pocus, and who did not doubt that some plot against their faction lay hidden behind it. Some young upper-class ladies and gentlemen made a show of mocking the purported miracle and planned outings to attend the newfangled dirge in Latona's frog pond that night. But the high priest's scheme had the full desired effect on both the common people and a large part of the better classes, who tend to act like commoners themselves in matters of this kind. The "Pheu! Pheu! Elelelelelu!" of Latona's frogs suddenly interrupted all public and private business. Young and old, women and children gathered in the streets and tried to explain the miracle with terrified looks on their faces. Almost all said they had heard about it directly from eyewitnesses, and the visible effect that such stories have on their audience seems a natural incentive for their narrators to add a little something to make them more interesting. In less than an hour and throughout the city, the miracle was therefore embellished with such frightful details that just hearing it made people's hair stand on end. Some asserted that the frogs had craned human heads out of the pool when they broke into their fatal song; others, that they had fiery eyes the size of walnuts; some, that ghosts had been seen roaming around the grove and uttering ghastly wails just then; others, that it had thundered and lightninged terribly over the pond in broad daylight; and finally, earwitnesses swore that they had very clearly distinguished the words "Woe to you, O Abdera!" over and over again. In short, the tale (as usual) grew taller and taller, the wider it spread. The more absurd, contradictory, and incredible reports of it were, the more readily people believed it. And when the Decemviri were seen hurrying toward the temple of Latona at an unusual hour, in great haste and with meaningful looks on their faces, no one any longer doubted that events of the greatest importance were brewing in the Abderites' fateful cup. The whole city suspensefully trembled in expectation of things to come.

The collegium of the Decemviri consisted of the archon, the four eldest councillors, the two eldest guildmasters, the high priest of Latona, and two overseers of the sacred pool, and it constituted the most honored of all Abderite tribunals. It had jurisdiction over all matters immediately concerning religion, and its prestige was nearly unlimited.

It has often been said that reasonable people grow wiser with age, while fools simply become sillier. An Abderite Nestor therefore seldom gained much by having seen two or three new generations come and go. And one could thus safely assume that the Decemviri, on the average, formed a committee of the emptiest heads in Abdera. These good people were so willing to take the high priest's story for an absolutely indisputable fact that they seemed to regard hearing witnesses as a mere formality that they should try to dispense with as quickly as possible. Now since Strobylus found these gentlemen already so convinced in advance that the miracle was true, he believed to risk very little by getting straight to the point of the story that he had gone to so much trouble to invent.

"From the first moment that my very own ears witnessed this miraculous sign," he began, "the likes of which (I may well say) have never been seen in the annals of Abdera, the thought occurred to me that it could be a warning from the goddess about the consequences of her revenge, which might be hanging over our heads for some secret, unpunished crime. And this obliged me to prevail upon His Grace the archon to call this meeting of the right honorable Decemviri. What was then just a hunch has been confirmed as certain within the last hour. The culprit has already been found, and the crime can be proved by eyewitnesses whose veracity is all the more beyond doubt because the perpetrator is a man of too great repute for anything less than fear of the gods to make common people come forth and testify against him. Would you ever have thought it possible, my lords, that someone in our midst could be insolent enough to scorn our ancient religion and its rites and relics, which were bequeathed to us by the first founders of our city and have been kept undefiled for so many centuries? And that he could willfully abuse what we all hold most dear and sacred, without respect for either the law or religious belief and our local customs? In a word, can you believe that right in the middle of Abdera, despite the explicit letter of our law, there lives a man who keeps storks in his garden and daily feeds them frogs from Latona's pool?"

Horror and disgust were written on every face at these words. So as not to be the only exception, the archon himself at least had to seem as shaken as the rest of his colleagues really were. "How can that be?" screamed three or four of the eldest all at once. "Who is the scoundrel guilty of such a crime?"

"Forgive me," replied Strobylus, "if I ask you to soften that harsh expression. I for one would prefer to believe that the source of this apparent disdain for our holy rites and orders is not godlessness, but rather mere thoughtlessness and what one nowadays calls philosophy, especially since Democritus has sown such weeds among us. I will and must believe this all the more because the man who can be convicted of this crime by the unanimous testimony of more than seven credible witnesses is himself a man of the cloth, himself a priest—in short, because he is Agathyrsus, the Jasonite."

"Agathyrsus?" cried the astonished Decemviri with one voice. Three or four turned pale and seemed to be embarrassed to see a man of such importance, with whom they had always been on good terms, mixed up in such nasty business.

Strobylus gave them no time to recover. He ordered the witnesses called. They were heard one after the other, and it turned out that Agathyrsus had indeed kept two storks in his garden for some time, that they had often been seen hovering over the sacred pool, and that they really had devoured one of its croaking occupants just about to sun himself on its bank.

This seemed to prove the truth of the accusation beyond all doubt, but to avoid unpleasant consequences, the archon Onolaus nonetheless thought it wise to proceed carefully with a man like Jason's archpriest. He therefore moved that it would be enough for the Decemviri to let him know in a friendly way that for now they were inclined to believe that this regrettable incident had taken place without Agathyrsus's prior knowledge; that they would nonetheless expect a man of his sound and well-known principles not to hesitate for a moment to surrender the criminal storks to the overseer of the holy pool; and that both the Decemviri and the entire city would consider this sufficient proof of his respect for their local laws and religious customs.

Three votes out of nine supported the archon's motion, but Strobylus and the others very vigorously opposed it. Apart from the fact that such extreme lenience should never be shown a citizen of Abdera convicted of such a heinous crime, they argued, due process stipulated that he could not be condemned before he had been given a hearing and allowed to testify. Strobylus therefore moved that the archpriest be summoned to appear immediately before the Decemviri and to answer the charge against him. And this motion passed by six votes to four, despite all the minority's objections. The archpriest was accordingly summoned with all the formalities customary in such cases.

Agathyrsus was not unprepared when the delegates sent by the Decemviri appeared at his door. He kept them waiting for more than an hour, then finally had them led into a hall where he sat in all his priestly splendor on a raised ivory chair. He quite calmly listened to their speaker's stammered message. When they had finished with that, he motioned to a servant who stood off to one side behind his chair. "Take the gentlemen into the garden," he said, "and show them the storks in question, so that they can tell their masters that they have seen them with their own eyes. Then bring them back here again."

The delegates' eyes bulged, but respect for the archpriest tied their tongues, and they followed the servant in silence, like people who were rather ill at ease. When they had come back, Agathyrsus asked them if they had seen the storks. And when they all answered yes, he added, "Then go now, pay my respects to the worthy court of the Decemviri, and remind whoever sent you that those storks, like everything else that lives in the circuit of this temple, are under Jason's protection. And you can also tell them that their insolence in summoning an archpriest of this temple and in wanting to try him according to Abderite law is simply ridiculous." He then motioned to them that they might withdraw.

This answer—which the Decemviri certainly should have expected, since they must have known that the temple of Jason and its priests were entirely exempt from the municipal jurisdiction of Abdera—threw them into indescribable confusion. The high priest Strobylus fell into such a violent fit on hearing it that he no longer knew what he was saying for rage. In the end, he threatened the entire republic with destruction unless someone humbled the overweening pride of such a puffed-up little lackey (as he said), who could not even be called a proper priest, and the offended goddess Latona were rendered complete satisfaction.

The archon and three councillors allied with him, however, replied that Latona (whose frogs, by the way, they honored with all due respect) had nothing to do with the Decemviri overstepping the bounds of their jurisdiction. "I told you all this would happen," spoke the archon, "but you refused to listen. If my proposal had been accepted, I'm certain that the archpriest would have given us a polite and agreeable answer, for a kind word is always well received. But the worthy Strobylus thought he had found an opportunity to let out his old grudge against Agathyrsus, and now it's plain that he and those who let themselves be carried away by his untimely zeal have stained the court of the Decemviri with shame that all the water

in the Hebrus and the Nestus will not wash away in a hundred years.
I confess," he added more passionately than anyone had seen him
for many years, "that I'm tired of being the head of a state that lets
itself be ruined by frogs and ass's shadows, and I'm sorely tempted
to resign my office before the day is done. But as long as I still hold
it, Mr. High Priest, you shall be responsible for any and all disorder
that occurs on the streets of Abdera from this minute on." And with
these words, which were accompanied by a very stern glance at the
astounded Strobylus, the archon proceeded to depart with his three
followers and left the others standing in speechless amazement.

"Well, what do we do now?" wondered the high priest at last,
becoming quite upset by the unexpected turn that this scheme of his
had taken. "What do we do now, gentlemen?"

"We don't know," said the two guildmasters and the fourth councillor, who then went away, too, so that only Strobylus and the two
overseers of the holy pool were left. After all three had talked at the
same time for a while, without really knowing themselves what they
were saying, they finally agreed first of all to take their midday meal
at the home of one of the overseers. After that, they would confer
with their friends and followers about how the motion that the
masses had been set into that morning could be guided toward a
goal that would clinch their faction's victory.

Chapter 11

*Agathyrsus Convenes His Followers. The Substance of
His Speech to Them. He Invites Them to a Grand
Sacrificial Feast. The Archon Onolaus Wants to Resign
His Office. Unease of the Archpriest's Faction at This
Plan. By What Cunning They Foil It.*

Meanwhile, as soon as the deputies sent by the Decemviri had gone,
Agathyrsus promptly summoned his most distinguished adherents
in the Council as well as the town, along with all the Jasonites. He
told them what the Decemviri had just done to him at the behest of
Strobylus the priest, and he showed them how necessary it was to
both the prestige of their faction and the honor of Abdera—indeed,

its very survival—to frustrate the designs of that devious man and to give the people a push back in the opposite direction, after Strobylus had upset them with such a ridiculous story about the lament of Latona's frogs. All could plainly see, he said, that Strobylus had devised this shabby fairy tale solely to trump up the equally absurd charge that he had leveled at him, Agathyrus, before the Decemviri. That charge was nonetheless serious, given the people's superstitious biases, and Strobylus was acting as if it concerned the welfare of the entire republic. But this, too, was all just a straw that he had clutched in desperation, in order to put his sagging faction back on its feet and to cause civil unrest that he might turn to his advantage in affecting the imminent decision about the ass's shadow. For this same reason, it was easy to foresee that the troublesome priest would also try to use what had happened that morning with the Decemviri to make him, the archpriest, unpopular with the people and, if need be, even to provoke a second, more dangerous revolt. Agathyrsus had therefore thought it necessary to put his own most trusted and civic-minded friends in a position to give the people, and anyone else who needed it, a better idea of the day's events and their possible consequences. As far as the storks were concerned, he claimed that they had come of their own accord, through no fault of his own, and had built themselves a nest in a tree in his garden. He had not thought himself entitled to disturb them there, in part because storks had enjoyed a kind of divine right to hospitality among all civilized peoples since time immemorial, in part because Jason granted freedom and protection to all things, dead or alive, within the walls of his temple. The law that the Decemviri had passed several years ago to ban all storks from Abderite territory did not apply to him because the jurisdiction of that tribunal extended only to the ways and means of worshiping Latona. Besides, it was well known that Jason's temple was connected to the republic only insofar as the latter, back when the temple was founded, had promised to protect it against all acts of aggression by domestic or foreign enemies. Otherwise, however, it was fully and forever exempt from all legal obligation to Abderite tribunals and all sovereignty vested in the republic. He had therefore done no more than what his station required of him when he rejected the unauthorized summons. But the Decemviri, by this thoughtless step that Strobylus misled the majority of them to take, had grossly infringed on his archpriestly privileges and forced him to demand strict and complete satisfaction from the republic, in the name of Jason and all the Jasonites. The matter was more important than Guildmaster Pfriem's hangers-on or Strobylus and his frog keepers seemed to realize. The Golden Fleece, which the Jasonites preserved in their temple as their most important legacy, has been regarded and revered for centuries as Abdera's palladium. The Abderites would thus do well neither to take nor to allow steps that could willfully rob them of what the fate and survival of their republic was bound to by an ancient and religiously held belief.

After this speech, the archpriest received the strongest assurances of support from all present, both for their common cause and for the rights and privileges of Jason's temple. They discussed various measures that they would take to reinforce the citizens' sympathies for them and to win back those either led astray by the alleged miracle of Latona's frogs or agitated by Strobylus about the archpriest's storks. All those gathered then dispersed, and everyone took up their posts after Agathyrsus had invited them all to a solemn sacrifice that he would make to Jason in his temple that evening.

While this was going on in the archpriest's palace, the archon had gone home, extremely displeased by the none-too-honorable role that he had been forced to play against his will. He called together all his relations—brothers and brothers-in-law, sons and sons-in-law, nephews and cousins—to announce to them that he was firmly determined to lay down his office before the Great Council the very next day and to retire to a country estate that he had bought some years ago on the island of Thasus. His eldest son and several other relatives were not present at this family convention because they had been summoned to the archpriest half an hour earlier. The rest saw that Onolaus firmly stuck to his resolution, despite all their begging and pleading. One of them therefore slipped away to notify those gathered at Jason's temple and to seek their aid against such a sudden piece of ill luck.

He arrived just as the meeting was about to adjourn. Those well acquainted with the archon's way of thinking found the matter more serious than it seemed to most at first glance. "This must be the first time in ten years," they said, "that the archon has decided anything for himself. It can't have just occurred to him all of a sudden! He's been brooding about it for a long time now, and the events of today have only cracked a vessel that had to break sooner or later. In short, this decision is his own doing, and you can bet that it won't be so easy to make him change his mind."

At these words, the whole assembly was seized with anxiety. All found that this blow, at such an unstable point in time, could be harmful to both their entire faction and the republic itself. They therefore unanimously resolved to reveal as much news of the archon's plan as was needed to sow fear and uncertainty among the people. At the same time, though, they would see to it that the most respected councillors and citizens of both factions betook themselves to the archon before the sacrifice in Jason's temple and implored him in the name of all Abdera not to abandon the rudder of the republic in the middle of a storm, just when they most needed such a wise helmsman.

The need to unite the foremost members of both factions for this purpose was clear because everyone foresaw that all their work on the archon would otherwise be fruitless. For though he had been passionately devoted to the aristocracy ever since his youth, he had nonetheless made it a matter of principle to avoid seeming so. And it was precisely the popular role he had therefore played so long it finally became second nature with him that made the people like him more than almost any of his predecessors. Especially since the city found itself divided into opposing factions of Asses and Shadows, he had made it a regular point of honor to act in a way that gave neither reason to think that he was on their side. And even though nearly all his friends and relatives were avowed Asses, the Shadows remained convinced that they lost—and the Asses gained—nothing by this circumstance. Indeed, the latter were obliged to hide all their actions from him, and they could be sure that for every advantage they won, he would incline to favor the Shadows, so as to bring things back into balance, even though he did not care for a single one of them personally.

Making the archon's decision public had the full effect that they all had wanted. It dismayed the people anew. Most said that no one needed to inquire any further into what the lament of the sacred frogs portended—if the archon abandoned the republic in its current, sorry state, then all was lost.

Word of the great sacrifice that Agathyrsus was making and rumors of the archon's decision to resign his office reached

Strobylus and Guildmaster Pfriem both at the same time. They foresaw the consequences of this double blow at once, and they hastened to counter the one and prevent the other. Strobylus had the people invited to an expiation that would be performed with great ceremony in the temple of Latona that evening in order to purify the city of its secret crimes and to avert the evil portent of the sacred frogs' "Eleleleleleu!" Master Pfriem meanwhile went to see the councillors, guildmasters, and most respected citizens of his faction and to confer with them about how the archon might be made to change his mind. Most were already prepared by agents secretly working for the other side, who had made no secret of the fact that they knew for sure how the Asses had gone to all conceivable lengths to reinforce the archon's resolution under the table. The Shadows were therefore convinced that the Asses meant to elevate someone from their midst to the highest office in the land and that they must thus already be very certain of a majority in the Great Council, with which this choice lay. This observation alarmed the Shadows so greatly that they hurried to Onolaus's house with a large crowd of common folk coming right behind them. While the rabble shouted "Long live Onolaus!" over and over again, the Shadows went in and most humbly begged His Grace, in the name of the whole city, to give up all unfortunate thought of resigning and never to abandon them, least of all at a time when his wisdom was indispensable to keeping the city calm.

The archon appeared very pleased by this public demonstration of his worthy fellow citizens' love and trust. He did not hide from them the fact that the greater part of the Council, the Jasonites, and all the other patricians in Abdera had been to see him barely a quarter of an hour earlier and had made this same request in equally gracious and urgent terms. Whatever reasons he had to be tired of the onerous burden of governing and to wish that it might be placed on shoulders stronger than his own, he did not have the heart to resist the confidence so warmly expressed by both factions. In this, their unanimity regarding his person and his office, he saw a good omen for restoring public order soon, to which he, for his part, would gladly contribute everything possible.

When the archon had finished this pretty speech, the Shadows stood gaping at each other and, to their most acute displeasure, found themselves suddenly much wiser than before. For now they realized that the Asses had deceived and misled them into a false step. Thinking to take this step by themselves, they had hoped it would win the archon over to their side. Now it turned out that he was just as obliged to their opponents, which was as good as saying that he was not obliged to themselves at all. But that was not the worst. The Asses' devious behavior obviously proved how much it meant to them that the archon's position not become vacant. Now the Asses could not possibly think much of Onolaus himself, for he had never done the least thing for their faction. If they so eagerly wanted him to keep his job, it could only be because they were sure that the Shadows would dominate the election of his successor. This insight, which now came to the poor Shadows in a flash, was so annoying that they could barely hide their disappointment and hastily took their leave. The archon was delighted to see them go, but it never occurred to him to wonder why they left so suddenly or to notice how the expressions on their faces had changed.

This had been a great day for the wise and rather portly Onolaus, and he was now fully reconciled with Abdera again. He therefore ordered his door closed to visitors and retired to his gynaceum, where he plopped into his favorite chair, chatted with his wife and daughters, ate dinner, went to bed early, and slept until late the next morning, greatly relieved and unconcerned about the fate of Abdera.

Chapter 12

Decision Day. Measures Taken by Both Factions. The Four Hundred Assemble and the Trial Begins. Philanthropic-Patriotic Dreams of the Editor of This Curious History.

The various engines of war ranged against the Abderite body politic by both sides that day had delivered blows that drove it in opposite directions and—despite the appearance of great internal movement—brought it to a kind of vacillating standstill. When the Four Hundred convened to decide the case of the ass's shadow, everything was therefore just about the same as it had been a few days earlier. That is, the Asses had the greater part of the Council, the patricians, and the most prominent and wealthiest citizens on their side, while the Shadows' strength lay largely in greater numbers. For since the solemn procession around Latona's frog pond, which Strobylus had staged the night before and which all the Shadows had very devoutly attended, with the nomophylax Gryllus and Guildmaster Pfriem in the lead, the mob had declared itself firmly for the Shadows again.

It would have been easy for Strobylus and the other heads of the Shadows to cause much trouble in Abdera after that procession. They were respected by a fanatical mass of people, most of whom had more to gain than to lose from the complete destruction of the republic. But Strobylus had again been most emphatically instructed, in the name of the archon, to keep the rabble in line and to see that the temple and all entrances to the sacred pool were closed before sundown. Unless it were absolutely necessary, moreover, the leaders themselves were far from wanting to take matters to extremes or to murder and burn the entire city. And though they were Abderites in every other respect, they were smart enough to see that it would no longer be in their power to put a stop to the rabble's violent fury, once such a blindly rapacious beast had torn the reins out of their hands. When the procession was over and the gates of the temple were shut, the guildmaster was thus content to tell the lingering crowd that he hoped all upstanding Abderites would come to the marketplace the next morning at nine o'clock to hear the verdict in the case of their fellow citizen Struthion and do as much as they could to help carry his just cause on to victory.

Despite the mild and (in his opinion) very cautious terms in which he had extended it, this invitation was nothing less than the highly illegal action of an insurgent guildmaster who, if necessary, would use the immediate threat of mass riot to coerce judges into seeing things his way. But then this was a risk that the Shadows were firmly resolved to take. And since the other side was completely convinced of this, it had taken all possible measures on its part to prepare itself for the worst that could happen.

As soon as the trial began, Agathyrsus ordered all entrances to Jason's temple occupied by a band of hefty tanners and butchers armed with strong clubs and knives. And in the homes of the most prominent Asses, all had steeled themselves as if to outlast a siege. The Asses themselves appeared in court with daggers under their robes, and some of those who spoke loudest had even taken care to wear armor underneath their tunics so that they could all the more safely expose their patriotic bosoms to blows struck by enemies of their righteous cause.

The ninth hour now approached. All Abdera stood trembling in expectation of the outcome that such an unprecedented dispute would have. No one had eaten a decent breakfast, though all had been up since dawn. The Four Hundred assembled on the raised terrace in front of the temples of Apollo and Diana (the usual place where the Great Council met outdoors), which lay opposite the marketplace and which they reached by climbing a wide flight of fourteen steps. The plaintiff and the defendant, too, had come and taken their proper places along with their closest relatives and their respective sycophants. Meanwhile, the entire marketplace filled up with a crowd of common folk who betrayed their sympathies clearly enough by giving a loud cheer whenever one of the Shadows' councillors or guildmasters came striding in and ascended the steps.

Everyone was now waiting for the nomophylax, who, according to custom in the city of Abdera, presided over the Great Council in all cases not concerned with the routine business of the commonwealth. Since a new law was supposedly at issue, the Asses had tried everything to persuade Onolaus, the archon, to weigh into the ivory chair (which was raised three steps above the councillors' benches and reserved for the president) with his own personage. But he declared that he would rather die than agree to preside over a trial about an ass's shadow. They thus saw themselves forced to yield to his sense of delicacy.

The nomophylax—a great stickler for etiquette, he liked to keep people waiting for him on such occasions—had seen to it that the assembly would meanwhile be entertained and (as he said) prepared for such a solemn rite by music of his own composition. This idea, though an innovation, was very well received and had a very soothing effect (contrary to the intentions of the nomophylax, who meant it to reinforce and excite his faction's feelings of courage and zeal). For the music led the Asses to make quite a few wisecracks, which were greeted from time to time with great laughter. One said, "This allegro sounds a lot like a battle hymn." "For a cock fight," quipped another. "But then the adagio," said a third, "sounds like a funeral march for that jawbreaker Struthion and his patron, Master Shoelace." "The whole piece," added a fourth, "is fit to be made by Shadows and listened to by Asses." As stale as these jokes were, it took nothing more with such a jovial and easily infected little people to put the whole assembly back into their naturally funny mood—a mood that subtly drew the venom out of the partisan spirit just barely still possessing them and that probably did more than anything else to save the city at this critical moment.

Finally, the nomophylax appeared with his bodyguard. These poor, emaciated, and sickly artisans, armed with dull halberds and a harmless kind of rusty sword, looked more like comical scarecrows meant to frighten birds away from a garden than like men of war whose duty it was to instill the rabble with respect and fear for the court. But happy is the republic that needs no other heroes to protect itself from enemies at home and abroad!

The sight of this grotesque militia, which had not been easy to disguise in its warlike attire, and the droll, ungainly way that it behaved gave the crowd of spectators a new shot of mirth. Indeed, the herald had great difficulty making the people quiet down and pay the respect that they owed the highest court in the land.

The president then opened the session with a short speech, the herald yet again commanded silence, and both parties' sycophants were called upon to make their complaints and answers in oral argument.

The sycophants passed for great experts in their field, and the chance to display their art in the case of an ass's shadow had to be extremely exciting for them all by itself. One can therefore easily imagine how completely they had gathered their wits, since this ass's shadow had become a topic that concerned the entire republic and had split its citizens into two opposing factions, each of which took its client's case to heart. For as long as there had been an Abdera on the face of the earth, no one had ever seen a lawsuit that was so ridiculous in itself yet so serious in the way it was handled. Only a sycophant with no talent whatsoever and with no idea of what it meant to ply his trade would not have outdone himself on such an occasion.

It is all the more regrettable that the notorious tooth of time, which so many other great works of genius and wit have failed to escape—or ever will—unfortunately did not spare the originals of those two famous speeches. As far as we can tell, that is. For who knows whether some future Fourmont, Sevin, or Villoison who sets out in search of old manuscripts might not succeed in tracking down a copy of those speeches in some dusty corner of an old monastic library? Or, if that would be asking too much, who can say whether Thrace itself might not in the course of time fall back into the hands of Christian princes who would think it an honor to be powerful patrons of science, to found academies, to have sunken cities excavated, etc.? Who knows if this history of the Abderites itself (as imperfect as it is) might not then be translated into the language of this future, better Thrace and have the honor of inspiring such a neo-Thracian musagete to raise the city of Abdera from its rubble? For then both the chancery and the archive of this famous republic would doubtless be found, and in them all the original documents from the trial of the ass's shadow, including the two speeches that we now lament are lost. At least it is pleasant to soar into the future on the wings of such patriotic-philanthropic dreams and to anticipate one's part in the bliss that still awaits our descendants—bliss so obviously guaranteed by the ever-growing perfection of the arts and sciences and by the enlightened thoughts, refined tastes, and sublime manners that such perfection bestows on all flesh.

For now, we take some solace in knowing that the papers from which the present fragments of the Abderites' history are taken allow us to furnish at least an excerpt of those speeches. Their authenticity is all the more reliable since no reader with a nose will mistake the distinctly Abderite air rising from them—an internal argument that in the end always seems the best that can be made for the work of any mortal, be he Ossian or an Abderite Figaro!

Chapter 13

Speech of the Sychophant Physignatus.

As attorney for the dentist Struthion, the sycophant Physignatus spoke first. He was a man of moderate size, strong muscles, and powerful lungs. He thought highly of himself for having been a pupil of the famous Gorgias, and he claimed to be one of the greatest orators of his time. But on this score, as on many others, he was obviously an Abderite. His greatest skill consisted of elaborately modulating his voice, so as to make his verbose delivery more lively and expressive, by jumping around like a squirrel from one interval to another within the range of an octave and a half. All the while, he would grimace and gesticulate so much that he seemed able to communicate with his audience only through sign language.

But there is no denying that he had a highly polished knack for wrapping judges around his little finger, for confounding their reason and describing his opponent as odious, and generally for making a thing seem better than it was. On occasion, he also knew how to paint pretty pictures with words, as the discerning reader— even without our reminder—will best gather from his speech itself.

Physignatus stood up with all the impertinence of a sycophant relying on the fact that his listeners are Abderites, and he began thus:

"Noble, Firm, and Wise! Magnificent Four Hundred!

"If ever there was a day when the excellence of our republican constitution revealed itself in all its splendor, and if ever I stood among you feeling what it means to be a citizen of Abdera, it is on this great occasion today. Before this worthy and supreme tribunal, before this expectant and solicitous multitude, before this imposing confluence of foreigners, whom the fame of such an extraordinary spectacle has drawn in droves, a lawsuit is about to be decided that in a less liberal, less well-ordered state—even in a Thebes, Athens, or Sparta—would not have been thought important enough to occupy the proud trustees of the commonwealth even for a moment. Noble, laudable, thrice-happy Abdera! You alone, protected by legislation that holds sacred even the least, even the most dubious and captious rights and claims of its citizens, you alone enjoy a kind of freedom and security by which other republics (whatever virtues their patriotic vanity might justly boast) are far overshadowed.

"Or tell me in what other republic a lawsuit between a common citizen and one of the lowest among the people, a suit that at first glance amounts to barely two or three drachmas, about an object that seems so insignificant that the laws completely overlooked it when naming the things that can become private property, a suit about something that a subtle dialectician might declare cannot be called a thing at all—in a word, a suit about the shadow of an ass— tell me in what other republic such a lawsuit would have become an object of universal interest, everyone's affair, and thus, if I may say so, an affair of the entire state, as it were? In what other republic are the laws of property so sharply defined, the mutual rights of citizens so secured from all arbitrariness of public officials, the slightest claims or demands of even the poorest regarded so highly and importantly in the eyes of the authorities that even the highest tribunal in the land does not consider it beneath its dignity to solemnly assemble and adjudicate the apparently doubtful right to an ass's shadow?

"Woe to the man who could sneer at this word and, with absurdly childish concepts of what is great and small, foolishly deride what is the highest honor of our judicial system, the glory of our government, the triumph of every good citizen and the entire Abderite way of life! Woe to the man, I'll say it again and again, who doesn't have the sense to feel this! And hail to the republic where as soon as citizens' rights and a doubt about mine and thine—the foundation of all law and order—are concerned, even an ass's shadow is nothing to be sneezed at!

"But while I, on the one hand, thus know and feel with all the patriotic fervor and all the righteous pride of a true Abderite what glorious witness this present case will bear for all posterity to both the excellent constitution of our republic and the impartial firmness and constant vigilance with which our renowned rulers hold the scales of justice—how much, on the other hand, must I deplore the waning of our ancestors' guileless simplicity, the disappearance of their civic-minded and good-neighborly spirit, their mutual assiduousness, their voluntary readiness to renounce some of our supposedly exclusive claims, out of love and friendship, out of a good heart, or at least for the sake of peace—how much, in a word, must I deplore the decline of good old Abderite customs, which is the true and only source of the shameful and disgraceful lawsuit that we are entangled in today! How will I be able to say it without turning crimson for shame? O you once so famous humility of our revered ancestors, have things gone so far that Abderite citzens—they whose patriotic loyalty and friendship for their neighbors should always prepare them to open their hearts to each other in love—are so selfish, so mean, so unfriendly—what am I saying!—so inhumane as to refuse each other even the shadow of an ass?

"But forgive me, worthy compatriots. I erred in my choice of words. Forgive me an inadvertent insult. He who was capable of such a base, such a coarse and barbarous way of thinking, is not our fellow citizen. He is an inhabitant merely tolerated in our city, a mere protégé of Jason's temple, a person from the deepest dregs of the mob, a person of whose birth, education, and way of life nothing better was to be expected, in short, an ass driver—who, except for the ground he treads and the air he breathes, has nothing in common with us that we do not also share with the wildest tribes of the Hyperborian wastelands. His disgrace stains him alone. It cannot sully us. An Abderite citizen, I daresay, could not have committed such a crime.

"But do I perhaps call it by too strong a name, this act? Put yourselves, I pray, in the place of your good fellow citizen Struthion—and see how it feels!

"He is traveling from Abdera to Gerania on business, the business of his noble art, which has to do solely with easing the pain of his fellow creatures. It is one of the sultriest days of summer. The extreme heat of the sun seems to have transformed the whole horizon into the hollow belly of a glowing oven. Not a cloud in the sky to soften its scorching rays! No gentle breeze to refresh the parched wayfarer! The sun flames over his skull, sucks the blood out of his veins, the marrow out of his bones. Parched, his arid tongue glued to his palate, his glassy eyes blinded by the heat and the glare, he looks around for a shady spot, a single compassionate tree, in the shelter of which he could rest, inhale a breath of fresh air, be safe for a moment from pitiless Apollo's searing arrows.

"In vain! You all know the stretch between Abdera and Gerania. Two hours long and—let it be said to the shame of all Thrace—no tree, no bush that could refresh a wayfarer's eye on this horrid plain of meager fallows and fields of corn, or that could offer him refuge from the midday sun!

"At last, poor Struthion slumped down off his animal. Nature could endure it no longer. He brought the ass to a halt and sat down in its shadow. Poor, wretched means of relief! But though it was slight, it was something!

"And what a monster the unfeeling, hard-hearted man must have been who could then refuse his suffering fellow the shadow of an ass! Would you believe that such a man existed if we did not see him with our own eyes here before us? But there he stands, and—what is almost worse, more incredible than the crime itself—he freely confesses it, even seems to glory in his infamy. And to leave no possibility that someone like him might someday be born to rival his shameless insolence, he goes so far as to tell this supreme, majestic court of the Four Hundred that he was right, despite already being condemned by the worthy municipal court of the first instance. 'I did not refuse him the ass's shadow,' he says, 'even though, strictly speaking, I was not legally obliged to let him sit in it. I merely demanded fair compensation for letting him have the shadow, which he had not rented, along with the ass, which he had.' Wretched, disgraceful evasion! What would we think of a man who refused to let a half-starved traveler sit down for nothing in the shadow of his tree? Or what would we call a man who would not let a stranger dying of thirst slake it with the water flowing on his land?

"Remember, O men of Abdera, that this alone and nothing else was the crime of those Lycian peasants whom the father of gods and men made a dreadful example of for all time by changing them into frogs—revenge for the equally inhumane reception that those poor souls had given his beloved Latona and her children. A fearsome miracle, and its truth and memory are at once kept alive, immortalized, and daily renewed here among us in the holy grove and pool of Latona, reverend and divine patroness of our city! And you, Anthrax, you—an inhabitant dwelling in the city where this fearsome monument to the gods' anger for refusing common decency is an object of public faith and worship—you dare incur their wrath with a similar crime?

"But you stubbornly insist on your right of ownership. 'He who avails himself of his right,' you say, 'does no one wrong. I owe others no more than they rightfully deserve from me. If the ass is my property, so is its shadow, too.'

"Do you really mean that? And do you really believe—or does the sharp-witted, sweet-talking attorney in whose hands you have placed the most despicable case that gods or men were ever called upon to judge—does he believe that the magic of his eloquence or the webs of his sophistic fallacies will so overcome and entangle our reason that we will be persuaded to regard a shadow as something real, much less something to which one can have a direct and exclusive right?

"I would be abusing your patience and insulting your wisdom, grandiose sirs, if I were to repeat here all the evidence that I already placed into the record of the lower court to demonstrate the nullity of my opponent's specious reasoning. For now, I shall limit myself to saying only as much as is absolutely necessary. Strictly speaking, a shadow cannot be considered a real thing. For that which makes it a shadow is nothing real and positive, but just the opposite, namely the privation of whatever light lies on the other things surrounding it. In the case at hand, the only true cause of the shadow that the ass seems to cast, and that any other body would cast in its place, is the oblique position of the sun and the opacity of the ass (a quality that it does not possess insofar as it is an ass, but only insofar as it is a dense and dark body). For the shape of the shadow does not matter here. Strictly speaking, my client therefore sat down not in the shadow of an ass, but in the shadow of a body. And the fact that this body was an ass, and this ass a fellow traveler of a certain Anthrax from the temple of Jason in Abdera, concerned him as little as it matters to us today. For as I said, not the asininity (so to speak) but the corporality and opacity of the aforesaid ass is the cause of the shadow that it seems to cast.

"But even if we admit for the sake of argument that shadows are things, it is clear and known from countless examples throughout the world that they are to be considered public things, which one person has as good a right to as the next and which rightfully belong to whoever first takes possession of them.

"But I will do even more. I will even admit that the ass's shadow is as much an appurtenance of the ass as its ears. What does that gain my opponent? Struthion rented the ass, consequently its shadow, too. For it is understood in every rental contract that the lessor grants the lessee use of the thing in question with all its fittings and appurtenances. What a shady deal it would therefore be if Anthrax could demand that Struthion pay him separately for the ass's shadow! The dilemma is beyond all doubt: the ass's shadow either is or is not an appurtenance of the ass. If it is not, then Struthion and everyone else have just as much right to it as Anthrax. But if it is, then Anthrax, by renting the ass, also rented its shadow. And his claim is as nonsensical as if someone sold me a lyre and then, if I wanted to play it, demanded that I had to pay extra for its sound.

"But why so much reasoning in a case so clear to common sense that one need only hear it to see whose side right is on? What is an ass's shadow? How insolent of this Anthrax to arrogate a right that he does not have, just to practice usury! And even if the shadow really was his, how mean to refuse such a small thing, the smallest thing you can name, the smallest thing imaginable, a thing completely useless in a thousand other instances, to a human being, a neighbor and friend, refuse it in the one instance when it is indispensable!

"Never, O noble and magnanimous Four Hundred, never let it be said of Abdera that such malice, such crime was condoned by a court that (like the famous Areopagus in Athens) the gods themselves would not blush to have settle their quarrels! Dismissing the plaintiff and his inadmissable, unjust, and ridiculous claim and appeal; condemning him to bear all costs and damages that his unwarranted behavior in this case has caused the innocent defendant—this is the least that I can demand in the name of my client. The unlawful plaintiff also owes us satisfaction, truly immense satisfaction, if it is to be commensurate with the enormity of his crime! Satisfaction for the defendant, whose domestic peace, business, honor, and reputation he and his patrons have disturbed and attacked in countless ways over the course of this suit! Satisfaction for the worthy municipal court, the just decision of which he has spuriously appealed to this high tribunal! Satisfaction for this supreme court itself, which he has dared maliciously trouble with such a worthless suit! Finally, satisfaction for the entire city and republic of Abdera, which he has on this occasion caused unrest, discord, and danger!

"Am I asking too much, gentlemen? Are my demands unreasonable? See here all of Abdera, pressing innumerably against the steps of this high court and expecting satisfaction, demanding satisfaction in the name of a deserving, gravely offended compatriot, yea in the name of the republic itself. Respect may tie their tongues, but this just, this irrefusable demand flashes from their eyes! The citizens' confidence, the assurance of their rights, the restoration of our private and public order, the establishment of such order for the future—in a word, the welfare of our whole state depends on the verdict that you will render, depends on your meeting a just and universal expectation. And as an ass had the distinction, in the earliest days of the world, of waking the slumbering gods with its cries when the Titans attacked by night, and thereby of saving Olympus itself from ravage and destruction—may the shadow of an ass now be the occasion, and today the happy epoch when this inveterate city and republic calms down again after so many dangerous shocks, when the ties binding its rulers and ruled are tightly drawn together again, when all past dissension is sunk into the depths of oblivion, and when the whole state is saved and its prosperity assured to flourish forever by the just condemnation of a single, lawless ass driver!"

Chapter 14
Reply of the Sycophant Polyphonus.

As soon as Physignatus had stopped speaking, the people—or rather the mob—that filled the marketplace gave their approval with a fierce shout so loud and long that the judges eventually began to worry that it might permanently interrupt the proceedings. The archpriest Agathyrsus's Asses grew visibly upset. The Shadows, by contrast, though outnumbered in the Great Council, took fresh courage and hoped for a favorable outcome, given the impression that this prelude had to make on the Asses.

Meanwhile, the guildmasters did not fail to give signs admonishing the people to be still. And after the herald had silenced them again with three calls to order, Polyphonus, the ass driver's sycophant, stepped forward. He was a stocky and heavy-set man with short, curly hair and thick, pitch black eyebrows. Raising a bass voice that echoed through the whole marketplace, he held forth as follows:

"Magnificent Four Hundred!

"Truth and light surpass everything else in the world because they need no outside help to be seen. I willingly concede my opponent all the advantages that he thinks to have gained by his rhetorical tricks. It befits a man in the wrong to throw dust in the eyes of children and fools with figures and tropes and feints and the whole hocus-pocus of scholastic rhetoric. Sensible people are not blinded so easily. I will not try to explain how much honor and fame the republic of Abdera will gain by this suit about an ass's shadow. I will neither try to bribe the judges with crude flattery nor try to intimidate them with veiled threats. Still less will I make inflammatory speeches giving the people license to riot and rebel. I know why I am here and to whom I speak. In short, I shall limit myself to proving that the ass driver

Anthrax is right, or—to put it more properly and precisely, as might be expected of an attorney—less wrong than his unlawful adversary. The judge will then know well enough where his duty lies, without my having to remind him."

At this point, a few among the rabble that stood next to the steps of the terrace started to interrupt the speaker with shouts, curses, and threats. But when the nomophylax rose from his ivory throne, the herald once more commanded silence, and the militia standing on the steps lifted their long spears, all were suddenly quiet again. The speaker, who could not be made to lose his composure so easily, continued thus:

"Grandiose sirs, I stand here not as attorney for the ass driver Anthrax but as plenipotentiary of Jason's temple and on behalf of the illustrious and reverend Agathyrsus—its current archpriest and superintendent, guardian of the true Golden Fleece, supreme authority over all its institutions, possessions, courts, and territories, and chief of the eminent race of the Jasonites—to request of you in the name of Jason and his temple that the ass driver Anthrax be rendered satisfaction because he is simply and fundamentally more right. And that he is right is something I hope to prove so clearly and distinctly that the blind shall see and the deaf shall hear it, despite all the ruses that my opponent prides himself on having learned from his master Gorgias. Without further preliminaries, then, let's get straight to the point!

"Anthrax rented his ass to Struthion for a day, not to use any way the latter pleased, but rather to carry the dentist and his carpetbag halfway to Gerania, which everyone knows lies a good eight miles away from here.

"Neither of the two, of course, thought about the ass's shadow when renting the ass itself. But when the dentist dismounted in the middle of a field and forced the ass, which had actually suffered more from the heat than he, to stand in the sun so that he could sit down in its shadow, it was only natural that ass's lord and master did not remain indifferent.

"I do not wish to deny that Anthrax did a foolish and asinine thing when he demanded that the jawbreaker pay him for the ass's shadow just because he had not included it in their contract. But then he is only an ass driver like his ancestors before him, i.e., a man who grew up surrounded by asses and spends more time with them than with honorable people. For this same reason, he has inherited and acquired a kind of right not to be much better than an ass himself. Fundamentally, it thus was all just an ass driver's antics.

"But to what class of animals should we assign the man who took such antics seriously? Had Mr. Struthion acted like a reasonable man, he only would have had to tell the ruffian: 'Good friend, let's not argue with each other on account of an ass's shadow. Since I didn't rent the ass from you to sit down in its shadow but to ride it to Gerania, it's only fair that I reimburse you for the few minutes' time that you lose due to my dismounting, especially since the ass will be no better off for having to stand in the sun that much longer. Here's half a drachma, brother. Let me catch my breath here for a minute, and then —in the name of all frogs!—we'll be on our way again!'

"Had the dentist taken this tone, he would have spoken like a just and honest man. The ass driver would have thanked him for the half-drachma by saying 'May God repay you,' and the city of Abdera would have been spared the dubious fame that my opponent promises this ass's trial will earn her, as well as all the troubles that were bound to occur, once so many high and mighty lords and ladies got themselves mixed up in it. Instead, the man makes an ass of himself, insists on his unfounded liberty of contract to sit down in the ass's shadow as often and as long as he likes, and thus so outrages the ass driver that the latter runs to the city magistrate and lodges a complaint that is just as absurd as the defendant's answer.

"My client, the illustrious archpriest, leaves it to this incisive and supreme court of the Four Hundred to decide whether it would not be wise to set a useful example by clipping the ears of Physignatus, my esteemed colleague, and perhaps sewing on a pair of ass's ears in their place, in everlasting memory of the service that he has performed for the Abderite commonwealth. His agitation is the one and only reason why the jawbreaker did not enter into the equitable settlement suggested by Philippides, our worthy city magistrate. Similarly, my client leaves it to you to decide what kind of public thanks the worthy Guildmaster Pfriem and the other gentlemen who fanned the flames with their patriotic zeal might deserve for their trouble. For his part, as the hereditary overlord and judge of the ass driver Anthrax, Agathyrsus will not fail to give him twenty-five lashes, as soon as this trial is over, as the well-earned reward for the lack of judgment that he has shown in this dispute. But this selfsame ass driver's right to demand satisfaction for the improprieties that he suffered thanks to the dentist Struthion, for the abuse that the latter made of his ass, and for the refusal of fair remuneration for the loss of time and deterioration of his beast of burden nonetheless still remains in full force. The illustrious archpriest therefore desires and expects this high court of justice to award his subject proper, full compensation and satisfaction without further delay.

"You, though," he added, turning around to face the people, "shall know in the name of Jason that all those who improperly and seditiously aided the jawbreaker's evil cause are and shall remain excluded from the alms given to the poor at Jason's temple every month."

Chapter 15

Commotion Caused by Polyphonus's Speech. Addendum by the Sycophant Physignatus. The Judges' Perplexity.

This short and unexpected speech evoked a few moments of utter silence. The sycophant Physignatus seemed sorely tempted to lash out at the passage regarding him personally, but he saw the chilling effect that the gist of his opponent's final lines seemed to have on the common people, so he contented himself with objecting to the defamatory passage about cutting off his ears and other innuendos, *quaevis competentia,* shrugged his shoulders, and fell silent.

The light in which Polyphonus had put the true *statum controversiae* had such a beneficial effect that there remained barely twenty of the entire Four Hundred who did not observe the Abderite custom of insisting that they had seen things the same way all along. And they used rather vivid expressions to speak against those who were guilty of letting such a simple matter become so complicated. Most seemed to favor not only awarding the archpriest the damages and satisfaction that he had sought for his dependant but also forming a commission drawn from the Great Council to find out just who had actually first provoked and instigated this business.

The guildmaster and those who had thrown their lot in with him for better or worse from the start bridled at this suggestion. Their sycophant Physignatus therefore took courage again and demanded that the nomophylax give him the floor once more because he had something new to say in response to his opponent's speech. And since he could not legally be denied this request, he then held forth as follows:

"If placing legitimate trust in a court as worthy as this deserves the name of venal flattery, as my opponent has not shied from calling it, then I must resign myself to bearing blame that I cannot avoid. In any case, I believe to sin less in my all-too-high opinion of you, magnanimous sirs, than my opponent does in imagining that your righteousness and judgment will fall into as obvious a trap as he has set for you. The appearance of common sense with which he glosses over his crude way of framing the case, and a tone of voice that he seems to have lent from his client, cannot do more than momentarily take you by surprise. But that they might be able to wholly overturn the wisdom of the highest deliberative body in Abdera would be blasphemy for me to fear and nonsense for him to hope.

"What? Instead of vigorously representing his client, as he did in the worthy municipal court and has always stubbornly done up to now, Polyphonus himself all at once admits that the ass driver acted wrongly and absurdly by basing his claim against the dentist Struthion on his presumed ownership of the ass's shadow? He publicly admits that the plaintiff has brought an inadmissable, unfounded, and frivolous suit? And he dares blather about a right to indemnification and to demand satisfaction in an ass driver's defiant tone of voice? What new and unique kind of jurisprudence would we have if the guilty party were to get off in the end, when it saw no other way out, by admitting itself to be wrong, and then could win a right to damages and satisfaction with twenty-five lashes that it accepts as punishment and that a fellow like Anthrax can easily bare his back to! Even assuming that the ass driver's mistake lay solely in not instituting the proper legal action, what does that matter to his innocent opponent or to the judge? The former must prepare his answer according to the complaint, and the latter judges a case not as it might appear in a different light and from a different point of view, but as it has been presented to him. In the name of my client, and despite all my opponent's hot air, I therefore expect the present case to be tried according to the rules of procedure and evidence, not to the new twist that Polyphonus has tried to give it, which runs counter to all prior proceedings. The ultimate issue in this dispute is not the loss of time and deterioration of the ass, but the ass's shadow. The plaintiff claimed that his ownership of the ass extends to its shadow, but he has not proved it. The defendant claimed that he has as much right to the ass's shadow as its owner, or that he in any case obtained full use of it by their rental contract, a claim that he has proved.

"I thus stand here, gentlemen, and demand a judicial ruling on that which has hitherto been the object in dispute. This supreme court has convened for its sake alone! It alone constitutes the case in which the court must find. And I daresay in front of all the people listening to me here: either there is no justice in Abdera any more, or my demand is legal and the rights of every citizen stand and fall with my client's!"

The sycophant stopped, the judges started, the people murmured and squirmed anew, and the Shadows once again held their heads high.

"Well," said the nomophylax, turning to Polyphonus, "what does the plaintiff's counsel have to say to that?"

"Nothing, Your Honor," replied Polyphonus, "except, word for word, everything that I already said. This trial about an ass's shadow is such ugly business that it cannot be settled soon enough. The plaintiff is wrong, the defendant is wrong, the lawyers are wrong, the judge on the lower court was wrong, all Abdera is wrong! One would think that some evil wind had come upon us all and that we have not been quite as right in the head as we should be. If we absolutely had to prostitute ourselves any longer, I could stand here and give you a speech about my client's right to his ass's shadow that would last from dawn till dusk. But, as I've said, even if the comedy that we have performed could be excused as long as it was nothing more than that, it doesn't seem at all right to me to keep pretending before a court as worthy as the High Council of Abdera. At least that is not my mandate, and I leave it to you, mighty lords, reminding you once again of all that I have rightly asked in the name of the illustrious and honorable archpriest, to settle this suit once and for all, however the gods may inspire you."

The judges were greatly perplexed, and it is hard to say what means they finally would have found to extricate themselves and save face, if chance, which has always been the Abderites' great patron, had not taken pity on them by giving this subtle civic drama a denouement that no one either had or could have foreseen a moment earlier.

Chapter 16

Unexpected Denouement of the Entire Comedy and Restoration of Peace and Quiet in Abdera.

The ass whose shadow caused such an odd obfuscation in the Abderites' thick skulls (as the archon Onolaus put it) had long ago been led off to the public stable and barely fed while the case was pending. The best that one can say is that it had hardly grown fatter.

Now this same morning it had occurred to the stable hands of the republic, who knew the case was going to end, that it was only fair that the ass—which, after all, played one of its leading roles—should go and join the party. They had therefore brushed it and adorned it with garlands and ribbons, and they now brought it out with great pomp, to the cheers of countless street urchins. As chance would have it, they arrived in the side street nearest the market just as Polyphonus had finished his addendum and the poor judges no longer knew what to do. The people, though, wavered in an uncertain and ill-humored kind of vacillation between fear of the archpriest and the new blow that Physignatus's second speech had given them.

The racket that those street urchins made about the ass turned everyone's head to see where it was coming from. Many people were startled and pushed their way forward. "Ha," one of them finally cried, "here comes the ass itself!" "It probably wants to help the judges reach a decision," another said. "That damned ass," cried a third, "it's ruined us all. I wish the wolves had devoured it before it saddled us with this ungodly mess!" "Hurrah!" screamed a tinker who had always been one of the most ardent Shadows. "All true Abderites, storm the donkey! Make it pay for all this! Don't leave a single hair hanging on its shabby tail!"

The whole crowd pounced on the poor beast at once, and in no time at all it was ripped to shreds. Everyone wanted a little bit. They tore, beat, pulled, scratched, tussled, and fought over the carcass with truly unique vehemence. With some, the rage went so far that they gobbled up their share, raw and bloody, right on the spot. Most, though, ran home with whatever they had taken, and since each was chased by a screaming crowd that tried to snatch his quarry, the marketplace was soon as empty as at midnight.

The Four Hundred were so alarmed at the outset of this uproar, the cause of which they could not immediately see, that without knowing what they were doing, they all drew forth the murderous implements secretly carried under their robes. And the gentlemen stared at each other in no little amazement when, all of a sudden, a dagger flashed in every hand, from the nomophylax down to the lowliest assessor. But when they finally saw and heard what was the matter, they quickly stuck their knives back into their bosoms and all burst out into unquenchable laughter, like the gods in the first book of the *Iliad*.

"Thank heaven!" laughed the nomophylax at last, after the right honorable gentlemen had come to their senses again. "For all our wisdom, we could not have brought the case to a more fitting conclusion. Why should we now rack our brains any longer? As often happens, the innocent cause of this sorry dispute, the ass, has become its victim. The people have vented their rage on it, and now all we have to do is reach the right decision for this day, which seemed about to come to a bitter end, to be a day of joy and a return to peace and quiet. Since the ass itself is no more, what good would it do to argue any longer about its shadow? I therefore move that we declare this whole asinine case officially over and done; that both parties be reimbursed for all costs and damages from the public treasury; that they be sworn to eternal silence; and that a monument be erected to the poor ass at public expense, so that we as well as our descendants may always be reminded how close to ruin a great and flourishing republic came for no better reason than an ass's shadow."

Everyone applauded the nomophylax's motion as the best and brightest way out, given the current state of things. Both parties could be satisfied with it, and it was a small price for the republic to pay for restoring order and preventing greater harm and disgrace. The Four Hundred therefore unanimously issued a decree based on this motion, though it took some doing to persuade Guildmaster Pfriem not to be the odd man out. With its martial militia guarding it front and rear, the Great Council escorted the nomophylax back to his house, where he invited his gentlemen colleagues, one and all, to a grand concert that evening, which he would give for them to confirm their reestablished harmony.

The archpriest Agathyrsus not only spared the ass driver the promised twenty-five lashes but—on top of that—even presented him with three fine mules from his own stable, explicitly forbidding him to accept any indemnification from the Abderites' public coffers. The following day he gave a splendid banquet for all the Shadows from both the Great and Small Councils, and in the evening he had half a drachma handed out to every citizen, no matter what guild, to drink to his health as well as that of all good Abderites. This generosity regained him their favor at once. And since (as we know) it did not take much for people like the Abderites to go from one extreme to the other anyway, it is hardly surprising, given such noble gestures by the former head of the stronger faction, that the names "Asses" and "Shadows" soon were heard no more. Even the Abderites themselves laughed at their foolishness as an attack of feverish frenzy that now—thank goodness—had passed. One of their balladeers (they had very many and very bad ones) hastened to do what he could to set the whole story to a popular song that was soon sung throughout the streets. And the dramatist Thlaps did not fail to write a whole comedy about it within a few weeks, with music composed by the nomophylax himself.

This nice little piece was performed in public to great applause, and both former factions laughed at it as hard as if the whole thing had nothing at all to do with them.

Democritus, who had let the archpriest persuade him to come along to this play, said while leaving: "At least one has to admit that Abderites are like Athenians in that they can laugh very heartily at their own foolish escapades. They are none the wiser for it, but there is still much to be said for a nation that can bear honest people laughing at its folly and that laughs along with them, instead of becoming spiteful, like apes."

It was the last time in his life that Democritus went to an Abderite comedy. For he soon afterwards simply packed his bags and left town, without telling a soul in Abdera and its surroundings where he was going. And from that time on, no one has ever heard from him again.

Translated by Ellis Shookman

Glossary

Abdera. Town in Thrace, founded c. 650 B.C. Its inhabitants were considered stupid by the ancient Greeks, and *Abderite* became a term of reproach. In the early part of his "history," Wieland tells how such silly people came to Thrace from a colony in Ionia, an ancient district, like Lycia, in western Asia Minor. His own fictional Abderites eventually abandon their city when it is overrun by frogs, rats, and mice.

Ab ovo. From the egg—i.e., from the very beginning.

Accessorium. "Accessory" in the legal sense of anything that is joined to another thing as an ornament, or to render it more perfect, or which accompanies it, or is subordinate to it, or which belongs to or with it.

Anacreon's wild Thracian maiden. Anacreon (fl. c. 521 B.C.) was a Greek lyric poet whose graceful, elegant, and sometimes erotic verse celebrates the joys of wine and love. His "Ode to a Thracian Maiden" begins "Thracian filly, coyly looking / At me with coquettish glances" (tr. J. F. Davidson). Earlier in his story, Wieland writes that the poem combines a "wild Thracian tone" with "Ionic grace," supporting his theory that Anacreon came to Abdera from Ionia.

And as an ass had the distinction . . . In the earliest published version of his story, Wieland described this ass as that of Silenus, the oldest of the satyrs—part human, part bestial creatures that belonged to the wine god Dionysus's entourage—who usually rode on an ass because he was too drunk to walk. The event cited here rather ironically shows such an ass saving the Olympian gods.

A non posse ad non esse valet consequentia. It logically follows that nothing is that cannot be.

Apollo. In Greek religion, god born (along with his twin sister Artemis, see **Diana**) of Leto (see **Latona**) and Zeus. Among many other roles, Apollo was often associated with archery and the law. As Phoebus Apollo, god of light, he was sometimes identified with the sun. As patron of music and poetry, he bore the name "Musagete" and was connected with the Muses, the mythological goddesses of the arts, whom he was said to lead.

Archon. Officer of the state in ancient Athens and other Greek cities. Elected or chosen by lot, archons served their terms and usually entered the Areopagus. The name of Wieland's archon, "Onolaus," means "the people's ass" in Greek.

Areopagus. A hill (near the Acropolis) that was the sacred meeting place of the prime legislative and judicial council of ancient Athens. This council itself was also called the Areopagus.

Aristophanes (c. 448–after 388 B.C.). Athenian comic poet and greatest ancient writer of comedy. He directly attacked historical persons in political, social, and literary satire. His *Wasps* (422 B.C.) is a satire on the Athenian passion for litigation, and his *Frogs* (405 B.C.) is a literary satire involving two other great Athenian playwrights, Aeschylus and Euripides. *Wasps* mentions fighting "for an ass's shadow," an ancient Greek proverb meaning "for a mere trifle." So that his chorus in *Frogs* sounds like its title characters, he has them make the noise "Brekekekek ko-ax ko-ax."

Athos, Mount. Mountain at the southern tip of the Athos peninsula in Macedonia, in northeastern Greece.

Attic talent. Attica was the region of ancient Greece around Athens, its chief city. A talent was an ancient unit of weight equal to six thousand drachmas or of value equal to a talent of gold or silver.

Citra praejudicium. Without precedent, being an exception (to the rule).

Daric. A small gold coin of ancient Persia, probably named after King Darius I of Persia (d. 486 B.C.)

Decemviri. A council or ruling body consisting of ten members.

Democritus (c. 460–370 B.C.). Greek philosopher from Abdera. His theories about the physical world, which he thought consisted of imperceptible atoms, were radically mechanistic and scientific for his day. In the first book of Wieland's story—"Democritus among the Abderites"—his clear thinking and cosmopolitan knowledge set him apart from his foolish fellow citizens.

Denouement. Final outcome, result, or unraveling of the main dramatic complication in a play or other work of literature; the outcome or result of any complex situation or sequence of events.

Diana. In Roman religion, the goddess originally associated with forests and women. She was identified with the Greek goddess Artemis, a virgin huntress who was the daughter of Zeus and Leto (Latona) and the twin sister of Apollo.

Drachma. An ancient Greek silver coin and basic unit of value.

"Eleleleleleu!" In ancient Greek, a loud cry.

Elysium. According to the Greeks and Romans, the dwelling place of happy souls after death.

Euripides (480 or 485–406 B.C.). Greek tragic poet whose plays show a rational, iconoclastic attitude toward the gods and a realistic interest in unheroic characters. "Cupid, prince of gods and men" is a quotation from his *Andromeda,* a play performed twice in the third book of Wieland's story—"Euripides among the Abderites"—just before *The Case of the Ass's Shadow* begins. The second performance, which Euripides himself oversees, is so moving that the Abderites cite this passage in a kind of frenzy, proof of Euripides' superiority to their own national literature and taste.

Ex consensu et consuetudine generis humani. According to the consensus and (established) custom of humankind.

Facti species. The shape of events; the nature of the affair.

Fates. In Greek religion, goddesses who controlled the lives of human beings. Clotho spun the web of life, Lachesis measured its length, and Atropos cut it.

Figaro. Hero of *The Barber of Seville* (1775) and *The Marriage of Figaro* (1784), comedies by P. A. Caron de Beaumarchais (d. 1799). For an explanation of the "fig" contained in this name, see **Sycophant.**

Fourmont, Sevin, Villoison. Michel Fourmont (1690–1746) and François Sevin (1682–1741) were French philologists sent on a scholarly expedition to the orient. Jean Baptiste Gaspard d'Ansse de Villoison (1750–1805) wrote on Greek language and literature, ancient and pagan religion, and deciphering ancient writings and inscriptions.

Golden Fleece. See Jason.

Gorgias (c. 485–c. 380 B.C.). Greek Sophist who taught and practiced rhetoric in Athens. His rhetorical art of persuasion rested on serious skepticism about the possibility of knowing objective truth. Plato wrote a dialogue bearing his name.

Gyneceum. Women's rooms in an ancient Greek house; boudoir.

Hebrus. The principal river of Thrace.

Hercules. Greek hero famous for his strength and courage shown in numerous labors and adventures. He was initially one of the Argonauts who sailed with Jason in search of the Golden Fleece, but he soon got sidetracked and never rejoined the expedition.

Hyperborean. From or relating to an extreme northern region. In Greek mythology, Hyperboreans were people living in a state of perfect bliss in the far north.

Iliad. The ancient Greek epic (ascribed to Homer) about the Trojan War. At the end of book 1, Zeus seems about to strike Hera, his wife. Hephaistos—her lame son, the gods' smith and comic craftsman—averts such divine domestic violence by first drawing the other gods' attention to himself and then not too gracefully serving them nectar, making them laugh out loud: "And quenchless laughter / broke out among the blissful gods / to see Hephaistos wheezing down the hall" (tr. Robert Fitzgerald).

In petto. In (the) breast; secretly, in private.

In statu quo. In the same (or former) state in which something is (or was).

Interveniendo. By intervention (as a third person, not originally a party in a lawsuit, but claiming an interest in its subject matter).

Inter vivos. Between the living, from one living person to another.

Iris. In Greek mythology, goddess of the rainbow who was often represented as a messenger of Zeus and Hera.

Jason. In Greek mythology, hero who led expedition seeking the Golden Fleece, the magic fleece of a winged ram. His fellow heroes were called the Argonauts.

Latona. Roman name for Leto, in Greek mythology the daughter of Titans and the mother of Apollo and Artemis. Wieland's remarks on the appearance of her temple in Abdera are somewhat confusing, since Ionic architecture was lighter and more graceful—but actually less simple—than the Doric order or style.

Lycian colony. See **Abdera.**

Lycian peasants . . . Lycia was an ancient country in southwest Asia Minor. Latona changed some peasants there into frogs for refusing to let her drink water from their pond. This story—in Ovid's *Metamorphoses,* book 6, lines 317ff.—bears some resemblance to Wieland's about the ass's shadow when the tired, faint, hot, and thirsty Latona asks the peasants why they will not let her drink: "Why am I kept from the water? The use of water / Is free to all, or should be. Nature never / Made the sun private, nor the air, nor water, / Whose gentle blessing I have come for, asking / Nothing that all men do not own" (tr. Rolfe Humphries).

Megara. Important town in ancient Greece, known for its wealth.

Meum et tuum. Mine and thine—i.e., what is my property and what is yours.

Milesian. From Miletus, flourishing ancient Greek seaport in western Asia Minor.

Mortis causa. By reason or in contemplation of death.

Musagete. See **Apollo.**

Nemesis. In Greek mythology, personification of the god's retribution for violation of sacred law; the avenger.

Nestor. In Greek mythology, wise Greek king. In the *Iliad* and the *Odyssey,* he is respected for his physical vigor in old age and his prudent advice.

Nestus (also Nestos or Mesta). River in southwestern Bulgaria and northeastern Greece.

Nomophylax. Guardian of the law. In Wieland's story, a high public official who leads the chorus in religious services and oversees the extremely active musical life of Abdera. As these functions came to outweigh all others, the best singer in Abdera always became nomophylax, despite his ignorance of its actual laws. The name of Wieland's nomophylax, "Gryllus," sounds like Greek words for *pig* and *caricature.*

Objectum litis. The thing sought to be attained in a lawsuit.

Ob paritatem rationis. For the same or a similar reason.

Olympus. Mountain in Thessaly that was considered the abode of the chief gods of ancient Greece.

Onoskiamachia. Battle of the ass's shadow. This compound noun recalls two other battles. The Titans, primeval deities in Greek religion, were overthrown by the Olympian gods, led by Zeus, in a battle called the Titanomachia. A less-serious struggle is recounted in the *Batrachomyomachia* (fifth century B.C.), a pseudo-Homeric epic about a mock-heroic battle of frogs and mice.

Ossian. Legendary Gaelic poet and Irish bard of the third century. In 1765, the Scottish author James Macpherson (1736–96) published *The Works of Ossian,* an edition of fragments and other supposedly ancient Scottish poetry that he claimed merely to have translated but that turned out to be largely of his own composition. Although thus exposed as forgeries, Macpherson's poems inspired many writers in the emerging Romantic movements, especially in Germany.

Palladium. Something that affords security or protection, named after a statue of Pallas (the goddess Athena) supposedly assuring the safety of ancient Troy.

Pcto. "Puncto," in point of, in the matter of, with regard to.

"Pheu! Pheu!" Cry (of woe) in Ancient Greek.

Philip. Greek coin named after (and depicting) the Macedonian king Philip II (382–336 B.C.), father of Alexander the Great.

Priapus. In Greek religion, fertility god of gardens and herds, represented as a grotesque little man with an enormous phallus.

Quaevis competentia. As suitable, appropriate, or rightfully due in one's station.

Rationes dubitandi et decidendi. Reasons for and against, decisive factors.

Res nullius. The full legal phrase (and basic concept) is *res nullius naturaliter fit primi occupantis*—"A thing that has no owner naturally belongs to the first finder."

Salvis tamen melioribus. Yet notwithstanding better evidence or findings.

Seladon. Celadon, sentimental lover in *L'Astrée* (1607–27), a pastoral novel by the French writer Honoré d'Urfé (1567–1625).

Statum controversiae. Present state of the controversy.

Stentorian. Extremely loud. From "Stentor," a Greek in the Trojan War famed for his powerful voice.

Stygian marshes. In Greek mythology, the Styx was one of four rivers separating Hades, the underworld of the dead, from the land of the living. Marshes around the Styx—and thus "Stygian"—are mentioned in Aristophanes' *Frogs*.

Summa appellabilis. Minimum sum of money required to be at issue in order for the decision of a lower court to be appealed to a higher court for review.

Sycophant. Literally, "fig-shower" (one who brings figs to light by shaking the tree on which they grow) or "fig-informer" (one who informed against persons illegally exporting figs from Attica). Alternatively, from using the "gesture of the fig" (one of contempt, such as thrusting the thumb between two fingers) to denounce a culprit in ancient Athens, where the term also meant "talebearer." Modern usage implies slanderous accusations and self-serving flattery, the same mendacious qualities shown by Wieland's fictional lawyers.

Thasos. Greek island off Macedonia in the northwestern Aegean Sea.

Themis. In Greek religion, a Titan sometimes identified as an earth goddess but more often associated with law, order, and justice.

Thlaps. Fictional Abderite poet whose plays Wieland elsewhere describes as being neither comedies, nor tragedies, nor farces, but rather "living portraits of family life in Abdera." As such hybrid "Thlapsodies," those plays seem merely silly, but this new genre recalls serious attempts to start a German national theater in the city of Mannheim with realistic plays about the moral and sentimental life of characters drawn from contemporary, eighteenth-century bourgeois families. With "Thlaps"—a name much like a Hungarian (and German) word for *clumsy* or *awkward*—Wieland thus satirizes certain, new aspects of literary life in his own day.

Thrace. Region now largely in northeastern Greece. The ancient Thracians did not absorb Greek culture, and the Greeks regarded them as barbarians. At the time Wieland wrote, modern Thrace was still ruled by the Ottoman Empire.

Virtuosi. People who are interested in the pursuit of knowledge or in objects of fine art or who excel in the technique of such an art, especially music.

"Wrek-kek-kek-koax-koax." See **Aristophanes**.

Karl Philipp Moritz

From
ANTON REISER

A PSYCHOLOGICAL NOVEL

This psychological novel might equally well be called a biography, as the observations in it are for the most part taken from real life. Anyone who is acquainted with human affairs and knows that what at first seemed petty and insignificant may become highly important as life goes on will not be offended at the apparent triviality of many circumstances here related. Further, in a book that is mainly to describe a human being's inner history, no great variety of characters will be expected. The object is not to distract the imaginative faculty but to concentrate it and to enable the soul to see clearer into its own being. The task is not an easy one, nor is it bound always to succeed; but from the pedagogic point of view it can never be lost pains to direct our attention more to human beings themselves and make them feel the importance of their own individual existence.

In Pyrmont, a place famous for its mineral spring, there was living on his own estate in 1756 a nobleman who was head of a sect in Germany known under the name of Quietists or Separatists, whose tenets were mainly drawn from the writings of Madame Guyon, a well-known enthusiast who lived in France at the time of Fénelon, her intimate friend.

Herr von Fleischbein, for that was his name, lived as completely secluded from all the other inhabitants of the place, and from their religious manners and customs, as his house was cut off from them by a high wall that surrounded it on every side.

This house formed a little republic of its own, governed by a constitution quite different from that of the countryside around it. The whole household down to the meanest servants consisted wholly of persons who made or professed to make it their sole endeavor to return again into their "nothingness," to use Madame Guyon's phrase, to "kill" all passions and eradicate all "individuality."

Everyone was obliged to assemble once a day in a large room of the house for a sort of religious service, which had been instituted by Herr von Fleischbein and which consisted in all sitting round a table for half an hour with closed eyes and their heads resting on the table, waiting to hear the voice of God or the "inner word." If anyone heard it he made it known to the rest.

Herr von Fleischbein also regulated the reading of his household and any of his servants, male or female, who had a quarter of an hour of leisure was to be seen sitting and reading with an air of reflection one of Madame Guyon's works on "silent prayer" or the like.

Everything down to the most trifling household occupations wore a serious, severe, and solemn air. In every face was to be read, so it seemed, "mortification" and "self-denial," and in every act the effort to "pass out of self" and "enter into nothingness."

Herr von Fleischbein after the death of his first wife had not married again but lived with his sister Frau von Prüschenk in this retirement, in order to devote himself entirely and without interruption to the great task of spreading the doctrines of Madame Guyon.

A steward called H. and a housekeeper and her daughter formed the intermediate grade in the household, and below them came the humbler servants. The household was closely united and all had unbounded respect for Herr von Fleischbein, who really led a blameless life, though the inhabitants of the place busied themselves with the most mischievous stories about him.

Every night he got up thrice at fixed hours to pray, and he spent most of the day time translating from the French the works of Madame Guyon, which fill many volumes; he then had them printed at his own expense and distributed them gratis to his dependents.

The doctrines contained in these writings are largely concerned with what I have already mentioned: the complete mortification of all so-called "self-hood" or "self-love," and a completely disinterested love towards God with which not an atom of self-love may mingle, if it is to remain pure; from this arises finally a state of perfect and blessed "tranquillity," which is the goal of all these efforts.

As Madame Guyon devoted almost all her life to writing books, they are so surprisingly numerous that even Martin Luther can hardly have written more. Among others there is a mystic interpretation of the whole Bible in some twenty volumes.

This Madame Guyon had to suffer much persecution, and as her principles were considered dangerous, she was put in the Bastille, where she died after ten years' imprisonment. When her head was dissected after her death, her brain was found to be almost dried up. She is still regarded by her followers as a saint of the first order, and almost worshiped as divine, and her sayings are put on the same level with those of the Bible; for it is assumed that by her complete mortification of "self" she was so completely united with God that all her thoughts were necessarily divine.

Herr von Fleischbein had become acquainted with Madame Guyon's writings on his travels in France, and the dry metaphysical extravagance that prevails in them had such a strong attraction for his habit of mind that he devoted himself to them with the same enthusiasm with which he would probably have devoted himself in other circumstances to the loftiest stoicism, with which the doctrines of Madame Guyon, with their complete mortification of all desires, often have a striking similarity.

He was accordingly revered by his followers as a saint, and they really believed that at the first glance he could see into the innermost soul of a person.

Pilgrimages were made to his house from all sides, and among those who visited the house at least once a year was Anton's father.

Brought up without proper education, he married his first wife very early, and always led rather a wild and wandering life, during which he felt religious emotions from time to time, but paid little attention to them. Suddenly on the death of his first wife he withdrew into himself, became reflective, and, as they say, quite a changed man, and during a stay at Pyrmont became acquainted first with the steward of Herr von Fleischbein and then through him with Herr von Fleischbein himself.

The latter gave him Madame Guyon's books to read one after the other, he was drawn to them, and soon became a professed follower of Herr von Fleischbein.

Notwithstanding, he took it into his head to marry again, and he made acquaintance with Anton's mother, who soon consented to marry him, which she would never have done had she foreseen the hell of misery she was to find in the married state. She promised herself more love and regard from her husband than she had enjoyed before with her relations, but how terribly did she find herself deceived!

While Madame Guyon's doctrine of complete mortification and suppression of all, even the gentle and tender passions, harmonized with the hard and insensible nature of her husband, she could never reconcile herself to these ideas, against which her heart revolted.

This was the germ of all the subsequent discord in their marriage.

Her husband began to despise her religious opinions because she would not grasp the high mysteries taught by Madame Guyon.

This contempt was extended afterwards to her other opinions, and the more she felt this, the more their affection as man and wife was bound to decrease, and their mutual discontent with one another to grow daily greater.

Anton's mother was well read in the Bible and had a pretty clear idea of its religious system. For instance, she could talk in a very edifying way on the doctrine that faith without works is dead.

She read her Bible at all hours with intense pleasure, but as soon as her husband tried to read the writings of Madame Guyon to her, she felt a sort of anxiety, probably due to the idea that she might be diverted from the true faith.

So she sought to escape by whatever means she could. A further reason was that she attributed the cold and unamiable behavior of her husband in great measure to the Guyon doctrine, which she began to curse more and more in her heart and to curse aloud when the discord of their marriage broke out openly.

Thus the domestic peace and tranquility and welfare of a family were disturbed for years by these unhappy books, which probably neither of them could understand.

Such were the circumstances in which Anton was born, and it can be said of him with truth that he was oppressed from his cradle.

The first tones his ear heard and his first glimmering intelligence understood were mutual curses and execrations of the indissoluble marriage tie.

Though he had father and mother, yet he was forsaken by both in his earliest boyhood because he did not know which to turn to, on which to depend, for both hated one another, and yet both were equally near to him.

In his earliest boyhood he never enjoyed the caresses of affectionate parents, nor the reward of their smile after some little effort.

When he entered his parents' house he entered a house of discontent, anger, tears, and complaints.

These first impressions were never obliterated from his mind, and they made it a place where gloomy thoughts collected that no philosophy enabled him to expel.

As his father was on service during the Seven Years' War, his mother went with him for two years to a little village.

Here he had comparative freedom and some compensation for the miseries of his childhood.

The impressions of the first meadows that he saw, of the cornfield that stretched up a gentle slope crowned with green underwood, of the blue mountains and the individual shrubs and trees that cast their shadows on the green grass at its foot and spread closer and closer as you climbed—these impressions still mingle with his pleasantest thoughts and form as it were the foundation of all the illusory pictures his fancy paints.

But how soon these two happy years fled!

Peace came, and Anton's mother went with him to the town to join her husband.

The effect of the long separation was a short-lived illusion of married harmony, but the deceptive calm was soon followed by a storm that was in fearful contrast.

Anton's heart melted in distress when he had to put one of his parents in the wrong, and yet it often seemed to him as if his father, whom he merely feared, was more in the right than his mother, whom he loved.

Thus his young spirit wavered to and fro between love and hate, between fear of his parents and trust in them.

When he was not yet eight years old, his mother bore a second son, on whom were concentrated the few remains of a father's and a mother's love, so that he now felt almost completely neglected, and when he was spoken of it was in a tone of depreciation and contempt that pierced his heart.

How was it that the ardent longing could arise in his heart for affectionate treatment to which he had never been used, and of which therefore he could hardly form a conception?

In the end, to be sure, this feeling was pretty well deadened; he almost felt as if it was the natural thing to be continually rebuked, and a friendly look, which he once received, seemed something quite strange that could not be reconciled with his other impressions.

He felt most intensely the need of friendship with his kind, and often when he saw a boy of his own age, his whole soul went out to him, and he would have given anything to make friends with him; but the depressing feeling of the contempt that he suffered from his parents and the shame he felt because of his wretched, torn, and dirty clothes kept him from venturing to address a more fortunate boy.

Thus he went about almost always sad and solitary because most boys of the neighborhood were more neatly and respectably dressed and in better clothes and would not associate with him; and he in his turn would not associate with those who were not, because of their loose character and also perhaps from a certain pride.

So he had no one to make a companion of, no playmate of his childhood, no friend among big or little.

But in his eighth year his father began to teach him to read, and for this purpose bought him two small books, one of which contained instruction in spelling and the other a discourse against spelling.

In the former Anton had to spell a good many hard biblical names—Nebuchadnezzar, Abednego, etc., which conveyed to him no shadow of an impression. This therefore was rather a slow process.

But as soon as he became aware that intelligible ideas were actually expressed by the combination of letters, his eagerness to learn to read became stronger every day.

After his father had given him barely a few hours instruction, to the surprise of all his relations he learned in a few weeks for himself.

To this day he remembers with intense pleasure the lively delight he then enjoyed when, with much spelling, he made out with difficulty a few lines that meant something for him.

But he could not understand how it was possible that other people should read as quickly as they spoke; he despaired at that time of ever being able to achieve it.

All the greater was his surprise and delight when he could do this too after a few weeks.

Moreover, his success seemed to bring him some attention from his parents, still more from his relations. This he did not fail to notice, but it never became the true reason that spurred him on to diligence.

His appetite for reading was insatiable. Luckily in his spelling book, besides verses from the Bible, there were stories of good children, which he read through a hundred times, though they were not very attractive.

One was the story of a six-year-old boy who at the time of persecution would not abjure Christianity, and instead preferred horrible torture and death with his mother as a martyr for his religion; the other of a wicked lad, who was converted in his twentieth year and died soon after.

Then came the turn of the other little book, containing the discourse against spelling, and he read to his great surprise that it was harmful and even soul-destructive to teach children to read by spelling.

In this book he also found a direction to teachers how to teach children reading and a treatise on the production of the several sounds by the vocal organs. Dry as this seemed, he read it through from beginning to end with the greatest persistence for want of anything better.

Through reading a new world was now opened up for him once and for all, in the enjoyment of which he could compensate himself in some degree for all that was unpleasant in his actual world. When nothing but noise and quarreling and domestic discord prevailed around him or when he looked in vain for a playmate, he hurried off to his book.

Thus he was driven quite early from the natural world of children into the unnatural world of imagination, where his spirit was put out of tune for a thousand joys of life that others can enjoy with a full heart.

In his eighth year he got a kind of wasting illness. He was quite given up and constantly heard himself spoken of as one regarded as dead. This he thought laughable, or rather death, as he pictured it to himself then, seemed something laughable rather than serious. His aunt, who seemed to have more affection for him than his parents, took him to a physician, and a cure of a few months restored him.

He had hardly been well for a few weeks when, while walking with his parents in the fields—a pleasure all the greater for its rarity—he began to feel a pain in his left foot. This was his first walk after his recovery and was to be his last for a long time.

On the third day the swelling and the inflammation in the foot had become so dangerous that they wished to amputate next day. Anton's mother sat and cried and his father gave him a halfpenny.

These were the first signs of compassion he remembered his parents showing him, and they produced all the stronger an impression on him from their rarity.

On the day before that fixed for the amputation, a compassionate shoemaker came to Anton's mother and brought her an ointment by the use of which the swelling and inflammation were reduced in a few hours, so no amputation took place, but the trouble nevertheless lasted four years before it could be cured, during which our Anton again, often suffering inexpressible pain, was cut off from all the joys of childhood.

This hurt sometimes kept him indoors for three months at a time, now healing and again breaking out afresh.

Often he was obliged to whimper and moan the whole night long and endure the most horrible pains almost every day from being bandaged. This naturally removed him still farther from the world and from commerce with his kind and tied him still closer to reading and books. Most frequently he read while rocking his younger brother's cradle, and if he had no book then he felt as though he missed a friend: for the book had to be friend and comforter and everything to him.

In his ninth year he read all the narrative part of the Bible from beginning to end, and when one of the leading characters—Moses, Samuel, or Daniel—died, he would mourn over them for a whole day and felt as though a friend had died, so dear to him always were the characters who had done much in the world and made a name for themselves.

Joab was his hero, and he was pained whenever he had to think ill of him. In particular the traits of generosity in David's story, when he spared his worst enemy though he had him in his power, moved him to tears.

Then the *Life of the Early Saints* fell into his hands, which his father prized very highly, quoting these saints as authorities on every occasion. Thus his speeches on conduct commonly began: "Madame Guyon remarks," or "St. Makarius or St. Antony says."

The saints, however absurd and full of adventure their story might be, were for Anton the patterns most worthy of imitation, and for a long time he knew no higher wish than to grow like his great namesake St. Antony, and like him forsake father and mother and fly into a desert, which he hoped to find not far from the gate. And indeed he once began a journey thither, going more than a hundred paces' distance from his parents' dwelling, and perhaps would have gone farther had not the pains in his foot compelled him to go back again. At times he also actually began to prick himself with needles and torture himself in other ways, in order to grow like the saints in some degree, though he had plenty of pains besides.

While he was reading thus he had a little book given him, the proper title of which he does not remember, but which dealt with piety in the young and gave directions how to grow in piety from the sixth to the fourteenth year. The sections in this book were entitled "For Children of Six Years," "For Children of Seven Years," and so on. Anton read the section "For Children of Nine Years" and found that there was still time to become religious, but that he was three years behind.

This gave a shock to his whole being, and he firmly resolved to be converted, such as grown-up people can rarely do. From this hour he most carefully obeyed all that the book contained on prayer, obedience, patience, order, etc., and treated almost every step too quickly taken as a sin. "How far I shall get," he thought, "in five years if I persevere!" For progress in piety was made an object of ambition in the little book, like the pleasure of being promoted at school from one class to another.

If, as was natural, he sometimes forgot himself, and jumped or ran about when he felt the pain in his foot relieved, he felt the most violent twinges of conscience and thought he had fallen several steps back again.

This little book long exercised a strong influence over his actions and thoughts, for he tried at once to practice what he read. Thus he read the evening and morning blessing for every day in the week because the catechism said one must read them; and he did not forget to cross himself and to say "Amen!" as the catechism commanded.

Otherwise he did not see much piety, though he constantly heard talk of it, and his mother blessed him every evening and never forgot to make the sign of the cross over him before he went to sleep.

Herr von Fleischbein had among other things translated the spiritual songs of Madame Guyon into German, and Anton's father, who was a bit of a musician, set tunes to them, most of which went to a quick cheerful time.

If it ever happened that he came home again after a long separation, his wife let herself be persuaded to sing some of these songs to the accompaniment of his zither. This generally happened soon after the first joy of meeting, and these hours were perhaps the happiest in their married life.

Anton was then most cheerful and joined as well as he could in these songs, which were a sign of the rare event of harmony and agreement between his parents.

His father, thinking him old enough, let him read these songs and made him learn some of them by heart.

Indeed these hymns, in spite of their stiff translation, had such a power to move the heart, such incomparable tenderness of expression, such light and shade, and so much that was irresistibly attractive for a sensitive nature that the impression that they made on Anton's feelings has remained indelible.

Often in lonely hours, when he thought himself forsaken by all the world, he comforted himself by one of these hymns of the blessed escape from self and the sweet annihilation before the source of existence.

Thus, even then, his childish thoughts often bestowed on him a kind of heavenly tranquillity.

One evening his parents had been bidden to a little family festival by the landlord of the house where they lived. Anton had to look on from the window and see the neighbors' children, finely dressed, coming in, while he had to stay behind alone in the room because his parents were ashamed of his shabby clothes. Evening came on and he began to be hungry, and his parents had not left him a morsel of bread.

While he sat upstairs in his loneliness and tears, the sound of the joyous tumult floated upwards. Utterly forsaken, he felt at first a kind of bitter self-contempt, but suddenly it changed to an inexpressible feeling of sadness, for he chanced to open the songs of Madame Guyon and found one that seemed exactly to suit his condition. Such a sense of nothingness as he felt at this moment must, according to Madame Guyon's poem, be felt in order to lose oneself, like a drop in the ocean, in the abyss of eternal love. But, as his hunger began now to be irresistible, the consolations of Madame Guyon could help him no longer, and he ventured to go downstairs where his parents were feasting in a large company, opened the door a little, and begged his mother for the key of the larder and for leave to take a little bread as he was very hungry.

This roused first the laughter and then the compassion of the company, not without some feeling against his parents.

He was brought to the table and treated to the best dishes, which gave him quite a different kind of enjoyment than the poems of Madame Guyon.

But that melancholy tearful joy still had its attraction for him, and he gave himself up to it by reading the poems of Madame Guyon whenever a desire was disappointed and something sad was impending, when for instance he knew beforehand that his foot was to be bandaged and the wound rubbed with caustic.

The second book his father gave him to read with the poems of Madame Guyon was a book called *Directions for Silent Prayer* by the same writer.

The book showed how it was possible to arrive by degrees at the point of communing with God in the true sense of the word, and of hearing His voice, the true "voice within," clearly in the heart. The process was first to get free so far as possible from the senses and occupy oneself with oneself and one's own thoughts, or learn to meditate; but this must cease and one must forget oneself before one was capable of hearing God's voice within one.

This injunction Anton obeyed with the greatest zeal because he was really eager to hear within him such a wonder as the voice of God.

He therefore sat for half an hour at a time with eyes closed to abstract himself from the sensual world. His father did the same, to the great distress of his mother. But she paid no heed to Anton because she thought him incapable of doing it for any serious purpose.

Anton got so far that he thought himself pretty well withdrawn from the senses and began really to converse with God, and presently on a footing of confidence. The whole day long, in his lonely walks, his work and his play, he talked with God, always with a kind of love and trust, but still as one speaks to one of his own kind, without any inconvenience; and then he always felt as if God gave him this or that answer.

It nonetheless sometimes happened that a disappointment about some amusement or desire made him discontented. Then he would say: "What! Not grant me this trifle!" or "You might have let this happen, if it had been at all possible!" And Anton did not scruple at times to be a little angry in his own way with God; for though he found nothing about this in Madame Guyon's writings, he thought that it was part of his familiar converse.

All these changes went on in him from his ninth to his tenth year. During this time his father took him, on account of his aching foot, to the waters of Pyrmont. What a joy it was to him to think of making the personal acquaintance of Herr von Fleischbein, of whom his father had constantly spoken with such reverence as of a super-human being, and how glad he was to be able to give an account there of his progress in inward godliness. His imagination painted for him a sort of temple, in which he too would be consecrated as a priest and would return as such, to the surprise of all who know him.

So he took his first journey with his father, during which his father was rather kinder to him and devoted himself more to him than at home. Anton here saw nature in indescribable beauty. The mountains around in the distance and near at hand and the lovely valleys enchanted his spirit and melted it to tenderness, which partly sprang from expectation of the great things that were to happen to him here.

His first walk with his father was to the house of Herr von Fleischbein, where his father first spoke to the steward Herr H., embraced and kissed him, and had a most friendly welcome from him.

In spite of the severe pain which Anton suffered in his foot from the journey he was beside himself with joy at entering the house of Herr von Fleischbein. Anton remained during this day in the room of Herr H., with whom he was in the future to sup every evening. Otherwise, not nearly so much notice was taken of him in the house as he had expected.

He continued his exercises in silent prayer with great diligence, but they did not fail at times to take a very childish turn. Behind the house where his father lodged in Pyrmont was a great orchard; here he happened to find a wheelbarrow and amused himself by wheeling it about the orchard.

But to justify this, as he began to count it a sin, he imagined a whimsical excuse. He had read a good deal in Madame Guyon's writings and elsewhere of the Child Jesus, of whom it was said that he was everywhere, and that it is possible to converse with him continually and in all places.

Thanks to the word *child,* he imagined a boy somewhat smaller than himself, and as he conversed so familiarly already with God himself, why should he not do so even more with this son of His? He trusted that he would not refuse to play with him and therefore would not object if he wished to wheel him about on the wheelbarrow.

He prized it as a great piece of good fortune, to be able to wheel about so great a person and to give him pleasure in this way, and as this person was a creature of his own imagination, he could do with him what he chose, and so made him find pleasure in riding for a longer or shorter time and even sometimes said, in all reverence, if he was tired of wheeling: "I should be glad to give you a longer ride, but I cannot do it now."

Finally he regarded it as a sort of worship and no longer held it a sin to busy himself half a day with the wheelbarrow.

But now, with the consent of Herr von Fleischbein, he got hold of a book that carried him again into a new and quite different world. This was the *Acerra Philologica.* In this he read the story of Troy, of Ulysses, of Circe, of Tartarus and Elysium, and was soon familiar with all the heathen gods and goddesses. Soon afterwards, also with the consent of Herr von Fleischbein, he was given *Telemachus* to read, perhaps because the author, Fénelon, was a familiar friend of Madame Guyon.

The *Acerra Philologica* had been an excellent preparation for reading *Telemachus,* as it had made him pretty familiar with mythology and had given him an interest in most of the heroes whom he found again in *Telemachus.*

He read these books several times, one after the other, with the greatest eagerness and genuine delight, especially *Telemachus,* in which for the first time he tasted the charm of a fine artistic narrative.

The passage in *Telemachus* that roused his liveliest feeling was the moving address of old Mentor to the young Telemachus, when the latter on the island of Cyprus was about to exchange virtue for vice, and his faithful Mentor, whom he had long given up for lost, suddenly reappeared, his sorrowful gaze moving him to his inmost being.

This tale indeed had now more attraction for him than the Bible story and all that he had hitherto read in the *Life of the Saints* or in the writings of Madame Guyon, and as he had never been told that these were true and the others untrue, he was inclined to believe the stories of the heathen gods with all that they contained.

At the same time he could not reject what he found in the Bible, especially as this had given him his earliest impressions. The only thing he could do then was to try to combine the different systems in his mind as well as he could, and in this way to fuse the Bible with *Telemachus,* the *Life of the Saints* with the *Acerra Philologica* and the heathen world with the Christian.

The first person of the Trinity and Jupiter, Calypso and Madame Guyon, Heaven and Elysium, Hell and Tartarus, Pluto and the Devil, formed the most extraordinary combination of ideas that ever existed in the brain of man.

This made such a strong impression on him that long afterwards he retained a certain reverence for the heathen deities.

From the house where Anton's father lodged to the springs and the avenue near it was a fairly long walk. Nevertheless Anton dragged himself there with his painful foot and his book under his arm and sat on a bench in the avenue, and as he read gradually forgot his pain and soon found himself no longer on the bench at Pyrmont, but on some island with high castles and towers or in the midst of the wild turmoil of war.

With a kind of melancholy pleasure he read how heroes fell; it pained him, but still it seemed to him they had to fall.

This too had a great influence on his games as a child. A field full of rank nettles or thistles was to him so many enemies' heads, among which he many a time raged furiously, cutting down one after another with his stick.

When he walked in the meadow he drew an imaginary line and made two armies of yellow or white flowers march against each other. He named the tallest after his heroes and sometimes named one after himself. Then he impersonated a sort of blind fate, and with closed eyes cut them down wherever his stick fell.

Then, when he opened his eyes again, he saw the fearful destruction; here lay one hero and there another, stretched on the ground, and often with a peculiar feeling, half-pleasant and half-sad, he saw himself among the fallen.

Then for a time he mourned for his heroes and left the fearsome battlefield. At home, not far from his parents' house, was a churchyard, in which he ruled with iron scepter over a whole generation of flowers and plants and let no day pass without holding a sort of review of them.

When he returned home from Pyrmont he cut out paper figures of all the heroes of *Telemachus,* painted them from the engravings with helmet and breastplate, and set them up for some days in battle array, till at last he decided their fate and raged among them with cruel strokes of his knife, cut open one hero's helmet and another's skull, and saw nothing but death and destruction around him.

Even his games with cherrystones and plumstones all ended in death and destruction. These too had to be controlled by a blind fate, as he made two sorts march against each other and then with closed eyes made his iron hammer fall on them, to strike where it would.

When he killed flies with the flyswatter he did it with a kind of solemnity, sounding the knell for each with a piece of brass he held in his hand. It gave him the greatest pleasure to set fire to a little town he built of paper houses and then to gaze in solemn and serious sadness on the ashes that were left.

Indeed when once, in the town where his parents lived, a house really was on fire in the night, amid all the fright he felt a kind of secret wish that the fire might not be put out quickly.

This wish was anything but mere malicious joy; it arose from a dim presentiment of great changes, migrations, and revolutions, in which everything takes a new form and in which previous uniformity would come to an end.

Even the thought of his own destruction was not only agreeable to him, but even caused him a kind of cheerful feeling, when in the evening, before he fell asleep, he often vividly imagined the dissolution and disintegration of his body.

Anton's three months' stay at Pyrmont was in many ways of great advantage to him, for he was almost always left to himself and had the good fortune once more for this short time to be away from his parents, as his mother stayed at home and his father had other business in Pyrmont and concerned himself little about him, though he behaved much more kindly to him here, when he saw him from time to time.

Besides, there was lodging in the same house with Anton's father an Englishman, who spoke German well and associated with Anton more than anyone had done before, in that he began to teach him English by conversation and delighted in his progress. He talked to him, went on walks with him, and at last could hardly be out of his company.

This was the first friend Anton had in the world, and he was sad at saying farewell to him. The Englishman, when he went away, pressed into his hand a silver medal, which he was to keep as a memento until he came to England, when his house would be open to him. Fifteen years later Anton did come to England, and brought his medal with him, but the first friend of his boyhood was dead.

On one occasion Anton was called on to deny this Englishman to a stranger, who wished to see him, and to say that he was not at home. But nothing would induce him to do so, because he would not tell a *lie*.

This was considered much to his credit, but it was just one of those cases when he wanted to seem better than he really was, for on other occasions he had made little of telling a convenient lie. His real inward conflicts, when he often sacrificed his most innocent wishes because he imagined them displeasing to God, passed unnoticed.

Meantime, the affection shown to him at Pyrmont was very encouraging and did a little to relieve his depression. Sympathy was shown him because of his foot, and he had a friendly welcome in the house of von Fleischbein, who kissed him on the forehead when he met him in the street. He was not used to such greetings, and they moved him greatly. An open brow, a clear eye, and a cheerful spirit once more came back to him.

Now he also began to turn to poetry and put what he saw and heard into verse. He had two stepbrothers, who were both learning to be shoemakers at Pyrmont under a master who was also a disciple of Herr von Fleischbein. He took his leave of them and also of the household of Herr von Fleischbein in very affecting verses that he composed and learned by heart.

It is true that he returned home from Pyrmont not quite in the state he had expected, but still he had in this short time become quite a different person, and his world of ideas was greatly enriched.

But at home the renewed quarrels of his parents, to which the arrival of his two stepbrothers probably contributed, and the interminable scolding and storming of his mother soon effaced the good impressions he had received at Pyrmont—especially in the house of von Fleischbein—and once more he found himself in the same hateful position, which made his spirit gloomy and misanthropic.

When Anton's two stepbrothers soon went away on their travels as journeymen, domestic peace was for a time restored, and Anton's father sometimes read aloud to him out of *Telemachus* instead of Madame Guyon's writings or told him some episode of ancient or modern history, with which he was really pretty familiar (for besides his music, in which he was accomplished on the practical side, he made it his special study to read instructive books, until finally the writings of Madame Guyon drove out everything else).

His talk therefore was a sort of bookish language, and Anton can still remember clearly how in his seventh and eighth year he often listened very attentively to his father's talk and was surprised that he did not understand a syllable of the words ending in *-hood, -ness,* and *-ing,* through he could understand anything else that was said.

Anton's father, out of his house, was also a very sociable man and could converse agreeably with all sorts of people on all sorts of subjects. Perhaps the marriage would have been a happier one if his mother had not had the misfortune to regard herself often as an injured person and to *enjoy* the feeling, even when she was not really injured, in order to have a reason for being vexed and afflicted, and to cherish a sort of self-pity, which gave her great pleasure.

Alas! She seems to have bequeathed this infirmity to her son, who now often has to fight against it in vain.

Even as a child, when everyone received something, and his share was assigned him without his being told that it was his, he preferred to let it alone, though he knew that it was meant for him, merely to feel the pleasure of being injured and to be able to say, "Everyone else has something, and I am to get nothing!" As he felt imaginary wrongs so keenly, he was bound to feel real ones even more. And certainly no one has a stronger sense of injustice than children, and to no one can injustice be done more easily: a fact all teachers ought to take to heart every day and every hour.

Often Anton would reflect for hours, nicely weighing argument against argument, whether a punishment inflicted by his father was just or unjust.

In his eleventh year he enjoyed for the first time the inexpressible pleasure of forbidden reading. His father was a sworn enemy of all romances and threatened to burn any book of the kind if he found it in his house. In spite of this Anton, through his aunt, got hold of *The Beautiful Banise, The Arabian Nights,* and *The Island of Felsenburg,* which he read secretly and by stealth, though with his mother's knowledge, in his bedroom and devoured with insatiable eagerness.

These were some of the happiest hours of his life. Whenever his mother came in, she merely warned him that his father might come but did not forbid him to read the books, in which she had once found enchantment herself.

The story of *The Island of Felsenburg* made a very great impression on Anton; for a long time his thoughts were directed to nothing less than the idea of playing a great part in the world and of drawing round him first a smaller and then a larger circle of persons of whom he should be the center. This idea expanded till his extravagant imagination made him finally draw animals, plants, and inanimate things, in a word, everything around him, into the sphere of his existence, till he grew dizzy at the thought.

With such a playful imagination, he often enjoyed more blissful hours then than he ever has since.

Thus it was that his imagination created most of the sorrows and joys of his childhood. How often on a dull day, when to his vexation and disgust he was shut up indoors, a chance sunbeam shining through the window awakened pictures of paradise, Elysium, or the island of Calypso, which enchanted him for hours!

But from his second or third year he could also remember the torments of hell the stories of his mother and his aunt conjured up for him, sleeping or waking. Now he would see himself in a dream surrounded by friends who suddenly looked at him with faces horribly transformed; or again he climbed a high and gloomy staircase and a horrible figure barred his retreat, or the Devil himself appeared on the wall in the shape of a spotted cock or a black curtain.

Even in the early days, when his mother lived with him in the village, every old woman inspired him with fear and horror, so continually did he hear of witches and magic; and when the wind blew through the cottage with a peculiar moan, his mother called it, in a figure, "the handless man," without thinking any more of it.

But she would not have done so, had she known how many a fearsome hour and how many a sleepless night this "handless man" was to give her son for years afterwards.

The last four weeks before Christmas in particular were a purgatory for Anton, to escape which he would gladly have given up his Christmas tree covered with candles and hung with silver-covered apples and nuts.

Not a day passed when some strange noise of bells or a scraping at the door or a hollow voice would not make itself heard, betokening St. Nicholas, the harbinger of Christ, whom Anton seriously took for a spirit or a superhuman being; and so all through this season not a night passed when he did not awake from sleep with terror and the sweat of fear on his brow.

This lasted till his eighth year, when his belief in the reality of St. Nicholas and of the Holy Christ finally began to waver.

His mother also gave him a childish fear of thunderstorms. His only refuge then was to fold his hands as firmly as he could and not to unfold them till the storm was past. This, besides crossing himself, was also his refuge and, as it were, his firm support whenever he slept alone, because he thought that then neither devil nor ghost could touch him.

His mother had a peculiar expression of anyone wanting to run away from a ghost, that "his heels grow long"; he felt this in the literal sense whenever he thought he saw something like a ghost in the dark. She also used to say of a dying man that "death sits on his tongue"; this too Anton took in the literal sense, and when his aunt's husband died he stood near the bed and watched his mouth very carefully to discover death, perhaps like a little black figure, on his tongue.

It was about his fifth year that he got his first idea of anything beyond his childish field of vision, when his mother was living with him in the village and was sitting alone in the room with an old woman, their neighbor, himself and his stepbrothers.

The conversation turned to Anton's little sister, who had died in her second year a little while ago, and for whom his mother remained inconsolable for over a year.

"Where can Julia be now, I wonder," she said after a long pause and then was silent. Anton looked at the window, where there was not a glimmer of light in the dismal night, and felt for the first time the wonderful limitation that made his existence at the earlier time almost as different from that of the present as being from not being.

"Where can Julia be now?" he thought, like his mother, and through his mind flashed the contrast of near and far, confined and open, present and future. No pen can describe his feeling at that moment. It came back again a thousand times, but never with the first vividness.

What a blessing is this limitation we are always using every effort to escape! It is like a little island of happiness in a stormy sea; happy is he who can sleep securely in its bosom. No danger wakes him, no storms alarm him. But woe to him who is driven by unhappy curiosity to venture beyond those dim mountain ranges that limit his horizon for his own good!

He is driven to and fro by unrest and doubt on a wild and stormy sea, seeks unknown regions in the shadowy distance, and his little island where he lived so securely has lost all its charms for him.

One of Anton's happiest memories in his earliest years is of his mother wrapping him in her cloak and carrying him through storm and rain. In the little village the world looked beautiful, but beyond the blue mountains, toward which his eager gaze was always turned, the troubles that were to embitter the years of his childhood were already awaiting him.

As I have gone back in my story to recapture Anton's first feelings and ideas of the world, I must here mention two of his earliest memories, which concern his sense of wrong.

He has a clear memory that in his second year, before he lived in the village with his mother, he ran from his own house to the one opposite and back again, and ran in the way of a well-dressed man, whom he pushed violently, because he wished to persuade himself and others that he was wronged, although he had an inward feeling that he himself was the offender.

This memory is remarkable because of its rarity and clearness; it is also genuine because the incident in itself is too trifling for anyone to have told him of it afterwards.

The second memory is from his fourth year, when his mother scolded him for some real naughtiness. As he was just undressing, it happened that one of his garments fell with a noise on the chair; his mother thought he had thrown it down in a temper and punished him severely.

This was the first wrong he felt deeply and never forgot; from this time he regarded even his mother as unjust, and at every fresh punishment this incident came back to him.

I have already mentioned how he thought of death in his childhood. This lasted till his tenth year, when a neighbor visited his parents and told them how her cousin, who was a miner, had fallen down from a ladder into the pit and had crushed his head.

Anton listened attentively, and the crushed head made him imagine a complete cessation of thought and feeling and a kind of annihilation and blankness of his being, which filled him with fear and horror as often as he fixed his thoughts on it again. From that time onward he had a great fear of death, which caused him many a sad hour.

I must say a few words more of the earliest ideas which he formed of God and the world in about his tenth year.

Whenever the sky was cloudy and the horizon narrowed, he had a sort of conscious feeling that the whole world was enclosed by a ceiling like that of the room in which he lived, and if his thoughts traveled beyond this vaulted ceiling, this world seemed to him much too small, and he imagined that it must be enclosed in another world and so on *ad infinitum*.

He had the same experience with his idea of God when he wished to think of Him as the Supreme Being.

One dull evening he was sitting alone at the door of his house and, thinking of this, he gazed up to the sky again and again and then looked at the earth and noticed how black and dark it was against the dull sky.

Beyond the sky he imagined God, but any God, even the highest, whom his thoughts created, seemed to him too small, and he felt that He must have a greater God above Him, against whom He entirely disappeared, and so ad infinitum.

Yet he had never read or heard anything on this subject.

What was most singular was that his continual reflection and immersion in his own thoughts led him into an egoism that might almost have made him lose his reason.

For as his dreams were in general very lively and almost seemed to border on reality, he began to fancy that he was dreaming in broad daylight and that the people about him, with all that he saw, might be creatures of his imagination.

This was an appalling thought, which made him afraid of himself whenever it occurred to him and led him actually to try to distract his mind and set himself free from these thoughts.

After these digressions we will continue the story of Anton's life in chronological order. We left him at eleven years old reading *The Beautiful Banise* and *The Island of Felsenburg*. He was now given to read Fénelon's *Conversations of the Dead* with his *Stories,* and his writing master began to set him to write letters and compositions of his own.

This was a delight he had never felt before. He now began to make use of his reading and to introduce now and again imitations of what he had read, which won him the approval and regard of his teacher.

His father played in a concert where Ramler's *Death of Jesus* was performed and brought home a printed copy of the words. This attracted Anton so much and was so far beyond any poetry that he had hitherto read that he reread it so often and with such delight that he almost knew it by heart.

This one accidental piece of reading, so often repeated, gave his taste in poetry a form and fixity he never lost again, just as *Telemachus* had done in prose, for in *The Beautiful Banise* and *The Island of Felsenburg,* notwithstanding the pleasure he found in them, he felt the contrast and lack of dignity in the style.

In poetical prose Carl von Moser's *Daniel in the Lions' Den* came into his hands; this he read through several times and his father used at times to read passages from it.

The season for the waters came on again and Anton's father decided to take him back to Pyrmont, but this time Anton was not to enjoy it as much as in the previous year, for his mother went with him.

By incessantly forbidding him little things and continually scolding and punishing him out of season she gave him a distaste for all the nobler sensations he had had the year before; his feeling for praise and approval was so crushed by this that, almost against his nature, he found a sort of pleasure in associating with the dirtiest street urchins and making common cause with them, merely because he despaired of ever winning again in Pyrmont the love and respect he had lost through his mother, who constantly talked not only to his father, whenever he came home, but also to perfect strangers of nothing but the badness of his behavior. The consequence was that his behavior really began to be bad and his heart seemed to grow worse.

His visits to the house of Herr von Fleischbein were also rarer, and the time of his stay at Pyrmont went by very unpleasantly and sadly, so that he often thought with melancholy of the delights of the previous year, though this time he had less pain to bear in his foot, which began to heal again when the damaged bone was taken out.

Soon after his parents' return to Hanover Anton entered his twelfth year, which was to bring many changes, for in this year he was to be parted from his parents. But he had one great pleasure first.

On the persuasion of some acquaintances Anton's father sent him to a private Latin class in the public grammar school of the town, so that he might in any event at least learn his declensions. To the very great regret of his mother and his relations, his father absolutely refused to send him to the other classes in the school, where religious instruction was the main subject.

Thus one of Anton's most earnest desires, to be allowed to go to a public grammar school, was partially fulfilled.

On his first entrance the thick walls, dark vaulted rooms, century-old benches and worm-eaten desks, seemed to him like holy things that filled his soul with reverence.

The assistant principal, a cheery little fellow, in spite of some want of gravity in his face, inspired him with profound respect by reason of his black coat and bob-wig.

He treated his pupils on a fairly friendly footing. Indeed, he usually addressed everyone in the second person (you), but the four top boys, whom he called "veterans" in jest, he addressed with the complimentary third person (he).

Though he was very strict, Anton never had a rebuke, still less a blow from him; he therefore thought he found more justice in school than at home.

He now had to begin to learn Donatus by heart, but his accentuation was peculiar, as soon appeared when he declined *mensa* by heart at his second lesson. When he said *singulariter* and *pluraliter*, he laid the accent on the penultimate because in learning it by heart the similarity of the last syllable with that of "Amorites" and "Jebusites" made him imagine that there were two people, the Singularites who said *mensa* and the Pluralites who said *mensae*.

Such misunderstandings may often happen when the teacher is content with the first words of his pupil, without penetrating into his mind!

Now came learning by heart. *Amo, amem, amas, ames* was soon recited in rhythm, and within six weeks he had his *oportet* at his fingertips; at the same time he learned new words by heart every day, and as he never missed one he moved up the classes quickly and got nearer and nearer to the "veterans."

How happy he was! What a splendid career Anton had before him; for the first time in his life he saw a path to fame, which he had so long wished for in vain, open before him.

At home too he spent this short time pleasantly, having to read to his parents every morning, while they drank coffee, from the *Imitation of Christ* of Thomas à Kempis, which he enjoyed doing.

Then they talked about it, and he was allowed sometimes to give his opinion. Besides he was lucky enough not to be at home much, as he still attended the classes of his old writing master, whom, in spite of the many cuffs he had had from him, he loved so sincerely that he would have sacrificed everything for him.

For he often had friendly and instructive talks with Anton and his schoolfellows, and as in general he seemed rather severe, this kind and friendly attitude had all the more effect and won their hearts.

So for a few weeks Anton was doubly happy; but his happiness was soon destroyed. Lest his good fortune should make him too proud, severe humiliations were prepared for him.

Though he was now educated in the company of children of good standing, his mother made him perform the duties of the meanest servant.

He had to carry water, fetch butter and cheese from the shops, and go to market like a woman with a basket on his arm, to buy eatables.

I need not say how bitterly he felt it when one of his more fortunate schoolfellows passed him on such occasions with a malicious smile.

But he gladly put up with this in view of the good fortune of going to a Latin school, where after two months he had risen so high that he was able now to share the lesson of the top bench, the so-called four veterans.

It was about this time that his father took him to see a very remarkable man in Hanover, of whom he had often told him before. This man was called Tischer and was a hundred and five years old.

He had studied theology and finally had been tutor to the children of a rich merchant in Hanover, in whose house he still lived, and was maintained by the present occupant, an old pupil of his, and himself now an old man.

He had been deaf since his fiftieth year, and anyone who wanted to talk to him had to have pen and ink in hand and write down his thoughts, which the man answered orally in a clear and audible voice.

Even in his hundred and fifth year he could read his small-type Greek Testament without spectacles, and he spoke very correctly and coherently, though sometimes more slowly or loudly than necessary because he could not hear himself.

In the house he was known simply as "the old man." His food and what else was needed for his comfort was brought him, but otherwise no one troubled much about him.

One evening then, as Anton was sitting at his Donatus, his father took him by the hand and said: "Come and I will take you to a man in whom you will see united St. Anthony, St. Paul, and the patriarch Abraham."

And on the way his father prepared him for what he was going to see.

They entered the house. Anton's heart beat fast.

They went across a long yard and climbed a little winding stair that led them into a long dark passage, where they mounted a second stair and then went down a few steps. The passages seemed like a labyrinth.

At length a little view opened up on the left, where some light from another window came through some window panes.

It was wintertime and the door was hung with cloth outside. Anton's father opened it. It was twilight; the room was large and spacious, furnished with dark hangings, and in the middle, at a little table strewn with books, sat the old man in an armchair.

He came bareheaded to meet them.

Age had not bowed him; he was a tall man and his appearance, large and majestic. Snow white locks adorned his temples, and an ineffable kindliness beamed from his eyes. They sat down.

Anton's father wrote something for him. "Let us pray," began the old man after a pause, "and include our little friend!"

Thereupon he bared his head and kneeled down, with Anton's father on his right and Anton on his left.

Anton found that he was all and more than all his father had described. He imagined himself kneeling by one of the apostles of Christ, and his heart was uplifted in great devotion when the old man stretched out his hands and began to pray with deep fervor and continued his prayer in tones now loud, now soft.

His words were as the words of one who in all his thoughts and wishes has passed beyond the grave, and who by some chance alone is left to wait a little longer than he expected in this world.

All his thoughts as it were came from the next life, and as he prayed his eye and his brow seemed to light up.

They rose from prayer, and Anton in his heart now regarded the old man almost as a higher being, more than human.

And when he came home in the evening, he would not join some of his school-fellows in coasting about on a little sledge, because it seemed to be profane and to spoil the sanctity of the day.

His father often sent him to this old man, and he spent with him nearly all the time that he was not in school.

There he made use of his library, which consisted largely of mystical books, and read many of them from beginning to end. He also often gave the old man an account of his progress in Latin and of the exercises he wrote for his writing master. Thus Anton spent two months of extraordinary happiness.

Then like a thunderclap, almost at one and the same time, he heard the dreadful announcement that his Latin lessons were to end with the month and that he was to be sent to another writing school.

Tears and entreaties were of no avail, the decision was made. Anton had a fortnight's notice that he was to leave the Latin school, and his grief became greater, the higher he rose in class.

So to make his leaving less painful he adopted a means one would hardly have expected in a boy of his age. Instead of trying to get higher in class, he did the opposite and either deliberately abstained from saying what he knew or used some other device to go down a place every day. The assistant principal and his schoolfellows could not understand it and often expressed their surprise to him.

Anton alone knew the reason and carried his trouble with him to school and home again. Every place he chose to go down in class cost him a thousand tears, shed secretly at home. But bitter as the medicine was that he prescribed for himself, it had its effect.

He had arranged so that he was bound to be at the bottom on the last day. But this was more than he could bear. He begged to be allowed to sit in his place again that day, and next day he would gladly take the lowest place.

Everyone pitied him and gave way. The next day the month was up and he did not return.

How much this voluntary sacrifice cost him may be inferred from the eager efforts he had made to win his way up.

Often when the assistant principal looked out of the window in his dressing gown, as he went past, he thought "If only you could open your heart to him!" But the distance between him and his master seemed far too great.

Soon afterwards, in spite of all his entreaties, he was also taken away from his beloved writing master.

He had overlooked some carelessness in Anton's writing and sum book, which roused the anger of his father.

Anton most earnestly took all the blame and made vows and promises to do all in his power, but it was no good, he had to leave his faithful old master, and at the month's end begin to learn writing in the public grammar school.

These two blows together were too much for Anton.

He tried indeed to cling to his last support and got his former schoolfellows to tell him of each lesson assigned them, so that he might learn it at home and go forward with them; but when this became impossible his virtue and goodness gave way, and, for a long time, from a sort of discontent and despair, he became what may be called "bad."

He got himself flogged in school out of sheer mischief and bore the strokes with steady defiance, without giving any sign of pain, and this gave him a pleasant feeling that lingered in his memory. He fought and scuffled with street urchins, played hookey from school lessons, and tormented a dog that his parents had whenever he could.

In church, where hitherto he had been a model of reverence, he chattered to his companions through the whole service.

He often felt that he was going wrong, he remembered with sadness his earlier efforts to be good, but whenever he was on the point of reforming, a sort of self-contempt and a rankling discontent overpowered his better resolutions and made him try once again to forget himself in all kinds of wild distractions.

The thought that his dearest hopes and wishes were disappointed and that the career of honor on which he had started was forever closed to him rankled unceasingly, without his being clearly conscious of it, and drove him to all sorts of extravagance.

He became a hypocrite to God and to himself and others.

He read the morning and evening prayer regularly as before, but without any feeling.

When he came to the old man, his former frankness was changed to dissimulation; his pious air and the words he wrote were mere hypocrisy, in which he pretended a thirst and longing for God, in order to keep the respect of the old man.

Sometimes he would even laugh to himself as the old man read what he had written.

Then he began to deceive his father also. His father remarked one day that he had been quite a different boy three years ago when he refused to tell a lie and say "not at home" for the Englishman.

As Anton was conscious that he had done this more from a sort of affectation than from any horror of lying, he now reflected: "If this is all that is wanted to make me beloved, it will not cost me much." Thus in a short time by sheer hypocrisy, which he tried to conceal from himself as hypocrisy, he succeeded so well that his father corresponded about him with Herr von Fleischbein and gave him news of the state of Anton's soul in order to ask his advice.

Meanwhile, when Anton saw that the matter was taken so seriously, he became more serious too and sometimes resolved to give up his bad way of life because he could no longer hide his hypocrisy from himself.

But then he thought of the years he had neglected since the time of his previous genuine conversion and of what progress he might have made had he not done so. This made him extremely dissatisfied and sad.

Besides, he read a book at the old man's in which the whole

process of salvation by means of repentance, faith, and religious life was described in detail with all its signs and symptoms.

Repentance must include tears, contrition, sorrow, and dissatisfaction. All this he felt.

Faith involved an unwonted cheerfulness and confidence of the soul in God. This too he could manage.

Thirdly the religious life must follow of its own accord. But this was not so easy.

Anton thought that if once the will to live a good and religious life was there, one was bound to live it continuously and at every moment, in every look and movement, and even in every thought; one must never for a moment forget the will to be good.

But naturally he often forgot it. His face was not always serious, nor his bearing decorous, and his thoughts wandered to earthly and secular things.

And so he thought that all was over, that he had achieved practically nothing and must begin all over again.

He often felt this several times an hour, and his condition was one of great distress and anxiety.

He gave himself up again, but always uneasily and with a beating heart, to his former distractions.

Then once more he began the work of his conversion over again and so wavered to and fro and nowhere found rest or content; meantime the most innocent pleasures of his youth were embittered and yet he never made much progress.

This continual wavering is also an image of his father's whole way of life; in his fiftieth year it was no better, yet he always hoped to find the right way that he had so long striven after in vain.

Anton had at first begun pretty well. But when he found he was no longer to learn Latin, his piety suffered a great shock. It was only a timorous, constrained thing and could make no real progress.

Then he read somewhere how useless and dangerous self-improvement was and how one should be purely passive and let God's grace work in one. And so he often prayed very sincerely: "Lord, convert me and I am converted!" But all was in vain.

His father went to Pyrmont again that summer, and Anton wrote to him how little progress he made in self-improvement and that perhaps he had made a mistake, because God's grace must be everything.

His mother regarded the whole letter as a piece of hypocrisy, as perhaps it partly was, and wrote below it in her own hand: "Anton behaves like all godless boys."

Yet, as he was conscious of a real inward struggle, he was bound to feel deeply wounded at being put in the same class with all godless boys.

This depressed him so much that for a long time he willfully lived an irregular life with other wild boys and was confirmed in it by the scolding and the sermons, so called, of his mother; for these depressed him still more, so that at last he regarded himself as no better than a common street urchin and was all the more ready to keep company with them again.

This lasted until his father returned from Pyrmont. All at once quite a new outlook was opened up for him.

Early in the year his mother bore twins, only one of whom survived, and his godfather was a hatter in Brunswick called Lobenstein.

This man was one of the disciples of Herr von Fleischbein, and through this Anton's father had known him for several years.

As Anton was to be apprenticed to a master some day (for his two stepbrothers had learned their trade, and both were discontented with the handicraft they had been forced into by their father), and as the hatter Lobenstein wanted to have a lad, who at first would only lend a hand, his father thought this a splendid opening for Anton, like his two stepbrothers, to be put early under the care of such a good man, who was also a disciple of Herr von Fleischbein, and to be admonished by him in the path of true religion and piety.

This may have been a plan of some standing and was perhaps the reason why Anton's father had taken him from the Latin school.

Now ever since he had learned Latin, Anton had got the idea of study firmly into his head; for he had a boundless respect for anyone who had studied and wore a black coat, so that he regarded such people as almost superhuman beings.

What could be more natural than that he should strive for what seemed to him the most desirable thing in the world?

It was said that the hatter in Brunswick would take a friendly interest in Anton, that he should be treated as a child of his own and should do only light and suitable work, such as keeping accounts, running errands and the like; and further that for two years he should go to school until he was confirmed and then could make up his mind what to do.

This sounded very agreeable in Anton's ears, especially the last item about school; for he thought that if he could only achieve this, he would not fail to distinguish himself sufficiently for ways and means to be forthcoming of themselves.

He himself wrote along with his father to Lobenstein the hatter, whom he dearly loved already, and rejoiced to think of the splendid days he would spend with him.

And what a charm the thought of a change of scenery had for him!

Life in Hanover and the constant monotonous sight of the same streets and houses now became intolerable; visions of new towers, gates, ramparts, and castles rose in his mind, and one picture drove out the other.

He was restless and counted the hours and minutes till his departure.

At length the longed-for day arrived. Anton took leave of his mother and his two brothers, the elder of whom, Christian, might be five, and the younger, Simon, named after Lobenstein the hatter, scarcely a year old.

His father went with him and they traveled half on foot, half by coach, for which a cheap opportunity arose.

Anton now for the first time in his life enjoyed the pleasure of a walking expedition, of which he was to have enough and to spare in the future.

As they drew nearer to Brunswick, Anton became more and more eager. The tower of St. Andrew with its red dome rose majestically to the sky.

Evening was coming on. In the distance he saw the sentinel walking to and fro on the high rampart.

A thousand thoughts rose and faded in his mind: how would his future benefactor look, what would be his age, his walk, his features?

At last he drew such a picture of him that he fell in love with him beforehand.

One of the habits of his childhood had been to frame peculiar pictures and notions of persons and places suggested by the sound of their names, in which the high or low pitch of the vowels did most to determine the picture.

Thus "Hanover" always sounded especially splendid, and he pictured it, before he saw it, as a town with high houses and towers, of a bright and cheerful aspect.

"Brunswick" had long seemed to him darker and bigger, and "Paris" from some dim suggestion in the name, he imagined chiefly as a mass of bright whitish houses.

This is natural enough, for when one knows nothing of a thing but the name, the mind strives to form an image of it even through the remotest resemblances, and for want of any other points of likeness has to take refuge in the arbitrary name, noting the sounds, hard or soft, full or thin, high or low, faint or clear, and imagines a correspondence between them and the object, which is often accidentally correct.

The name Lobenstein made Anton think of a tall man, with an honest German face and an open brow.

But this time his reading of names completely deceived him.

As darkness fell, Anton and his father crossed the great drawbridge and walked through the arched gates into the town.

They went through many streets, past the castle and at last over a long bridge into a rather dingy street where Lobenstein the hatter lived opposite a long public building.

They stood in front of the house. It had a dark exterior and a great black door, thickly studded with nails.

Above hung a sign with a hat on it and the name Lobenstein.

An old woman, the housekeeper, opened the door and led them to the right into a large room with dark painted panels, where a half-effaced representation of the five senses could be discovered with difficulty.

Here the master of the house received them. A middle-aged man, rather short than tall, with a youngish but pale and melancholy face, which at rare moments assumed a forced smile; black hair, rather romantic eyes, a refinement in speech, movement, and manners rarely found in working people. His speech was pure, but very slow and dragging, with words long drawn out, especially when religious things were talked of. He had an insufferably intolerant air when he contracted his dark eyebrows over the depravity and wickedness of people, and especially of his neighbors or his own household.

When Anton first saw him he wore a green fur cap, a blue waistcoat with a brown jerkin, and black apron, his usual indoor wear, and at the first glance he felt that instead of the friend and benefactor he looked for he had found a stern master.

His preconceived affection was quenched, as water quenches a spark, when the first glance of his supposed benefactor, cold and imperious, made him feel that he was to be nothing more than his apprentice.

For the few days that his father stayed with him, some considera tion was shown him; but as soon as the former was gone he had to work in the workshop like the other apprentice.

He was employed for the meanest tasks—splitting wood, carrying water, and sweeping out the shop.

In spite of his disappointment the unpleasantness was somewhat compensated by the charm of novelty, and he even found a kind of pleasure in sweeping, chopping, and water carrying.

His imagination, which colored everything, stood him in good stead. Often the spacious workshop with its dark walls and awesome gloom, illuminated night and day by only the glimmer of some lamps, seemed to him a temple in which he ministered.

In the morning he lit the holy quickening fire beneath the great cauldrons, which kept everything at work and active all day long, and many hands busy. So he regarded his duties as a kind of office that had a certain dignity in his eyes.

Immediately behind the workshop flowed the Oker, over which was built out a projection of planks for drawing water.

He regarded all this in a way as his own domain, and sometimes when he had cleaned the shop, filled the great boilers set in masonry, and lit the fire beneath them, he could properly enjoy his work, as if he had given everything its due. His ever-busy imagination quickened the inanimate things about him and made them live creatures, with which he lived and talked.

Moreover the regularity he noticed in the course of the business processes gave him a kind of agreeable sense of pleasure in being a wheel in this machine that moved so regularly, for at home he had known nothing like it.

The hatter set great store by order in his house, and everything went by the clock: working, eating, and sleeping.

If an exception was made, it was in regard to sleep, which had to be left out when there was night work, which happened at least once a week.

Dinner was always punctually at twelve, breakfast and supper at eight in the morning and evening.

These were the fixed points they counted on as they worked. In those days Anton's life passed thus: from six in the morning, at work, he counted on his breakfast, which he tasted in anticipation and, when he got it, ate with the healthiest appetite a man can have, though it consisted of nothing but coffee grounds with a little milk and a roll.

Then he set to work again, and the hope of dinner again gave new interest to the morning hours if the monotony of the work was too wearisome.

In the evening he had, year in, year out, a glass of strong beer—stimulus enough to sweeten the afternoon's labors.

And then from supper till bedtime the thought of rest, soon to come and eagerly desired, again cast a gleam of comfort over his toilsome and disagreeable labor.

Of course he knew that next day the same cycle of life began again. But even this uniformity, wearisome as it was, was pleasantly interrupted by the hope of Sunday.

When the stimulus of breakfast, dinner, and supper was not sufficient to keep the joy of life and work going, he counted the days to Sunday, which was a whole holiday, when he could leave the dark workshop for the open fields and enjoy the free and open face of nature.

What charms, unknown to the higher classes, who can rest from their business when they like, has Sunday for the workman!

"That the son of thy handmaid may rejoice!" Only the workman can fully realize what a great, noble, humane meaning is embodied in this law!

If the thought of one day's rest from work was counted on for six days, it was well worthwhile to look forward for a third of the year to three or four holidays in succession.

If ever the thought of Sunday lost its power to lighten the burden of monotony, the joy of life was quickened again by the approach of

Easter, Whitsuntide, or Christmas.

And when these thoughts lost their power, there was always the hope of the completion of apprenticeship and of becoming a journeyman, a hope beyond all others, which made a new and great epoch in life.

Anton's fellow apprentice had no horizon beyond this, and certainly this made his position no worse.

It is a wise and beneficent disposal of things that gives to the laborious monotonous life of the artisan its divisions and periods, introducing a sort of rhythm or harmony, which makes it pass unnoticed without causing its possessor any feeling of weariness.

But Anton's romantic ideas put him out of step with this rhythm.

Just opposite the hatter's house was a Latin school Anton had hoped to attend, but in vain. When he saw the boys going in and out his thoughts went sadly back to the Latin school and its assistant principal in Hanover, and when he passed St. Martin's College and saw its grown-up students come out he would have given anything to be allowed to see the inside of this sanctuary.

In his present position he considered it almost impossible that he should ever be able to attend such a college, but he could not quite give up a faint glimmer of hope.

Even the choristers seemed to him beings from a higher sphere, and when he heard them sing in the streets, he could not help following them, to enjoy the sight of them and envy their brilliant lot.

When he was in the workshop with his fellow apprentice he tried to impart to him all the scraps of knowledge he had gained partly by his own reading, partly by the instruction he had enjoyed.

He told him about Jupiter and Juno and tried to explain the difference between adjective and substantive, so as to teach him when to put a capital letter and when a small one.

His companion listened attentively to him, and they often discussed moral and religious subjects. Anton's companion on such occasions was great at inventing new words to express his ideas. For instance he called following God's commands the "fulfillness of God." While he chiefly tried to imitate the religious phrases of Herr Lobenstein, mortification and the like, he often fell into strange confusion.

When he thought that the housekeeper or anyone else blackened or abused his character, he was ready to quote with special emphasis passages from the Psalms of David that expressed no gentle sentiments toward his *enemies.*

Nearly all the household servants were more or less infected with the religious enthusiasm of Herr Lobenstein, all except the journeyman. If his master talked to him too much of mortification and self-effacement, he cast on him such a withering and annihilating glance that Herr Lobenstein turned away with horror and said nothing.

Sometimes Herr Lobenstein could preach for hours against the whole human race, distributing blessing and damnation with a gentle gesture of the right hand. His expression then was meant to be compassionate, but intolerance and misanthropy were entrenched between his black eyebrows.

He was politic enough to turn his preaching to good purpose by warning his household to be zealous and faithful in his service, if they did not wish to burn for ever in hellfire.

His people could never work hard enough for him, and he made a cross over the loaf and the butter when he went out.

Anton, who certainly could not work hard enough for him, found his dinner spoiled by a thousand repeated instructions from Herr Lobenstein about how to hold his knife and fork and carry his food to his mouth, so that he often lost his appetite. At last the journeyman insisted on taking his side and he was able to eat in peace.

But he did not dare to utter a sound, as his master found fault with everything he said, with his looks and his least movement. Anton could never please him and at last was almost afraid to go into his presence, for he found fault with everything he did. His intolerance extended to every smile and every innocent outburst of pleasure that appeared in Anton's features or movements. For in these he gave himself free outlet, knowing that he could not be contradicted.

Meanwhile the faded five senses on the black paneling of the wall had been revarnished. The memory of the smell, which lasted some weeks, Anton ever afterwards associated with the idea of his position at the time. Whenever he smelled varnish, involuntarily all the unpleasant images of those days rose up in his mind, and conversely, when he happened to be in circumstances that resembled those days, he fancied that he smelled a smell of varnish.

A coincidence improved Anton's position.

The hatter was a hypochondriacal enthusiast; he believed in warnings, and had visions that often roused his fear and horror. An old woman, who had lodged in the house, died and appeared to him in dreams at night, so that he often woke in terror, and as he went on dreaming after he woke he fancied he still saw her shadow in a corner of the room. Anton now had to keep him company and sleep in a bed near by him. So he became in some degree necessary to his master, who became kinder to him. He often had conversations with him, asked him how he stood with God, and taught him that he must give himself wholly to God and that then if he was fortunate enough to be elected as one of the children of God, God would himself begin and complete the work of conversion in him. Before he went to bed Anton had to stand apart and pray in a low voice, and the prayer could not be very short or his master would ask him whether he had finished so soon, and had no more to say to God. This was a new incentive to hypocrisy and dissimulation, which were otherwise quite against his nature. Though he prayed in an undertone he tried to pronounce his words so clearly that he could be heard quite well by Lobenstein, and now his whole prayer was dominated not so much by the thought of God as how he could best ingratiate himself with Herr Lobenstein with expressions of repentance, contrition, yearning for God, and the like. Such was the fine result that this compulsory prayer had on Anton's heart and character.

But still Anton sometimes found a kind of secret pleasure in solitary prayer, when he knelt down in a corner of the workshop and prayed God to bring about in his soul, if it might be, even one of the great changes of which he had read and heard so much in his childhood. And so strong was the illusion of his imagination that he sometimes really had a sense of some special experience in his inmost soul; and then at once came the thought that he wanted to clothe his spiritual state in a letter to his father or Herr von Fleischbein, or describe it to Herr Lobenstein. Thus his imaginary feelings constantly served to feed his vanity, and the intense pleasure he felt arose chiefly from the thought that he could *say* he had felt such a divine and heavenly joy in his soul. It flattered him to think that old and grown-up people regarded his spiritual state as something important enough to trouble themselves about. That was the reason that he so often imagined a change in his spiritual condition, so that he might complain to Herr Lobenstein that he was in a state of emptiness and drought, that he could no longer find in himself any trace of yearning for God, and then ask advice on his condition from Herr Lobenstein, who gave it to him with great seriousness.

It even went so far that his spiritual state was discussed in correspondence with Herr von Fleischbein, a passage in whose letter, referring to it, was shown him. It was no wonder that in this way he was encouraged to keep up his importance in his own eyes and those of others by continual imaginary changes in his spiritual state, as he was regarded as a person in whom the guidance of God was revealed in a very special way.

Now he was also given a black apron, like the other apprentice, and this circumstance, instead of making him feel humble, rather added much to his content. He now looked on himself as a person who was beginning to have a position of his own. The apron brought him into line with others like him, whereas before he was lonely and isolated. For some time the apron made him forget his inclination for study and he began to find a kind of pleasure in the other customs of the trade, which made him wish for nothing more eagerly than to be able one day to share them. He was delighted when he heard the greeting of a journeyman coming in to ask for the usual gratuity, and he could imagine no greater happiness than to come in some day as a journeyman himself and then repeat the greeting in the prescribed words according to the custom of the trade.

Thus it is that the youthful mind always clings more to the symbol than to the reality, and little or nothing can be inferred from the early utterances of children in regard to the choice of a vocation. As soon as Anton had learned to read, he found inexpressible pleasure in going to church, and his mother and aunt were overjoyed. But what drew him to church was the triumph he always enjoyed when he could look at the blackboard, on which the numbers of the hymns were written, and could tell some grown-up man who stood by him what the number was, and when he could look up the numbers in his hymnbook as quickly or more quickly than his elders and join in the singing.

Herr Lobenstein's attachment to Anton seemed to grow stronger, the more Anton showed a desire for his spiritual guidance. He often allowed him to join in the conversations he held up to midnight with his most intimate friends, with whom it was his habit to discuss the apparitions seen by himself and others, some of them so horrible that Anton listened with hair on end. They generally went to bed late, and when the evening had been spent in such talk Herr Lobenstein would ask Anton when he got up next morning whether he had not noticed anything in the night or heard anything walking in the bedroom.

Often in the evening he also talked to Anton alone, and they read together in the writings of Tauler, John of the Cross, and such books. It seemed as though they would become lasting friends. Anton actually conceived a kind of love for Herr Lobenstein, but this feeling was always mixed with a bitter taste, with a certain sense of deadening, withering influence, produced by Lobenstein's sardonic smile.

Meanwhile Anton now was spared the hard and menial tasks he did before. Sometimes Lobenstein took walks with him, and he even engaged a master to teach him the piano. Anton was delighted at his position and wrote a letter to his father, in which he expressed the liveliest satisfaction.

But now Anton's fortune had reached its climax in Lobenstein's house, and his fall was at hand. Everyone looked at him with envious eyes from the day the pianist was engaged. Intrigues were contrived like those of a petty court. He was slandered and his downfall planned.

So long as Lobenstein was harsh and unjust to Anton, he enjoyed the sympathy and friendship of all the household; but as soon as it seemed as if he would make a friend and confidant of him, then enmity and distrust of him grew in proportion. And as soon as they had succeeded in reducing him to their own level and had got the piano teacher dismissed, they no longer had any feeling against Anton; they were friends as before.

But now it was not difficult to rob him of the goodwill of one so suspicious and distrustful as Lobenstein; it was only necessary to repeat a few of his vivid expressions or to call Herr Lobenstein's attention on every occasion to certain real faults of carelessness and untidiness in Anton in order to give his sentiments a different direction. This was very conscientiously done by the housekeeper and other dependents.

Meanwhile it took several months to attain this object, during which time even Anton's piano master took pains to be converted, a good and honest man, but one who in Herr Lobenstein's opinion had not yet quite resigned himself to God and did not behave himself passively enough towards Him.

This man often had to take a meal in the house, but in the end spoiled everything by spreading too much butter on his bread. The housekeeper called Herr Lobenstein's attention to this in order to gain her object of putting an end to Anton's piano playing, so that he might not be exalted above the rest of the household.

Besides, Anton had no great genius for music and consequently learned little by his lessons. A few tunes and chorales were all he could achieve with much pains, and the piano lesson was always disagreeable to him. Fingering too he found very difficult, and the teacher always found something to criticize in the position of his outspread fingers.

Meanwhile he did succeed on one occasion, as David did with Saul, in driving away the evil spirit of Lobenstein by the power of music. He had committed some small fault, and as his master's fancy for him was beginning to turn into hatred, the man had intended in the evening to give him a severe chastisement before bedtime. Anton was aware of this, and when the hour seemed to be approaching he had the courage to play a chorale, the first he had learned, on the piano and to sing to it. This took Herr Lobenstein by surprise. He confessed to him that he had fixed that very hour to give him a severe flogging, which he now spared him.

Anton then began to remonstrate with him on the apparent decline of his friendship and affection, whereupon Lobenstein confessed to him that it was true that his affection for him was not so strong as it had been and that this must be due to Anton's spiritual deterioration, which had built a dividing wall, so to speak, between him and his previous love. He had put the matter before God in prayer and received this solution.

This was very sad for Anton, and he asked what steps he must take to improve his spiritual condition. The answer was that the only means to save his soul was to walk his way in simplicity and commit himself to God. No further directions were given. Herr Lobenstein did not think it proper to forestall God, who seemed to have withdrawn from Anton. The emphasis laid on the words "walk his way in simplicity" referred to the fact that he had for some time begun to find Anton too clever for him; he talked and reasoned too much, and generally his satisfaction with his condition made him too lively. Lobenstein regarded this liveliness as the road to Anton's ruin; his cheerful countenance must mean that he was becoming a vicious, worldly minded man, of whom the only thing to be expected was that God would let him perish in his sins.

Had Anton better understood his own advantage, he might now have been able to put everything right by adopting a melancholy, misanthropic manner and pretending anxiety and uneasiness about his soul. For then Lobenstein would have believed that God was going to draw the wandering soul to Himself.

But as Lobenstein held the principle that he whom God will convert is converted even without his own cooperation and that God chooses whom He will and rejects and hardens whom He will in order to reveal His majesty, it seemed to him dangerous to interfere with God if it appeared that someone was rejected by Him.

And, to judge from Anton's lively and worldly ways, it looked to Herr Lobenstein as if he were really so with him. He thought it so important that he had corresponded about it with Herr von Fleischbein, and now he showed a passage in a letter from Herr von Fleischbein in which he asserted that, to judge by all signs, "Satan had now built his temple so firmly in Anton's heart that it could scarcely be destroyed again."

This was indeed a shock for Anton. But he examined himself and compared his present with his previous state and found it impossible to discover any difference between them; his imagination indulged in religious feelings and emotions just as often as before, and he could not convince himself that he had fallen entirely from grace and was to be rejected by God. He began to doubt the truth of Herr von Fleischbein's oracular answer.

So he lost his depression, which otherwise perhaps might have paved the way to the favor of Herr Lobenstein, whose friendship he now completely forfeited by the continuance of his cheerful air.

The first consequence was that Lobenstein removed him from his room; he had to sleep again with the other apprentice, who began to be friendly now that he envied him no longer. The second was that he had to begin doing the hardest and most menial jobs again, and always had to remain in the workshop and only rarely join Herr Lobenstein in the parlor. The piano master was only retained because Lobenstein wished to complete the work of conversion he had begun in him and so bring another soul to God in place of the lost one.

Winter came and Anton's position began really to be a hard one; he had to perform tasks that were far beyond his years and powers. Lobenstein seemed to think that as now nothing was to be done with Anton's soul, at least all possible use must be made of his body. He seemed to regard him as a tool to be thrown away when worn out.

Frost and hard work soon made Anton's hands quite unfit for piano playing. Almost every week he had to stay up twice at night with the other apprentice to pull the blackened hats out of the boiling dye-vat and then wash them immediately in the running stream of the Oker, for which purpose they had first to cut an opening in the ice. This repeated transition from heat to cold made Anton's hands chap till the blood ran.

But instead of this depressing him it rather increased his courage. He looked at his hands with a kind of pride, as a sort of badge of honor for his work, and as long as these hard tasks had the charm of novelty they brought him a certain satisfaction, chiefly consisting in the sense of his bodily strength. At the same time they gave him a pleasant sense of freedom he had not known before.

He felt as though he could indulge himself more after bearing the day's burden and heat like the rest. Under the heaviest burdens he experienced a kind of inward esteem that came from the exertion of his powers, and he often felt he would hardly have exchanged this for the irksome position he was in when he enjoyed the austere friendship of Lobenstein, which destroyed all freedom.

Lobenstein now began to treat him with still more severity. He often had to card wool the whole day long in the bitterest cold in an unwarmed room. This was a clever device of his master to increase Anton's diligence, for if he did not want to die of cold he had to bestir himself, so far as his strength allowed, so that often in the evening his arms were almost paralyzed, though hands and feet were frozen.

This occupation, from its constant monotony, made his lot most bitter, especially if, as often happened, his imagination failed to work. On the other hand, when once the quicker movement of his blood set it going, the hours often passed by unnoticed. Then he often lost himself in enchanting visions. Sometimes he expressed his

feelings in song, in recitative to tunes of his own. And when he felt
especially tried of work, crushed and exhausted by his labors, he
liked to lose himself in religious sentiments of "sacrifice," "utter
devotion" and the like; the phrase "altar of sacrifice" appealed to
him most deeply, and he wove it into all the little hymns and
recitatives that he invented.

The conversations with his fellow apprentice, August, now began
to have a new charm for him, and as they were equals again, their
talk became confidential. Their friendship was cemented still closer
by the nights through which they often had to sit up together. But
their most intimate times were when they sat together in the "drying
room." This was a pit dug into the earth and vaulted with brick,
where a man could just stand upright and two men could sit
together. In this pit a great brazier was placed, and on the walls
around it were hung the skins of hares treated with nitric acid, the
hair of which was here softened, to be used afterwards for the finer
kind of hats.

Anton and August sat in front of the brazier in the steamy
atmosphere of the half-subterranean pit, into which you had to
crawl rather than walk; this confinement of the place, faintly lighted
by the glow of the coals, made them feel so closely united by the
remote quiet and awesome character of this dark vault that their
hearts often overflowed in mutual outpourings. Here they revealed
their inmost thoughts to one another and spent their happiest
hours.

Lobenstein, like Herr von Fleischbein and all his followers, was a
seceder who did not hold with church and sacrament. So long as he
had been friends with Anton, Anton had hardly entered a church in
Brunswick. Now August took him to church on Sunday, and they
went sometimes to one, sometimes to another, for Anton took
pleasure in hearing different preachers.

Anton and August were sitting in the drying room together one
midnight and discussing different preachers when August promised
to take him to the Brothers' Church next Sunday, where he would
hear a preacher who surpassed anything he could think or imagine.
The preacher was called Paulmann, and August told him over and
over again how deeply he had often been moved and affected by his
sermons. Nothing had more attraction for Anton than the sight of a

public speaker who holds the hearts of thousands in his hand. He listened attentively to what August told him. Already in his mind's eye he saw Pastor Paulmann in the pulpit and heard him preach. His only wish now was for Sunday to come.

Sunday came. Anton rose earlier than usual, attended to his duties and dressed. When the church bells rang he had a sort of pleasant presentiment of what he would soon hear. They went to church. The streets that led there were full of a stream of people hurrying thither. Pastor Paulmann was preaching again for the first time after a long illness; that was why Anton had not been taken there by August already.

When they entered they found a place facing the pulpit, but with difficulty. Every bench and all the aisles and galleries were full of people, all trying to look over one another's heads. The church was an old Gothic building with thick pillars supporting the high vaulted roof and vast, long, arched windows of painted glass letting only a faint light through.

The church was full before the service began, and a solemn quiet reigned there. Suddenly the full-voiced organ was heard and the hymn that burst from that great congregation seemed to shake the roof. When the last verse ended, all eyes were fixed on the pulpit, and there was no less curiosity to see this idolized preacher than to hear him.

At last he came forward and knelt on the lowest stair of the pulpit before he went up. Then he rose and was soon standing before the assembled people—a man in the full strength of his years, his face pale, a gentle smile playing around his mouth and his eyes shining with heavenly devotion; even before he began, his attitude as he stood there with hands quietly folded made a deep impression.

And then, as he began, what a voice! what expression! First slow and solemn, then a rapid flow. As he warmed to his subject the fire of eloquence began to sparkle in his eyes, to breathe from his breast, and to scatter sparks from his fingertips. He was all movement; the expression conveyed by features, attitude, and gestures went beyond all rules of art, yet was natural, noble, and carried one away irresistibly.

There was no pause in the powerful outpouring of his feelings and thoughts; the first word was hardly spoken when the next was ready to be uttered. As one wave swallows another in the flowing tide, so each fresh emotion was merged with that which followed, and yet the new emotion was but a livelier presentation of the first.

His voice was a clear tenor, which as it rose was unusually rich; it had the ring of pure metal and vibrated through every nerve. He spoke, under guidance of the Gospel, against injustice and oppression, against luxury and extravagance, and in the fiery heat of his inspiration he addressed by name the sensual, luxurious town whose inhabitants were for the most part assembled in the church, laid bare their sins and crimes, reminded them of the time of war, when the town was besieged and all men were in danger, when necessity made all equal and brotherly unity reigned; when the luxurious inhabitants were threatened by hunger and want and prison chains instead of the tables groaning with plenty and the bracelets and jewelry of today. Anton imagined himself listening to one of the prophets chiding the people of Israel with holy zeal and rebuking Jerusalem for its sins.

Anton went home from church without saying a word to August, but wherever he was or wherever he went he thought of nothing but Pastor Paulmann. He dreamed of him by night and talked of him by day; his face, his features, his every movement were graven on Anton's mind. As he carded wool in the workshop or washed the hats, he busied himself all week with entrancing thoughts of Pastor Paulmann's sermon and repeated to himself many times over every expression that had affected him or moved him to tears. His imagination then reproduced the majestic old church, the listening throng and the voice of the preacher, which now in his fancy sounded even more heavenly. He counted the days and minutes to the next Sunday.

It came, and if ever anything made an indelible impression on Anton's soul, it was the sermon he heard that day. The crowd was if possible even larger than the Sunday before. A short chant was sung before the sermon, composed of the words of the Psalm "Lord, who shall abide in thy tabernacle? who shall dwell in thy holy hill? He that walketh uprightly and worketh righteousness and speaketh the truth in his heart. He that backbiteth not with his tongue, nor doth evil to his neighbor nor taketh up a reproach against his neighbor. In whose eyes a vile person is contemned, but he honoreth them that fear the Lord; he that sweareth to his own hurt and changeth not. He that putteth not out his money to usury, nor taketh reward against the innocent; he that doth these things, shall never be moved."

This short and moving chant made everyone thrill with expectation of what was to come. The heart was ready for great and exalted impressions when Pastor Paulmann came forward and, with earnest solemnity in his face and a look of deep absorption, began without prayer or introduction to speak with outstretched arm:

"He that oppresseth not the widow and the orphans; he that is not conscious of secret sins; that taketh not advantage of his neighbor with wrong; whose soul is burdened by no perjury; let him lift up his hands with me to God full of confidence and prayer. 'Our Father.'"

Then he read from the Gospel the passage where John the Baptist is asked whether he is the Christ. "And he confessed and denied not, and confessed I am not the Christ." And from these words he took occasion to preach on perjury, and after he had read the words of the Gospel in a solemn, subdued voice he began after a pause:

> Oh, woe to thee, by sin beguiled,
> Thy Lord, oh shame! denying!
> How canst thou lift thy face, defiled
> By perjury and lying?
> Thou hast been false to Him and so
> In depth of sin thou liest low,
> His name profanely scorning.
> When thou before Him show'st thy face
> He knows thee not, so lost to grace;
> Yet, if thou wilt take warning,
> It may be, wretchedest of men,
> That tears may quench the guilty flame
> Within thy breast, now dead to shame,
> So lift thy heart in hope again!
> Contrition, in the length of years,
> May wash thy guilt away in tears.
> Thou who the path of sin didst choose,
> If thou canst weep, the stain may lose,
> God helping thine endeavor.
> He dooms not sinners all to death,
> He turns His face and pardoneth,
> His promise stands forever.

These words, spoken with frequent pauses and the most exalted feeling, produced an incredible impression. When they were ended all present breathed more freely; they wiped the sweat from their brows. Then he went on to examine the nature of perjury—to put its consequences in a more and more appalling light. The thunder rolled down on the head of the perjurer, destruction approached him like an armed man, the sinner trembled in the innermost depth of his soul, he cried, "Ye mountains fall on me and ye hills cover me!" The perjurer received no mercy, he was annihilated before the wrath of the Eternal.

He was silent, as if exhausted. A panic terror seized all hearers. Anton hastily ran through all the years of his life to see if he had ever been guilty of perjury.

But then began the note of consolation. Mercy and pardon were announced to the despairing sinner, if he atoned tenfold for what he had stolen from the widow and the orphan, if, his whole life long, he tried to wash away his sin with tears of repentance and other good works.

Mercy was not easily vouchsafed to the criminal: it had to be won by prayer and tears. And then it seemed as though he wished to win it by his own prayer and tears, in God's sight before all the people, putting himself in the place of the contrite sinner.

He appealed to the despairing: "Kneel down in dust and ashes, till your knees are sore, and say, 'I have sinned against heaven and before Thee.'" And so every period began with "I have sinned against heaven and before Thee." And then followed a series of confessions: "I have oppressed the widow and the orphan, I have robbed the weak of his only stay, the hungry of his bread," and so through all the list of crimes. And every period closed with "Lord, is it possible that I should find mercy?"

The whole company melted in sorrow and weeping. The refrain in each period had an incredible effect; it was as if men's feelings each time received a fresh electric shock, which raised them to the highest pitch. Even the final exhaustion, the hoarseness of the orator (it was as though he cried to God for the sins of the world), contributed to the spreading flood of emotion caused by the sermon; there was not a child who did not join in the sighing and weeping out of sympathy.

Two and a half hours had passed like minutes. Suddenly he stopped and after a pause he ended with the same verses with which he had begun. With a voice exhausted and subdued he read the general confession and the absolution promised to such as repent; then he prayed for those who wished to come to the Sacrament, himself among the number, and then with uplifted hands he gave the blessing. The contrast of his lowered voice with the tone that prevailed in his sermon had a solemn and moving effect.

Anton did not leave the church. He first had to see Pastor Paulmann go to the Sacrament. His every step was sacred to him. With a kind of reverence he went to the place where he knew that Pastor Paulmann had gone. What would he not have given to be able to go to the Sacrament with him? Then he saw the pastor go home, accompanied by his son, a boy of nine. Anton would have given his whole existence to be that lucky boy. As he watched Pastor Paulmann, surrounded by people on all sides, cross the street and saw him giving friendly thanks to those who greeted him on all sides, he imagined that he saw a sort of halo around his head, as if he were a superhuman being walking among mortals. His dearest wish was to win a look from him by lifting his hat, and when he succeeded he hurried quickly home, so as to preserve this look, as it were, in his heart.

The next Sunday Pastor Paulmann preached on love of the brethren, and this sermon was as tender in feeling as that against perjury had been powerful. The words flowed like honey from his lips, all his movements were different, his whole being seemed altered to suit his subject. Yet there was not the least affectation. It was natural to him to merge his personality with the thoughts and emotions his subject matter suggested to him.

That morning Anton had listened with amazing weariness to the other preacher of this church. Once or twice he got quite angry with him because, just when he seemed about to say amen, he began over again in the same tone. Now more than ever it was Anton's greatest torment to listen to a wearisome sermon like this, because he could not help making constant comparisons, when once he had conceived as his highest ideal the sermon of Pastor Paulmann, which seemed to him unattainable by anyone else.

When the morning sermon was over, it was Pastor Paulmann's turn to perform the consecration at the Sacrament, which Anton now heard him do for the first time. And what a venerable figure he seemed to him at that moment! He stood at the far end of the church, before the high altar, and chanted the words "Oh, thank the

Lord, for He is gracious, and His mercy endureth forever" with such a heaven-uplifting voice and such powerful expression that Anton thought himself for the moment rapt into higher regions. The whole ceremony seemed to happen behind a curtain, in the holy of holies, which his feet dared not approach. How he envied everyone who could go up to the altar and receive the Sacrament from the pastor's hands! A very young woman, dressed in black, with pale cheeks and an air of heavenly devotion, who went up to the altar, made an impression on Anton's heart such as he had never felt before. He never saw her again, but her image was never effaced from his memory.

His imagination now found a new field. The idea of the Sacrament occupied him at his rising and his lying down and at every moment when he was alone at his work, and the form of Pastor Paulmann hovered before his mind, with his gentle, rising voice and his eyes turned heavenwards with a light of more than earthly devotion. Sometimes the figure of the young woman in black also came back into his vision, with her pale face and her air of devout worship.

All this so inspired his imagination that he would have counted himself the happiest man under the sun if he could have gone to the Sacrament the next Sunday. He promised himself such celestial solace from the Sacrament that he shed tears of joy beforehand. At the same time he had a feeling of mild self-compassion, which sweetened everything unpleasant and bitter in his lot when he reflected that, once he had become a journeyman, no one could rob him of this consolation. He resolved to go to the Sacrament at least once a fortnight, once he had got to this stage, and then there blended with this desire the secret hope that perhaps this frequent attendance would finally attract the notice of Pastor Paulmann. And it was this thought above all that made these ideas so inexpressibly sweet to him. Thus even here, where perhaps it was least to be expected, vanity lay in ambush for him.

He found it impossible to believe that he would always be misunderstood and neglected, as he was now. Certain romantic ideas that he had got into his head led him to think that one day some generous man who met him in the street would notice something remarkable in him and would take notice of him. A certain sad and melancholy air, which he assumed for this end, would, he thought, best attract attention, so he affected it more than was natural to him.

Often indeed, when the face of some gentleman of quality inspired confidence, he nearly went so far as to address him and reveal his circumstances. But he was always deterred by the fear that the gentleman might perhaps take him for a fool.

Sometimes, as he went along the street, he would also sing in a plaintive voice some of Madame Guyon's hymns that he had learned by heart, hymns in which he thought he found allusions to his own lot; and then, as in romances sometimes a plaintive song sung by somebody works wonders, he thought he might succeed in giving a new turn to his fortune by thus drawing the attention of some humane person to himself.

His reverence for Pastor Paulmann was too profound for him ever to dare to address him. If he was near him, he felt a thrill as if he were near an angel.

He could not imagine, or tried to rid himself of the thought, that this pastor was like other men, getting up and going to bed and performing all natural functions like them. It was quite impossible to picture him in dressing gown and nightcap, or he avoided the thought, as though it would have made a breach in his soul. The thought of a nightcap, especially, in connection with Pastor Paulmann, was more than he could bear; he felt it would bring discord into all his other ideas.

But it happened once that Anton was standing at the church door just as Pastor Paulmann came in and was telling the sacristan in Low German that there was a baptism afterwards.

If ever Anton felt a contrast it was this: to have a man, whom he had thought of as never speaking except in the most solemn and moving tones, speak to the sacristan in *Low* German, like the simplest workman, on such a solemn thing as baptism, and that in a tone that was anything but solemn, the tone in which one might say to anyone that he must not forget to bring the washing basin.

This single incident in some degree moderated Anton's idolatry of Pastor Paulmann. He worshiped him less and loved him more.

Meanwhile he had modeled his ideal of happiness entirely on him. He could imagine nothing more noble or more attractive than to be able to speak publicly before the people like Pastor Paulmann and like him now and again to address the city by name. This personal address was to him a great and moving thought, which often occupied his mind for days on end. Even when he went along the street, to fetch beer perhaps, if he saw a couple of boys fighting, he could not help repeating the pastor's words to himself, warning the wicked city against destruction and lifting his arm to heaven to threaten it. Wherever he was, wherever he went, he delivered speeches in his imagination, and when he was worked up to high passion he gave the sermon against perjury.

He lived for some time amid these pleasant fancies, which almost made him forget the woolcarding in the cold room, the icy hat washing, and the want of sleep when he had to sit up several nights on end. Sometimes as he worked, the hours flew by like minutes, when he succeeded in imagining himself in the character of a public orator.

But either the unnatural strain on his mental faculties or the physical effort of work that was beyond his years proved too much for him, and he became dangerously ill. His nursing was not the best. He was delirious with fever and often lay all day with no one to trouble about him.

At last his good constitution won the battle, and he was restored. The illness, however, left behind a certain languor and depression, and the humane Herr Lobenstein very nearly gave him a fatal relapse by one of his gentle admonitions.

It was one evening in the twilight, when Lobenstein was taking a warm bath of herbs in a dark and distant room, when Anton had to wait on him. As he sweated in his bath and was in great tribulation, he said to Anton in a voice that pierced his marrow "Anton, Anton, beware of hell!" And he stared into the corner.

Anton trembled at these words, a sudden shudder went through all his body. All the terrors of death fell upon him, for he had not the least doubt that at that moment Lobenstein had seen a vision portending Anton's death and that this had moved him to the awful cry "Beware, beware of hell!"

Immediately afterwards Lobenstein suddenly came out of the bath, and Anton had to light the way to his room. He went in front of him with trembling knees, and Lobenstein looked paler than death when he left him.

If ever prayer was made to God in genuine piety and fervor, it was offered by Anton now, as soon as he was alone. He threw himself, not on his knees but on his face, into a corner of the workshop and prayed to God for his life, like a criminal on whom sentence has been passed, for a respite for conversion, if he must indeed die. For he remembered that scores of times he had run and jumped and laughed wildly in the streets, and now all the torments of hell he would have to endure forever in punishment weighed heavily on him. "Beware, beware of hell" still rang in his ears, as though a spirit from the grave had called to him, and he went on praying a full hour and would never have ceased all night, if he had found no relief from his anguish. But as one sigh of anguish after another issued from his breast, and his tears flowed at last, he felt as if God had vouchsafed to hear his prayer, God who, as at Niniveh of old, would rather have a prophet shamed than a soul destroyed. Anton had prayed away his fever but would probably have relapsed into it, if his excited spirits had not found this escape. Thus one delusion or folly drives out another: the devils are driven out by Beelzebub.

After this exhaustion Anton was refreshed by quiet sleep and rose next morning perfectly well, but the thought of death awoke with him. He fancied that at most a short respite was given him for conversion and he must make haste if he would save his soul.

And he did what he could. Many times a day he prayed on his knees in a corner and at last dreamed himself into such a firm conviction of God's mercy and such cheerfulness of spirit that he often fancied himself in heaven and many a time wished he might die before he could stray from this good path.

But amid all these wanderings of his fancy it could not but be that nature seized the moment to come back. And then the natural love of life for life's sake awoke again in Anton's soul. Then the thought of his approaching death was indeed sad and unpleasant, and he regarded these moments as moments when he had again forfeited divine mercy and fell again into fresh anxiety because he found it impossible to suppress the voice of nature within him.

And now he experienced with double force the evil consequences of the superstition that had been instilled in him from earliest childhood. Properly understood, his sufferings were those of a vivid imagination, but still they were to him real sufferings, and they robbed him of the joys of his youth.

He knew from his mother that it was a sure sign of death being near when the hands do not steam when washed—now he saw himself dying whenever he washed his hands. He had heard that if a dog howls in the house with his muzzle to the ground he scents a man's death—every time he heard a dog howl it was a prophecy. Even if a hen crowed like a cock it was a sure sign that someone would soon die in the house—and here was an evil-boding hen strutting about the yard and crowing constantly in unnatural fashion like a cock. No death knell seemed so fearful as this crowing, and this hen caused him more gloomy hours in his life than any misfortune he ever suffered.

Comfort and hope of life often returned to him when the hen was silent for a day or two, but when it began again all his fair hopes and plans were suddenly ruined.

As he went about with nothing but thoughts of death in his head, it so happened that for the first time after his illness he went again to Pastor Paulmann's church. The pastor stood up in the pulpit and preached on death.

This was a shock for Anton; for as he had learned to relate everything to himself, following the ideas of "special divine guidance" that he had imbibed, he felt the sermon on death could have been meant only for him. No criminal listening to his death sentence could feel deeper anxiety than Anton at this sermon. Pastor Paulmann added some grounds for consolation to weigh against the terrors of death, but that counted for little compared with the natural love of life, which in spite of all the fancies that filled Anton's head, was still the feeling that predominated.

He went home downcast and depressed, and for a fortnight the sermon made him melancholy, a sermon Pastor Paulmann would probably never have delivered if he had known it would have the effect on two or three men that it had upon Anton.

Thus Anton in his thirteenth year, thanks to the special guidance divine mercy through its chosen instruments had vouchsafed him, had become a complete hypochondriac, of whom it could justly be said that at every moment though alive, he was dead. Shamefully defrauded of the enjoyment of his youth, he was driven to madness by "prevenient grace."

But spring was coming again, and nature, which heals all, in him too began to restore what grace had ruined.

Anton felt a new power of life in him. He washed, and his hands steamed again, no dogs barked any more, the hen ceased to crow, and Pastor Paulmann preached no more sermons on death.

Anton began again to go for walks alone on Sundays, and it

chanced one day that, without knowing it, he came to the very gate through which he had walked in with his father a year and a half before. He could not refrain from going out and following the broad willow-lined highway that he had come by. Peculiar feelings rose in him as he went. At once his whole life came back to him, from the day when he first saw the sentinel walking to and fro on the rampart and formed all sorts of ideas of how the city would look inside and what sort of a house the Lobensteins' would be. It was as if he woke from a dream and found himself again on the spot where the dream began. All the changing scenes of his life, as he had lived in this year and a half in Brunswick, came crowding in on him, and every single scene seemed to grow smaller, measured by a bigger scale, of which he was now suddenly possessed.

So powerful is the effect produced by the idea of place, with which all our other ideas are connected. The individual streets and houses, which Anton saw day after day, formed the enduring core of his ideas, with which the constantly shifting scenes of his life were connected, which gave them unity and reality, by which he distinguished between waking and dreaming.

In childhood especially, all other ideas are bound to be connected with ideas of place because in themselves they are as yet too fluid and cannot yet hold together without support.

That is why in childhood it is also difficult to distinguish waking from dreaming. And I remember that one of our greatest living philosophers has told me a very curious story from his childhood years in this respect.

He had often been flogged for a certain bad habit that is very common in children. But he had always very vividly dreamed, as is also common, that he had gone up to the wall and. . . . When now he sometimes really went up to the wall for the same reason by day, he thought of the harsh punishment that he had so often suffered—and he often stood there a long time before he dared answer the urgent call of nature, because he feared it might be another dream for which he could expect severe punishment again—until he had first looked around on all sides and then also calculated backwards with respect to time, before he could fully convince himself that he was not dreaming.

On waking in the morning, one often goes on half dreaming, and the transition to waking is gradually made as one begins to get one's bearings; as soon as the bright light of the window gives a fixed point, everything else gradually falls into place.

So it was quite natural that Anton, after he had been some weeks in the Lobensteins' house in Brunswick, still thought he was dreaming in the morning when he was really awake, because the pivot, so to speak, to which he had been used to attach his ideas of the day before or of his previous life, and which gave them their unity and truth, was now disturbed, because the idea of place was no longer the same.

It is surprising then that a change in surroundings often contributes so much to make us forget like a dream what we do not like to think of as real?

As years go on, especially if we have traveled much, the association of ideas with place tends to diminish. Wherever we go we see either roofs, windows, doors, pavement, churches, and towers, or meadows, forest, plow land or heath. The striking differences disappear; the earth becomes everywhere the same.

When Anton walked along the street in Brunswick, especially in the evening as twilight began, he often suddenly felt as if in a dream. This would also happen to him if he went into some street that seemed to have a distant resemblance to a street in Hanover. For a few moments his circumstances in Hanover were present again; the scenes of his life were confused with one another.

In his walks he took a special delight in hunting out places in the town where he had never been. His soul expanded then, and he felt as though he had taken a bold leap out of the narrow sphere of his existence; everyday notions disappeared and wild and pleasant prospects, mazes of the future were opened up for him.

But he had never yet succeeded in grasping in one single, complete vision his whole life in Brunswick, with all its various changes. The place where he was at any time reminded him too strongly of some particular part of it to make room for a mental picture of the whole; his ideas always revolved within a narrow circle of his existence.

In order to obtain a distinct view of his present life as a whole, it was necessary that all the threads, so to speak, which fastened his attention on what was momentary, everyday, and fragmentary should be cut off, and that he should be put again at the point of view from which he regarded his life in Brunswick before it began, when it still lay before him in the twilight of the future.

To this point of vision he was now transported when he came by chance out of the gate through which about a year and a half before he had come in along the broad willow-lined high road and had seen the sentinel walking to and fro on the rampart.

It was precisely this place that, suddenly reminding him of a thousand little things, seemed to put him exactly in the position he was in before the beginning of his present life. All that lay between inevitably came crowding into his imagination, events melting into one another like shadows or a dream. His standing on the bridge now and looking up at the high rampart, where the sentinel stood, seemed quite near to his standing and looking upwards a year and a half before. The past, all the scenes of the life that Anton had led in Brunswick, he now called up again, just as he had thought of them a year and a half before as still in the future, and the more than vivid image and recollection of the place made his memory of the time that had passed between become faint or disappear. At least it is hardly possible in any other way to explain the mystery of that peculiar feeling that Anton then had and that everyone will remember to have had at least once in his life.

More than ten times Anton was on the point of not returning into the town, but of going straight to Hanover, if the thought of hunger and cold had not deterred him.

But from that day forward he firmly resolved not to stay any longer in Lobenstein's house, cost what it might. He therefore became more indifferent to everything, because he imagined it would not last much longer. Lobenstein himself began to become so dissatisfied with him that he wrote to Anton's father in Hanover, telling him that he might fetch his son back at any time, as nothing was to be made of him.

Nothing could have been more welcome to Anton than news that his father would fetch him home at once. He concluded that he would in any case be sent to school in Hanover before he was admitted to the Sacrament, and then his intention would be to distinguish himself so as to attract attention. Eagerly as he had striven before to go to Brunswick, he now hankered again for Hanover and indulged himself once more in pleasant dreams of the future.

Notwithstanding the hard conditions, he had become very fond of many things in Brunswick, so that his pleasant hopes were often tinged with sadness and a gentle melancholy. He often stood in solitude by the Oker and looked at some little passing boat, following it as far as he could with his eyes; and then he would often have a sudden feeling as if he had taken a look into the dark future, but just when he thought he grasped the delusive vision, it suddenly disappeared.

He now took pains to enjoy once more all the regions of the city that he had so far visited on his Sunday walks, and took a sad farewell of each in turn, as if he never hoped to see them again.

He heard several more sermons from Pastor Paulmann, many passages from which he has never forgotten.

He was extraordinarily moved in a sermon on the sufferings of Jesus by the intensity with which Pastor Paulmann said the words: "He looks down on his murderers in compassion, and prays and prays and prays 'Father, forgive them, for they know not what they do!'"

And in a sermon on confession, given on the gospel story of the leper who was to show himself to the priest, the address to the hypocrites, who conscientiously observe all the outward forms of religion but bear a malevolent heart within them, when every period began with "you come to the confessional, you show yourselves to the priest, but he cannot see into your heart." In this sermon he was also extraordinarily moved by an expression, frequently repeated, which sounded to him like "You'll go to heaven." The last word, which the preacher always swallowed, so that he could not understand it, sounded like "heaven," and this word or this sound moved him to tears as often as he thought of it.

There was another phrase that often came in Pastor Paulmann's sermons—"the heights of reason." This had an equal charm for him, but for special reasons, which it will be worthwhile to explain. The choir in the church, where the organ stood and the choristers sang, always seemed to him something out of reach. He often looked up to it with longing and desired no greater happiness than for once to be allowed to look closely at the wonderful structure of the organ and all that was up there, because he could now only admire it all at a distance. This fancy was connected with another he had brought with him from Hanover. There a certain tower had also been an extremely attractive object; he regarded it with ecstasy morning and evening and often envied the town musicians who stood above in the gallery making music morning and evening to those below.

For hours he could watch this gallery, which seemed to him from below so small that it would not reach to his knees, yet would hardly allow the musicians' heads to show over it; and the face of the clock too, which those who had been up assured him was as large as a wagon wheel, but from below seemed to him no bigger than the wheel of a wheelbarrow. All this roused his curiosity to the utmost, so that he often went about for days with nothing but the thought and the wish to be able for once to see the gallery and the face of the clock close at hand.

Now in the tower at Hanover it was possible, through the apertures above the gallery, to see the bells being played; and Anton almost devoured the strange spectacle with his eyes, when he saw the great metal machine, which caused the clang that shook the whole structure, swinging up on either side, under the feet of the ringers, who looked quite small as they stood high up and trod on the beams.

He felt as if he had looked into the very bowels of the tower and as if the mysterious mechanism of the wonderful peal, which he had so often heard with emotion, had now revealed itself in the distance. But his curiosity was only roused the more instead of being satisfied. He had only seen one-half of the bell, as it rose upwards with its huge concavity, and not its whole bulk. He had heard of the size of the bell from childhood, and his imagination multiplied the image many times over, so that he had the most romantic and extravagant ideas of it.

Amid all the pains he endured in his foot, amid all the oppression from his parents under which he sighed, what was his consolation? What was the pleasantest dream of his childhood? What was his dearest desire, which often made him forget everything else? It was that he might see the face of the clock and the gallery close at hand in the tower of the New Town in Hanover and the bells that hung in it.

For more than a year this play of his fancy cheered the dullest hours of his life, but alas! he had to leave Hanover without his dearest wish being gratified. Yet the image of the tower in the New Town never vanished from his thoughts, it followed him to

Brunswick and there often hovered before him in dreams at night as he climbed the tower, up high stairs through the labyrinthine windings, and stood in the gallery and touched the face of the clock on the tower with inexpressible pleasure, and then inside the tower saw close before his eyes not only the great bell but innumerable smaller ones, along with other more wonderful things, until perhaps he knocked his head against the edge of the big bell he could not look over, and so awoke.

Whenever Pastor Paulmann talked of "the heights of reason," Anton thought with rapture of the heights of his beloved tower, with its bell and clock-face, and then also of the organ gallery in the Brothers' Church, and then all at once his longing returned, and the phrase "the heights of reason" made him shed tears of sadness.

The strictly theoretical part of Pastor Paulmann's sermons, which he delivered with amazing speed, was indeed lost on Anton, who found it too quick for his thoughts to follow. But he listened to him with pleasure, in the hope of hearing the exhortation; it was then that he felt as if the clouds were gathering that would presently fall in a beneficent storm or gentle rain.

But the day came when he went to the church with the idea of writing down Pastor Paulmann's sermon when he got home, and he felt at once, as he listened, as though light dawned in his soul. His attention had received a new direction. Hitherto he had listened with the heart, now he listened for the first time with the intellect. He no longer wanted merely to be moved by single passages but to grasp the sermon as a whole, and he began to find the theoretical part as interesting as the hortatory. The sermon dealt with love of one's neighbor: how happy men would be if each tried to further the welfare of everyone else, and everyone else the welfare of each individual. He never forgot this sermon with all its divisions and subdivisions; he heard it with the purpose of writing it down, and did so as soon as he got home and very much astonished August, to whom he read it.

Writing down this sermon had, as it were, developed new faculties in his mind. For from this time on, his ideas began gradually to sort themselves out. He learned to reflect on a subject for himself, he tried to represent the succession of his thoughts externally, and as he could tell them to no one, he expressed them in written essays, which were often strange enough. Before, he had communed with

God orally; now he began to correspond with Him, and wrote long prayers to Him, describing his condition.

He felt himself all the more compelled to written expression because he was cut off from all reading, for Lobenstein had long ceased to allow him any book except a description of heaven and hell by Engelbrecht, a journeyman clothier of Winsen on the Aller, which he had given him.

There cannot be a worse braggart in the world than this Engelbrecht must have been. He had been taken for dead, and after his recovery he made his old grandmother believe that he had really been in heaven and hell; she had enlarged on his story, and so the precious book had come into being.

The fellow did not blush to assert that he had floated with Christ and the angels of God right up beneath heaven and had taken the sun in one hand and the moon in the other and counted the stars in heaven.

Nevertheless, his comparisons were sometimes rather naïve. He compared heaven, for instance, to a delicious wine-soup, of which one only tastes a few drops on earth, but there could take by spoonfuls. And heavenly music surpassed that of earth as a fine concert surpasses the droning of a bagpipe or the tootle of a night-watchman's horn.

And he could not find enough to say of the honor paid him in heaven!

For want of better nourishment Aton's soul had to content itself with this poor diet. At least it served to occupy his imagination. His intellect remained neutral, he neither believed nor doubted, he only pictured it all vividly.

Meanwhile, Lobenstein's anger and hatred of him frequently went as far as abuse and blows; he embittered his life most cruelly and made him do the meanest and most humiliating tasks. But nothing offended Anton more than having for the first time in his life to carry a load on his back, a pannier packed with hats, along the public street, while Lobenstein walked in front of him. He felt as if everyone in the street was looking at him.

Any load he could carry in front of him or under his arm or in his hands seemed to him honorable and no cause for shame. But to be obliged to go bent and bow his neck beneath the yoke like a beast of burden while his proud master walked in front bowed his whole spirit and made the load a thousand times heavier. He felt he would sink into the earth for weariness as well as for shame before he arrived with his burden at his destination.

This destination was the arsenal, where the hats, which were regulation hats, were delivered. Anton had eagerly desired to see the inside of the arsenal, which he had often passed without being able to gratify his wish, just as he had wished to see the bells and the clock face on the tower in the New Town at Hanover. But now his pleasure was completely spoiled by having to see it under these conditions.

This carrying on the back weakened his spirit more than any humiliation he had suffered and more than Lobenstein's abuse and blows. He felt as if he could not sink lower; he almost regarded himself as a despicable, godforsaken creature. This was one of the cruelest situations in his life; whenever he saw an arsenal he had a lively recollection of it, and its image ran in his mind whenever he heard the word *subjugation*.

When anything of this sort happened, he tried to hide from everyone. Every cheerful sound jarred on him; he hurried to the Oker behind the house and often looked for hours with longing at the stream below. If even there he was pursued by some human voice from one of the neighboring houses, or if he heard laughing, singing, or talking, he imagined the world was laughing him to scorn, so despised and good for nothing did he regard himself since he had bowed his neck beneath the yoke of a pannier.

He felt a kind of rapture in joining in the bitter laughter his gloomy fancy heard ringing over him. In one of those dreadful hours, when he burst into a wild laughter of despair over himself, his disgust at life was so strong that he began to tremble and shake on the weak plank he was standing on. His knees would support him no longer; he fell into the stream. August was his guardian angel; he had been standing behind him unnoticed for some time and now pulled him out by the arm. Nevertheless other people had come up, the whole house was astir, and Anton was from that moment looked on as a dangerous person, to be got rid of as soon as possible. Lobenstein reported the incident to Anton's father, who came to Brunswick a fortnight later in a bad mood to fetch back to Hanover his misguided son, in whose heart, according to Herr von Fleischbein's opinion, Satan had built an indestructible temple.

He stayed a day or two with the hatmaker, during which time Anton performed all his duties with redoubled zeal and found peace in doing all that lay within his powers. He now in thought took leave of the workshop, the drying room, the woodyard, and the Brothers' Church; the pleasantest idea he had was that when he got home to Hanover he would then be able to tell his mother about Pastor Paulmann.

The nearer the time of departure came, the lighter was his heart. He would now soon emerge from his narrow, oppressing situation. The wide world opened before him.

August took leave of him tenderly, Lobenstein was cold as ice. It was on a Sunday afternoon beneath a dull sky that Anton and his father left the house of Lobenstein. He looked once more at the black door studded with large nails and turned his back on it with satisfaction, to walk again through the gate, outside which he had lately had such an interesting stroll. The high ramparts of the city and the tower of St. Andrew had soon vanished from sight, and he could only just see the snow-covered Brocken disappearing in the distance in dim twilight beneath the thickening clouds.

His father's heart was cold and reserved towards him, for he looked at him entirely with the eyes of the hatmaker and Herr von Fleischbein as one in whose heart Satan had built his temple once and for all. There was little talk along the way, they walked silently on, and Anton hardly noticed the length of the road, so pleasantly did he converse with his thoughts of when he should see his mother and brothers again and be able to tell them his fortunes.

At last the four handsome towers of Hanover stood out again in the distance, and Anton looked on the tower of the New Town as a friend seen again after long separation, and at once his love for the bells awoke again.

So he saw himself again within the walls of Hanover and found everything new. His parents had taken a smaller and darker house in a remote street, and everything seemed so strange as he went up the steps that he felt he could not possibly feel at home there.

But if the behavior of his father was cold and repellent, the delight with which his mother and brothers ran to meet him was loud and demonstrative. They looked at his frost-chapped hands, and for the first time he felt himself pitied again.

When he went out next day he visited all the familiar places where

he had played in old days; he felt as if he had grown old and wished
to revive the memories of his youth. He met a troop of his old
schoolfellows and playmates, who all shook him by the hand and
rejoiced at his return.

As soon as he was alone with his mother he could not fail to tell
her about Pastor Paulmann. She had an unbounded respect for the
clergy, and she was ready to sympathize with Anton in his feelings
toward Pastor Paulmann. What blessed hours those were in which
Anton was able to unbosom himself and talk to his content of the
man whom he loved and respected above all men on earth!

He now heard the Hanover preachers, but how different they
were! Among them all he found no Paulmann except one called
Schlegel, who when he was deeply moved had some resemblance to
him.

No preacher could win Anton's approval unless he spoke at least
as fast as Pastor Paulmann; and if a preacher is viewed as an orator
only, I am not sure whether he was wrong. A teacher must speak
slowly, an orator quickly. The teacher has to enlighten the mind by
degrees, the orator to penetrate the heart irresistibly. The mind must
be approached slowly, the heart quickly, if any result is to be
achieved. No doubt he is a bad teacher who does not at times
become an orator, and he is a bad orator who does not at times turn
teacher; but when Fox speaks in the English Parliament, he does it
with unequaled spirit and carries everything away in the roaring
stream of his eloquence, as Pastor Paulmann did in his sermon on
perjury.

One Sunday Anton heard a preacher called Marquard at the
Garrison Church in Hanover with the greatest aversion because he
was not in the least like Pastor Paulmann, and indeed his slow and
easy speech was about the exact opposite. Anton, when he came
home, could not help expressing to his mother a feeling of dislike
toward this preacher, but how surprised he was when she told him
that he was to go to this very preacher for religious instruction and
confession and the Sacrament because he was her confessor and she
belonged to his congregation!

Anton could never have believed that he would one day come to
love this man, for whom he now felt an unconquerable aversion, and
that he would one day be his friend and benefactor.

Meanwhile an event happened that made Anton, who was already inclined to depression, still more melancholy. His mother became dangerously ill and for a fortnight hovered between life and death. It is impossible to describe Anton's feelings. His existence was so closely bound up with hers that he felt that his life would end with hers. He often wept all through the night on hearing that the doctor gave up hope of her recovery. He felt that it would be impossible for him to bear the loss of his mother. This was natural enough, for he felt forsaken by everyone and found himself again in her love and confidence.

Pastor Marquard came and gave his mother the Sacrament; he now thought all hope was gone and was inconsolable; he prayed to God for his mother's life and thought of King Hezekiah, who received a sign from God that his prayer was heard and her life prolonged.

Anton now looked for some such sign. Perhaps the shadow on the garden wall would go back? And at last the shadow did seem to go back, for a thin cloud had passed over the sun; or else his fancy put back the shadow. Anyhow, from that moment he took fresh hope and his mother really began to mend. So his life revived and he did everything to win his parents' affection. But with his father he had no success. Ever since he had fetched him from Brunswick, the man had taken a bitter, irreconcilable dislike to him, which he made him feel on every occasion. Every meal was grudged him, and Anton often had literally to eat his bread with tears.

His only comfort was in his solitary walks with his two younger brothers, with whom he arranged regular expeditions on the ramparts of the city, always fixing some point to which he pretended to make a journey with them.

This was his favorite occupation from earliest childhood; when he could scarcely walk he set himself a goal of this sort at the corner of the street where his parents lived, and this was the limit of his little walks.

He now converted the rampart he climbed into a mountain, the bushes through which he struggled into a forest, and a hillock in the town ditch into an island, and thus within a circuit of a few hundred paces he often took journeys of many miles with his brothers, lost his path and his bearings with them in forests, climbed high crags, and visited desert islands. In a word he enacted with them as well as he could the whole ideal world of romance.

At home he arranged all sorts of games with them, often rather rough ones. He besieged cities and captured fortresses built of the books of Madame Guyon with wild chestnuts, which he shot at them like bombs. Sometimes he preached and his brothers had to listen. The first time he had built himself a pulpit of chairs, and his brothers sat on footstools in front; he became violently excited, the pulpit collapsed, he fell down, and the chair he stood on struck his brothers' heads. The noise and confusion were general; meanwhile his father came in and began to punish him pretty severely for his sermon, and then his mother came and wanted to rescue him from his father's hands, but as she was unable to do so, her anger took just the opposite direction and she began to lay in to Anton with all her might, in spite of all his prayers and entreaties. Perhaps never was a sermon so unlucky as this sermon of Anton's, the first he gave in his life. The memory of this incident has often frightened him in dreams.

Meanwhile this did not deter him from often mounting his pulpit again and reading whole written sermons with text, subject, and headings. For since he had first begun to write down Pastor Paulmann's sermons, he found it easier to arrange his thoughts and bring them into connection with one another.

Not a Sunday passed now when he did not write down a sermon, and he soon acquired such facility that he was able to replace anything missing from memory and to reproduce at home on paper almost completely any sermon he had heard, if he had taken notes of the chief points.

Anton was now more than fourteen, and it was necessary, if he was to be confirmed and received into the bosom of the Christian church, that he should attend for some time a school where religious instruction was given.

Now there was an institution in Hanover where young people were educated to be village schoolmasters, to which was attached a free school, which served as a training college for the student teachers. This school existed rather for the sake of the teachers, than the teachers for the school, but as the pupils could pay nothing, it was a refuge for the poor, who could get their children taught there for nothing; and as Anton's father had never thought of spending much on a son who was so degenerate and so fallen from divine grace, he brought him at last to this school, where the boy saw at once an entirely new career opened to him.

It was a solemn sight for Anton when he saw gathered together in one class at the first morning lesson all the future teachers with their pupils, boys and girls. The inspector of this institution, who was a clergyman, had a catechism class every morning, which was to serve as a model for the teachers. The teachers all sat at tables, in order to take notes of the questions and answers, while the inspector walked up and down asking questions. In an afternoon lesson one or other of the teachers had to repeat with the pupils, in the presence of the inspector, the catechism he had given in the morning.

Anton by this time had learned to take notes very easily, and when the teacher repeated in the afternoon the lesson of the morning, Anton had taken much better notes in his notebook as he stood in class than the teacher had done, and could answer more than he was asked, which seemed to attract the notice of the inspector in a way very flattering for Anton.

But, that he should not be conceited with his fortune, a humiliation awaited him almost greater than what he felt at Brunswick when he had to carry a porter's basket for the first time.

A spelling exercise was fixed for the second lesson next morning, at which one boy had to spell a syllable alone and shout it out, and the others had then to repeat it with one voice. This clamor, which made the ears tingle, and the whole exercise, seemed to Anton sheer madness, and he was not a little ashamed, as he flattered himself that he could now read with expression, at being expected to begin to learn spelling again. Soon his turn came to shout, for it ran around the class like wildfire; and there he sat hesitating, and at once all the fine music was put out of time. "Go on!" said the inspector, and when he could not, he looked at him with supreme contempt and said, "Stupid boy!" and went on to the next boy to spell. Anton felt completely crushed at that moment, seeing himself suddenly sunk so low in the opinion of one on whom he had counted so much and who now would no longer believe that he could spell.

If in Brunswick his body had been subjugated by the load laid upon it, much more was his spirit crushed now by the weight with which the words "stupid boy!" of the inspector fell on him.

But this time his experience was that of Themistocles, of whom it is told that when once in his youth he suffered a disgrace in public, *non, fregit eum sed erexit.* From the day that he was thus humbled he exerted himself ten times more than before to win the respect of his teachers, so as to put to shame, as it were, the inspector who had so misunderstood him and to make him repent of the wrong he had inflicted on him.

Every morning the inspector in the early hours lectured dogmatically on the system of the Lutheran church, with refutations of the Papists as well as of the Calvinists, and took as his basis Gesenius's interpretation of Luther's smaller catechism. This filled Anton's head with a good deal of useless lumber, but he learned how to make logical divisions and subdivisions and to go to work systematically.

His notebooks grew bigger and bigger, and in less than a year he possessed a complete system of dogma, combined with passages from the Bible to prove it, and a complete polemic against heathens, Turks, Jews, Greeks, Papists, and Calvinists. He was able to talk like a book about transubstantiation in the Sacrament, about the five steps of the exaltation and humiliation of Christ, about the chief doctrines of the Koran and the chief proofs of the existence of God urged against freethinkers.

And he did actually speak like a book on all these things. He had then plenty of material to preach from, and his brothers' lot was now to hear all the contents of his notebooks delivered from the breakneck pulpit in the parlor.

Sometimes he was invited on Sunday to a cousin's who held a gathering of apprentices; here he had to stand at the table and deliver a formal sermon with text, subject, and headings before this assembly. He generally refuted the doctrine of the Papists on transubstantiation or refuted the Atheists, or enumerated with much feeling the proofs of the existence of God and exposed the doctrine of chance in all its nakedness.

It was the practice of the institute where Anton was taught that the adults who were being educated as schoolmasters had to distribute themselves on Sunday among all the churches and take notes of the sermons, which they then submitted to the inspector. Anton now found his pleasure in taking notes of sermons doubled because he saw that in this way he shared the occupation of his teachers, and those to whom he showed the sermons showed him increasing respect and met him almost as their equal.

He finally collected a thick volume of reported sermons, which he regarded as a precious possession, and two in particular were great treasures: one by Pastor Uhle, who came nearest to Pastor Paulmann in speed of delivery, given in St. Giles's church, was on the Last Judgment. Anton often delivered this to his mother with great delight. The destructive power of the elements, the crash of the universe, the trembling and shaking of the sinner, and the joyous awakening of the righteous were represented in a contrast that excited Anton's imagination in the highest degree, and this was just what he loved. He disliked cold appeals to reason. The second sermon he prized most highly was a farewell sermon delivered by Pastor Lesemann in the Castle Church, a sermon in which he was interrupted from beginning to end by tears and sobs, so much beloved was he by his congregation. The deep emotion with which this was actually delivered made an indelible impression on Anton's heart, and he could wish for no more blessed lot than to be one day allowed to give a farewell sermon like this before such a congregation, who all wept with him.

On such occasions he was in his element and found inexpressible pleasure in the melancholy feeling into which it transported him. No one perhaps has felt "the joy of grief" more deeply than he felt it on such occasions. To be so moved in spirit by such a sermon he reckoned more precious than any other pleasure in life, and he would have given up food and sleep for it.

His sense of friendship also now found fresh food. He really loved some of his teachers and felt a longing for their society. His friendship was specially directed to a teacher called R——, who to outward appearance was a hard and rough man, but really possessed the noblest heart that can be found in a future village schoolmaster.

He gave Anton a private lesson in arithmetic and writing, for which his father paid, for these were the only things he thought it worthwhile for Anton to learn. As he wrote quite correctly already, R—— soon made him write essays of his own, which received his approval. This was so flattering to Anton that at last he took courage to open his heart to him and speak to him with a frankness and freedom he had for long not been able to use with anyone.

So he revealed to him his invincible bent for study and the cruelty of his father, who kept him from it and wanted to make him learn nothing but a manual trade. The rough R—— seemed moved at this confidence and encouraged Anton to confide in the inspector, who might be able to help him to his object sooner than himself. This was the inspector who, when Anton did not wish to shout at the spelling lesson, had said "Stupid boy!" with a contemptuous face that he could not yet forget, and he therefore long doubted whether to reveal his bent for study to a man who had doubted his power to spell.

Meantime the respect won by Anton in the school grew daily, and he attained his desire to be at the head of the class and attract the most attention. This so fed his vanity that he often imagined himself a preacher already, especially if he had on a black waistcoat and breeches. Then he walked along with a dignified gait and more serious than usual.

On Saturday at the end of the week, after the hymn "So Far Hath God Brought Me" had been sung, a long prayer was read by one of the pupils. When the turn came to Anton, it was a real joy to him. He imagined himself in the pulpit, collecting his thoughts during the last verse of the hymn and then suddenly, like Pastor Paulmann with all the wealth of his eloquence, bursting into an earnest prayer. His declamation then was too emotional for a schoolboy and naturally sounded strange, so the teacher rarely let him read the prayer.

Indeed in the end the teachers became jealous of him. One of them assigned an exercise in which one of Hübner's Bible stories had to be told over again by the pupils in their own words. Anton adorned the story poetically with all his fancy and delivered it with oratorical embellishment. This offended the master, who remarked that Anton should tell his story more briefly. Next time he accordingly compressed the whole story into a few words and ended in two minutes. This the master found too short and was annoyed again, and finally he did not get him to tell stories in his own words any more. In the afternoon the masters who repeated the catechism class were afraid to question him, as his notes were always fuller than theirs. The result was that he had no chance to show his capacity, which was his dearest wish, so that he might attract attention.

Full of vexation at always having to sit dumb and unquestioned, he at last went with tears in his eyes to the inspector, who had often questioned him at morning lessons but seemed to have changed his mind about him. The inspector asked him what was the matter, whether one of his companions had wronged him. Anton answered that it was not his schoolfellows but his teachers who had wronged him. They neglected him now and no one asked him a question, though he knew the subject better than others. In this at least he might have justice!

The inspector tried to talk him out of that and excused the teachers on the grounds of the number of pupils, but from that time on he began to pay more attention to him and questioned him at the early morning lesson more frequently.

At one lesson a week an exercise on the Psalms was conducted. Every pupil had to draw lessons from them for himself, and these were written on a sheet of paper or a slate and then read aloud, which caused anguish to many. The inspector was present. Anton wrote nothing down, but when his turn came he went through the whole Psalm and gave a regular discourse or sermon on it, which lasted half an hour, so that at last the inspector said he was not to explain the Psalm, but ony draw some moral lessons from it.

In this way almost a year passed, in which Anton made such extraordinary progress in his diligence and behaved so blamelessly that he completely attained his object of attracting notice, while he even attracted the envy of his teachers.

He was now at the critical point when he had to choose some vocation, and the severity of his father, whose object was to get rid of him soon, increased from day to day, so that the school was a sort of sure refuge from the oppression and persecution of his home.

Meanwhile his beloved teacher R—— was promoted to be a village schoolmaster, and he now had no friend of his own among his teachers. His friend, when he went, once more advised him to appeal to the inspector, and as it was high time in any case to make a decision, he ventured one day with beating heart to ask the inspector for an interview, as he wished to talk to him of something important. The inspector took him to his room, and here Anton spoke more freely, told him his story, and opened his whole heart to him. The inspector pointed out to him the difficulties and the cost of a university education, but nevertheless did not rob him of all hope, and promised to do what he could to enable him to attend a Latin school. But all this was very remote because he could not hope for anything from his parents for his support, not even board and lodging, as his father had obtained a small office eighteen miles beyond Hanover and therefore had soon to leave Hanover.

Meanwhile the inspector had talked to Councillor Götten, under whose direction the Teachers' Institute was conducted, and he sent for Anton. The sight of this venerable old man at first discouraged Anton, and his knees shook as he stood before him. But when the old man took him kindly by the hand and talked to him quietly he began to speak frankly and to make known his desire to be a student. The councillor thereupon made him read aloud one of Gellert's spiritual odes, to hear what sort of voice and enunciation he had, if he should ever wish to devote himself to the ministry. Then he promised to procure him free instruction and supply him with books; this was all he could do for him. Anton was so overjoyed at this offer that his gratitude knew no bounds and he thought he had conquered all his difficulties at once, for it did not occur to him that besides free instruction and books he also needed food, lodging, and clothes.

He hastened home triumphantly and announced his good luck to his parents, but his delight was very much damped when his father coldly said to him that he could not count on a penny from him if he wanted to be a student. If he was in a position to procure himself bread and clothes he had no objection to his studying. He would be leaving Hanover in a few weeks, and if Anton by then had no master to go to, he might look around for shelter and wait as long as he liked to see whether any of the people who advised him so warmly to be a student would provide for his maintenance.

Sadly and pensively Anton now wandered about, reflecting on his fate. He clung to the idea of study even if many more difficulties stood in his way, and all sorts of plans went through his mind. He remembered that he had read that once in Greece there was a youth eager for learning who hewed wood and drew water for his maintenance, so that he might be able to devote his spare time to study. He wanted to follow this example and was willing to work as a day laborer for certain hours, if he might have the rest of his time to himself. But then he could not attend the school lessons regularly, so all his meditation and reflection only made him more melancholy and irresolute. Meantime the critical moment approached when he had to make a decision. He was now to leave the school he had hitherto attended, in order to go for a time to the garrison school, because he was to be confirmed by Marquard, the garrison preacher, whose preparation and catechism lessons he now began to attend, and whose notice he had attracted by his answers. But he would never have dared of his own accord to confide the troubles of his soul to this man in whom at first he could put no trust.

As no sure prospect opened up for Anton to become a student, he would probably in the end have had to resolve to learn a handicraft, had not a very trivial-seeming incident given a different turn to his fortune and affected his whole future life.

Translated by P. E. Matheson,
revised by Ellis Shookman

Glossary

Abednego. Biblical name given to the prophet Daniel's son Azariah. Daniel 1 : 6–7.

Abraham. Progenitor of the Hebrews, founder of Judaism. Muhammadans consider him ancestor of the Arabs.

Acerra philologica. Seventeenth-century humanistic collection of stories that introduce their readers to antiquity. After *Anton Reiser,* Moritz himself wrote a work surveying Greek mythology.

Ad infinitum. To infinity; without end or limit.

Amo, amen . . . Indicative and subjunctive conjugations of the Latin verb *amare,* "to love."

Amorites. A people of Canaan subdued and gradually absorbed by the Israelites.

"And he confessed not, and denied not. . . ." John 1 : 20.

Anthony, St. (251?–c. 350). Egyptian hermit said to have experienced but repelled every temptation that the devil could devise; father of Christian monasticism. He spent many years secluded in the desert.

Apostles. Prime missionaries of Christendom: Peter, Paul, Andrew, James (the Elder), John, Thomas, James (the Less), Jude (Thaddaeus), Philip, Bartholomew, Matthew, Simon, and Matthias.

Arabian Nights (or *Thousand and One Nights*). A series of stories in Arabic (among them those of Ali Baba, Sinbad the Sailor, and Aladdin) held together by the story of Scheherazade, who kept her husband, the legendary king of Samarkand, from killing her by telling these stories over the course of 1,001 nights.

Bastille. Fortress and state prison in Paris. Many political prisoners were held there, and it became a hated symbol of absolutism. Its storming by a Parisian mob on July 14, 1789, opened the way for the lower classes in the French Revolution.

Beautiful Banise. Courtly historic German novel, *Die asiatische Banise* (1689), by Heinrich Anselm von Ziegler und Kliphausen (1663–96).

Beelzebub. Nickname for the Devil. In the New Testament, the Pharisees, scribes, and some common people, too, argue that Jesus has exorcised devils not with the help of God, but only with that of Beelzebub, the "prince" or "chief" of the devils (Matthew 12:24, Mark 3:22, Luke 11:15).

Brocken (or Blocksberg). Peak in the Hartz Mountains, Saxony; popularly believed to be the site of the Walpurgis Night or Witches' Sabbath.

Calvinists. Adherents of the French Protestant theologian John Calvin (1509–64), the teachings that developed from his doctrine and practice, or of the Reformed—rather than Lutheran—Protestant churches. Calvinism preached doctrines stressing the sovereignty of God in the bestowal of grace, which resulted from divine election or predestination rather than atonement or good works.

Calypso. In Homer's *Odyssey,* a nymph who entertained Odysseus on the island of Ogygia for seven years. She offered to make him immortal if he would stay, but he spurned the offer and continued his journey.

Circe. In Greek mythology, enchantress who lived on an island, decoying sailors and turning them into beasts. In Homer's *Odyssey,* she changed Odysseus's fellow travelers into swine but was forced to break the spell.

Daniel (sixth century B.C.). Biblical prophet, central figure of the Book of Daniel.

Daniel in the Lions' Den. Religious-moral work by Friedrich Karl von Moser (1723–98), published 1763.

David (died c. 972 B.C.). King of the ancient Hebrews. His story is repeated several times in the Old Testament, and many of the Psalms are attributed to him.

Death of Jesus. Cantata written by the German poet Karl Wilhelm Ramler (1725–98) and set to music by C. H. Graun; published 1756.

Donatus. Latin grammar written by Aelius Donatus (fourth century A.D.).

Elysium. According to the Greeks and Romans, the dwelling place of happy souls after death.

Engelbrecht. Hans Engelbrecht (1599–1642); wrote *Engelbrecht's . . . Description of Heaven and Hell* (1625).

Enthusiast. A person inspired or possessed by a divine power or spirit; a person who is visionary, extravagant, or excessively zealous in matters of religion.

"Father, forgive them. . . ." Luke 23:34.

Fénelon, François de Salignac de La Mothe (1651–1715). French theologian and writer, archbishop of Cambrai, disciple and defender of Madame Guyon. As such, he gave mystical instructions in faith and helped found quietism. In his *Télémaque* (1699), he held up Ulysses as an example for young princes. He also wrote *Stories and Tales* (1690) and *Dialogues of the Dead* (1700).

Fox, Charles James (1749–1806). British statesman known for his oratoric genius.

Gellert's spiritual odes. Religious odes and songs by Christian Fürchtegott Gellert (1715–69), published 1757.

Gesenius. See **Martin Luther.**

Gospel story of the leper and the hypocrites. Matthew 8:1–4, Luke 17:11–21 and 18:9–14.

Greek Testament. The books of the New Testament were first transmitted in a form of popular Greek.

Guyon, Jeanne-Marie Bouvier de la Motte (1648–1717). French mystic and author of writings about quietism, including a religious, soul-searching autobiography, a collection of spiritual poems and songs, and a book of directions for silent prayer.

Hezekiah (d. c. 687 B.C.). King of Judah who reformed and purified the religion of Israel. In II Kings 20:8–11, Hezekiah asks the prophet Isaiah for a sign of God's promise to heal him. The sign is a shadow that recedes.

Hübner's Bible stories. Selected by Johann Hübner (1668–1731), published 1714.

Island of Felsenburg. Title of Johann Gottfried Schnabel's *Die Insel Felsenburg* (1731–43), a German novel written in the style of Defoe's *Robinson Crusoe*.

Jebusites. Name of a tribe that inhabited Jerusalem before the Jews and that was absorbed by them.

Joab. Son of King David's sister and commander of his armies, he defeated and slew David's rebellious son Absalom, an example of the cruelty that later caused David to curse him.

John of the Cross, St. (1542–91). Spanish mystic and lyric poet.

John the Baptist, St. (fl. c. A.D. 29). Jewish prophet and forerunner of Jesus, his cousin. He called for repentance to prepare for the Messiah, and he baptized his followers as well as Jesus himself.

"Joy of Grief." Phrase attributed to the English author Edward Young (1683–1765) and characteristic of the refined emotion and taste for the pathetic that were current in the eighteenth-century "Age of Sensibility."

Juno. In Roman religion, wife and sister of Jupiter; later identified with the Greek Hera, she was a goddess and the protector of women.

Jupiter. Supreme god in Roman religion, identified with Zeus, brother and husband of Juno.

Koran. Sacred book of Islam, believed to have been revealed by God to the prophet Mohammed.

Life of the Early Saints. Probably *Vitae Patrum, oder Das Leben der Altväter und anderer Gottseeligen Personen* (1700), by the pietistic theologian Gottfried Arnold (1666–1714). The German subtitle literally translates as *The Life of the Patriarchs and Other Revered Persons.*

"Lord, who shall abide . . ." Psalm 15.

Low German. Colloquial language and dialects of northern Germany.

Luther, Martin (1483–1546). Leader of the Protestant Reformation in Germany. His writings include two catechisms that are basic statements of the Lutheran faith. One was interpreted by Justus Gesenius (1601–73).

Mensa. In Latin, singular noun for *table. Mensae* is its plural.

Mentor. In Greek mythology, friend of Odysseus and tutor of Telemachus. His name is generally used to mean a faithful and wise advisor.

Moses. Hebrew lawgiver who led his people out of bondage in Egypt to Canaan in the thirteenth century B.C.

Nebuchadnezzar (d. 562 B.C.). King of Babylonia mentioned in the Book of Daniel.

Nicholas, St. (fourth century). His feast (December 6) is a children's holiday when gifts are given. Named Santa Claus by the English in New York, who associated him with Christmas.

Nineveh. Ancient capital of the Assyrian Empire, often mentioned in the Bible. Through the prophet Jonah, God announced his will to punish its inhabitants for their wickedness but then refrained from doing so when they repented. Jonah was still angry with them, but God taught him pity.

Non fregit eum sed exerit. "It did not crush him, but roused him instead."

Oportet. "It is necessary." Apparently the beginning of a Latin grammatical paradigm for remembering such impersonal verbal constructions.

Papist. A Roman Catholic who is a partisan of the pope; used disparagingly.

Paul, St. (died 67?) Apostle born as Saul, a Jew, who converted to Christianity, made many missionary journeys among the Gentiles, and wrote a number of epistles establishing Christian doctrine.

Period. A well-proportioned sentence consisting of several clauses.

Pluraliter. See *Singulariter.*

Pluto. In Greek religion, god of the underworld (Hades) who was associated with both the dead and the fertility of the earth.

Prophets. In the Bible, especially in the Old Testament, religious leaders of Israel who were believed to have been inspired by God to guide the chosen people.

Pyrmont. Spa in Lower Saxony with mineral springs and mud baths.

Quietists. Believers in a heretical form of mysticism founded in the seventeenth century. According to quietism, perfection lies in the complete passivity of the soul before God and the absorption of the individual in divine love to the point of annihilation, not only of will but also of all effort and self-consciousness. Since quietists often broke with established churches, some of them were also called separatists.

Samuel (flourished 1050 B.C.). Biblical prophet (or seer) who as the last "judge" of Israel anointed Saul and David as kings.

Seven Years' War (1756–63). Worldwide war fought in Europe,

North America, and India. It involved both the colonial rivalry between France and England and the struggle for supremacy in Germany between Austria and Prussia. Hanover sided with England and Prussia.

Singulariter. "Singular"; cf. *pluraliter,* "plural." Anton mistakes these two Latin words for the names of biblical peoples like the Amorites and Jebusites because these latter two words, in German, similarly end in *-iter: Amoriter, Jebusiter.*

"So Far Hath God Brought Me." Seventeenth-century German Protestant hymn.

Stoicism. School of philosophy founded in Ancient Greece. In ethics, Stoics held virtue to be the highest good in life. Freedom to practice such virtue came from putting aside passion, unjust thoughts, and indulgence and from performing duty with the right disposition.

"Substantive . . . small one." In German, all nouns (substantives) are capitalized.

Tartarus. In Greek mythology, the lowest region of the underworld. After death, the wicked were sent to Tartarus as punishment for their sins.

Tauler, Johannes (c. 1300–1361). German mystic and preacher whose sermons spread the idea of detaching oneself from the world and abandoning oneself to the Holy Spirit.

Telemachus. See Ulysses and Fénelon.

"That the son of thy handmaid . . ." Exodus 24:12: "Six days thou shalt do thy work, and on the seventh day thou shalt rest: that thine ox and thine ass may rest, and the son of thy handmaid, and the stranger, may be refreshed."

Themistocles (c. 525–c. 460 B.C.). Athenian statesman, naval commander, and hero of the Persian Wars.

Thomas à Kempis (c. 1379/80–1471). German monk and priest traditionally held to have written *The Imitation of Christ* (c. 1427), a great devotional work that encourages mystical devotion to Christ and distrust of human intellect.

Transubstantiation. Roman Catholic concept that the bread and wine used in the Eucharist are miraculously turned into the divinity, body, and blood of the crucified Jesus.

Trinity. In Christianity, the doctrine, revealed truth, or mystery that

God exists in three equal and indivisible persons—God the Father, God the Son (who became incarnate as Jesus), and God the Holy Ghost.

Troy. Ancient city (also called "Ilion" or "Ilium") in Turkey that was the site of the Trojan War.

Ulysses (or Odysseus). A Greek leader during the Trojan War, known in Homer's *Iliad* for his strategy and cunning. His legendary wanderings after the war—including the search for him by Telemachus, his son—are related in Homer's *Odyssey*.

Whitsuntide (or Whitsunday). An English name for Pentecost, derived from the white garments of ancient converts baptized then.

Wilhelm Heinse

From
ARDINGHELLO

AND THE FORTUNATE ISLES
AN ITALIAN STORY FROM THE
SIXTEENTH CENTURY

Genoa, November.

As I ascended from the great fertile valley of Lombardy, infused by a hundred rivers, which has no equal in the world, through the wild barren rocky bends of the Apennines, and finally emerged from the Bochette, playfully lapped by calm breezes, so that the locks fluttered around my hot temples, and saw from on high the deep broad sea glittering below me, surrounded by sweet beaming clouds of evening: God, how it seized my heart and all my senses! Like Homer's Thetis, I could have thrown myself into the eternal abundance of life with a single leap from Olympus and whirled about in it like a whale and cooled all my sorrows.

I spent the night there with an old shepherd, the chronicle of the region, and saw the stars rise and set and the light of the world appear again, and thus throned over Italy, this paradise with all its inhabitants from the very beginning of time, people and animals and plants and trees, and I, all peacefully at one, so pure and piously molten was my soul.

The next morning I descended and slept that afternoon in a charming coastal village not far from the city. Around midnight I reawoke to the sound of strings and to a voice that sweetly suffused my being. I hearkened and heard the words and leaped to the window. The music came from an old ruins built onto a hill that jutted out from the sea, covered with tall pines and cypresses and low fruit trees; they were stanzas from a fairy tale by Pulci, which I knew very well. When then a female voice also joined in with the male, I, too, took out my guitar, softly tuned it, and when they stopped, after striking a few chords in their sad harmony, sang in a happier key: "Who are you sweet singers there, who wake me from sleep so delightfully? Thanks, thanks be to you for thus giving people joy and touching their hearts in the quiet dawn."

"We are father and daughter, who are lulling a lovely child to sleep along with its father, whom the hot day has fatigued," echoed to me in answer as an old man with a long beard placed himself at the arch of the door.

"O you happy few!" I replied and sang, seized with enthusiasm, of Hesperia at the time of Saturn, when all lived this way, when no Phalaris tortured the golden island of the three capes and no Caesars dunged the fields with citizens' blood.

"And who are you, noble spirit?" he then asked me.

"A young pilgrim who seeks the excellent on earth and feasts his soul here on honey."

He came down, I went toward him; we welcomed each other and filled the cups. He was a grand man, about sixty, the very picture of a poet, much like the ideal Homer, only not blind; but then neither was that noble Ionian, who only did not see what is always present in the empty heads of ordinary people, which earned him that droll name "blind"; but the Greek artist who created his image conformed to public opinion.

We quickly became acquainted. He had been an architect and, since he found little to build, followed his inclination for poetry; and he was considered one of the best improvisatori far and wide, and as such he traveled about the country and entertained people. His wife had died young, and a few years ago he had given his only daughter in marriage to a worthy farmer, who had leased an estate here and with whom he resided most of the time. The farm was truly from the golden age, as I later learned with pleasure.

I said to him that I pursued painting in nearly the same way as he formerly had architecture. This delighted him heartily; he took my young head and pressed it into his gray beard and kissed me over and over; and then seized his instrument and sang the praises of poetry with such great enthusiasm, like a true priest of Apollo, that I stood transfixed. Half the village assembled and cooed quiet applause at the open doors and windows. And as he finished, the sea seemed to surge more strongly onto the shore, and all cried: "Long live Boccadoro!" Thus he was called.

For further amusement I then began an antistrophe and adapted Pindar's "Golden Lyre of Apollo" to the present time and place, in the end describing the old man in front of me true to life and elevating his state above that of a king. And as we parted toward morning, the crowd dispersed with a triumphant cry: "Long live the handsome young stranger and the divine old man!"

At dawn I took a walk up the hill and looked out over Genoa: a charming amphitheater, which had always spurred its inhabitants to rule the sea, and from which the greatest sea heroes have always come. Holy Columbus and you, Andrea Doria, who now walk hand in hand with the Themistocleses and Scipios in Elysium, you demigods among men I worship in the dust. Ah, that no such lot is fated for me! I looked out into the immeasurable sphere of the waters, and its vast majesty threatened to burst my breast; my spirit soared far above the middle of the depths and fully felt its own infinity in unspeakable bliss.

Nothing in the world so strongly and powerfully fills the soul; the sea is still the most beautiful thing that we have here below. Sun and moon and stars are only single brilliant points by comparison and, together with the blue mantle of ether above them, merely ornaments of reality. This is true life. Here people give themselves wings, which nature denied them, and combine in themselves the perfections of all other creatures. People who do not know the sea seem to me like birds that cannot fly or that do not use their wings, like ostriches, chickens, and geese. Here is eternal clarity and purity; and everything petty that nests in our urban nooks is scared away by the huge masses here. How the Ligurian Alps rise over there, like heroes with Aspasia and Phryne! How the tender line on the horizon curves so softly! I would out into the ocean; how my heart is pounding!

Boccadoro was already waiting for me when I returned to the inn. He said that I had to accompany him to a great feast today, which would last the entire week.

Marquis S—— was to be wed to a young Fregosi in all conceivable pomp; the groom, he explained, had to be one of the wealthiest private noblemen in Europe. Races would be held tonight, then a banquet and ball; tomorrow a bullfight, and so forth, every day a new amusement; theater, tightrope walking, and all kinds of arts would be seen onshore and at sea. Boccadoro had been called upon to sing at table between other music, and he earnestly made me, too, prepare myself to do so; we could think up a pretty theme for an alternating chorus along the way. The palace lay a few miles away from the city, on the other side of the sea; a couple of his son-in-law's servants would take us there in a barque along with himself and his daughter. But he believed that I already knew all this and presumably had come here precisely on account of it.

I assured him that I had descended without knowing the least thing about this wedding; that I could not sing extempore in such high society; and that besides, I always had to know a little about the nature of my audience in order to find the easiest way into its heart and imagination; otherwise even the most excellent thing often fails to have its full effect. Still, I would accompany him; just the idea of hearing his epithalamium excited me. He could introduce me at the banquet as the tuner of his zither.

I now met his daughter, an utterly good, happy young matron; and her husband, a cheerful excellent farmer; and a little angel of a son: together, the living picture of a beautiful whole. I found the old ivy-covered ruin of the small country castle comfortably furnished inside. Around noon I took a healthy, delicious, simple meal with them. After dinner we all slumbered a couple of hours and then departed; and the waves delighted me endlessly, so greenishly clear and soft and so fearfully charming and rough above the abysmal depths, where even in its smallness, each appeared majestically as a daughter of the immense ocean.

We arrived right at the racetrack just as the horses were being led forth. The seats were radiant and all aglow from the beautiful and splendidly dressed lords and ladies, surrounded by a crowd of common folk. There were only three horses; but all were spirit-snorting regal animals, so that it was hard to predict which one would carry off the prize. People had therefore placed large bets; most were for a divinely beautiful raven black horse that could barely be held back at the gate. A sorrel, by contrast, stood there quietly: yet the look in its eyes blazed down the track like a beam of sunlight, and it was light-footed, as if nothing but full nerved. When the rope fell, the black horse shot out in the lead; but in middle of the course, the sorrel swung out and overtook the others so fast that its gait was swifter than the speed of a storm blowing over amber grain; it flew along, and its movement was a joy to behold, even for those who had bet against it. In short, it won the prize, albeit with difficulty, and only later became intractable.

After the race came theater, and after the theater the nightly banquet. Toward the end of the latter, when wine and conversation had raised everyone's spirits, Boccadoro started to strum his instrument. A general stillness ensued; and the sounds of his chords were like quiet whispers of sea breezes in cool forests at high noon. His spirit then reeled through the old times of Greek heroes; and he sang the marriage of Peleus and Thetis, embellished the story with charming words and thence shifted to the present, described the bridegroom as a new Peleus, equally blessed by the gods, and his bride as a younger Thetis.

Then the old rascal all of a sudden turned to me, who was standing behind him in the corner among the other musicians, and introduced me as a second Apollo, if I may repeat his words, who had unexpectedly descended the Apennines to exalt this celebration still more—and handed me his zither.

I was taken by surprise and blushed with shame in the unfamiliar, brilliant company. A joyous murmur ran through the whole hall, and everyone's glances shot toward me. It was no use refusing, unless I wanted to become a laughingstock and be ruined. I therefore decided to make the best that I possibly could of the matter and chose the easiest meter for me, with the ever more strongly beating anapestic rhythm, like the melody that so often delighted you.

After a few simple chords I sang exactly what had happened, my surprise and confusion, and that I followed Boccadoro here to see the splendor and beauty of the feast, completely foreign and unknown, a mere wanderer here only for a few hours. Yet your renown, I continued, extends over sea and Alps; and who is the cold, envious person whom your happy love would not inspire? Kindly accept the few flowers that I hastily stole to strew about your table.

The son of Thetis now beams through all posterity because he had a Homer for his bard: but how much greater were Columbus and Doria? And how far can the fruit of your love exceed him in deeds more noble than running around the walls of Troy three times on account of a withered, eloped wife of a man whom nature destined to be a cuckold and who was neither his ally nor his friend, and thereupon stabbing the weary enemy in the throat! Than making a dreadful fuss on account of a rebuffed priest, and then, on top of that, patiently handing over his beloved and sitting down at the sea and crying!*

*One needs to remember here that poetry was and still is so popular in Italy that even artisans know Homeric stories and mythology.

Forgive me these slanders, best of friends; you know that I feel the Homeric spirit more deeply than the superficial beau monde, whose fashion it does not fit. But you know the saying: "When among wolves, one has to howl along."

I then described the region of Genoa and its inhabitants; extolled their heroic courage since the most remote times; and that it was situated better than even old Rome itself to rule the islands of the Tyrrhenian Sea and the coasts of Africa; raised in song the young Themistocles, his mother and father's happiness at him, and his citizens' golden age, and made all the guests' mouths water for the good life. All seemed to swear from the bottom of their hearts to behave differently than their ancestors had toward Columbus, whose inventive high spirit had brought them more scorn and contempt than honor.

I was interrupted during some happy stanzas of this song by loud jubilation and received great applause when I finished, which pleased me well only insofar as I had saved myself embarrassment.

Everyone now rose from the table, and it was time for the ball. As the bride was led past me, she greeted me with a firm, lewd glance and a voluptuous smile and called to me: "Bravo!" She still looked back at me after she was past, and her mien and gestures consented to kiss and embrace, if we were alone; the figure of a maenad, all lushness and ardor, full of physical charms, with a brazen soul— such women can please me only at certain moments. I felt little inclination to become more closely acquainted with her; much, though, with another young lady, whose mother, given the lines of her face, seemed to have confused her with the Apollo Belvedere, only without pride and anger, rather all holy goodness; a wonderful creature!

I learned from Boccadoro that she was a friend of the bride and was staying with her. Her parents had been failed merchants from Nice in Provence and died a few years ago. The bride is named Fulvia and her friend Lucinde; I asked to see the latter dance, but dance she did not.

Later, about two hours after midnight, when the ball was at its liveliest, we heard shots fired and, during the sudden silence that followed, anxious screaming and more shots and turmoil up the staircase leading to the hall. And in no time, before you could turn around, horrible men with sabers and guns in their hands broke in at the front door. People stood as if petrified and wanted to flee but could not and did not know where to go. Everyone thronged aside toward the windows and wherever there was an opening; and wailed and whined, and a deathly pallor blanched every face.

We were being attacked by pirates, to judge by their yellow, African figures; and there was little thought of resistance. Part of them occupied the door where they came in, others seized the bride at once and then reached for the young ladies and dragged them away. I stood at the end of the hall by the windows onto the garden; the first among the nobility jumped out at great peril. I was almost crushed by the turmoil and could barely tear loose a pistol, which I immediately fired off at the strongest fellow by the door. The bullet struck him so squarely in the left ear that he fell down on the spot. The bang gained me some room, so that I drew the other and my sword at the same time. Meanwhile, some other Genovese and servants had furnished themselves with guns or, lacking them, laid about with chairs. The pirates lashed out with their sabers and split several people's skulls and wounded those who were in front. Yet we finally drove them back out the door, though they continued to occupy it from the outside until their companions got down to the sea with their booty and loaded it on board. They then retreated, and we were too late to do them much damage since they had planned their attack so well.

The bridegroom himself received a serious wound; and a couple of the most distinguished guests lay helpless, struck down on the ground. The bravest set out for Genoa at once with Johann Andreas Doria, who, as you know, helped defeat the Turkish fleet, a descendant of the grand old man, to pursue the pirates; and I, too, wanted to go along. It was impudence without precedent since time immemorial.

We arrived there toward morning. Five triremes were outfitted, and we were an hour out of port at dawn, when the sun was still struggling with a fog that had fallen; the wind had shifted overnight, and a sirocco blew from the southeast! We did not know which way to set our course and held steady between both coasts. Finally, bit by bit, though slowly, the horizon grew wider and the mountains began to appear beneath the gray veil; yet only toward noon did the water world come more or less clearly into view, so encircled by mist, though, that we could discern nothing.

Doria now resolved to detach two ships and let them make for

Sicily. He himself would go with the others via Corsica into Provençal waters. Even before we set sail, corvettes had been dispatched in both directions; but none had returned. I remained on the ship where he himself was. All was now in full swing. We still did not know the enemy's strength; in the night and fog we had not been able to distinguish the number of their barques.

One corvette came back in the evening and announced that it had caught sight of the enemy near Monaco; the pirates were four galleys strong. We rowed the whole night; and the next morning, when the weather cleared up, we spotted their sails. O how my heart pounded to be in the thick of battle soon! After all, death there is nothing other than a clear path, the noblest of all, from this ignorant chaos into the spirit world.

They likewise detected us and redoubled their oarstrokes. Thus we vied with each other all day.

Just as the sun, as Stesichorus says, stepped from the skies into the golden chalice and swam down the ocean to the murky depths of holy night, we fired our first cannon shots at them; we had the wind in our favor, and they soon stopped because they could flee no farther. We attacked them in nearly a straight line and spread ourselves out somewhat, so that they could not come at us from our flanks. We inflicted several splendid broadsides on them and were far better supplied than they with heavy artillery. After tacking about various ways, as dusk was already falling, two of our ships closed with them in hand-to-hand combat, and our third tried to ward off the other two galleys, which wanted to board it.

I was on the first and fought with all the might and presence of mind that I could muster. As yet I luckily had no wounds, but bullets from small arms and saber cuts laid low many around me. We finally forced our way onto their largest galley, and I was among the first, with a stout dagger in my left hand, my sword in my right, and another loaded pistol in my belt. Before I jumped on board, I struck down one of their boldest, who was just about to cut through Doria's abdomen with his sickel-shaped Damascus sword, and thus saved the latter's life. After that, I soon finished off another one on the enemy barque, who fell upon me. But I could not ward off his two-fisted blow so completely with my dagger that he did not graze my left arm a little in crashing down. Meanwhile I struck him right in the throat, so that he stuck out his tongue.

They yielded and surrendered; only the one who appeared to be the ringleader ran down below deck, and I after him. And behold! Here was the bride hiding with the other booty. He wildly swung his saber at her, to chop her head from her body; but I got the better of him and stuck my blade into the hair under his raised arm with all my strength, so that he fell on his side, drew it out, and then finished him off for good.

The main galley was now overrun, but the other defended itself all the more fearfully. A young man, still beardless, fought desperately and had many dead lying next to him; and he would have freed himself, had not we others come to the aid of our comrades. This ship, too, then had to surrender. Meanwhile, the two others fled with our third vessel after they conquered it. We chased after them but lost them in the dark; and the next morning they were out of sight, and we could not tell which way they had gone.

Doria returned home, angry that things had not turned out better. Perhaps he would not have attacked at all, however, if one of his relatives, whom he now freed again, had not been dragged off from the dance hall. We were hard pressed, and the greatest danger lay in delay. He admittedly should not have sent the two other ships to Sicily; but who can foresee all? Who knew that the pirates were so strong? After the fact every fool is smarter than Hannibal and Caesar.

I, however, was happy as a god; it seemed to me that I had not tasted true life until now. The stern Doria, despite all his displeasure, warmly sang my praises and publicly said: "You are off to a fine start, young man; if you live longer and go on this way, you will make a famous hero." Fulvia, whose guardian angel I had been, thanked me with tears full of tenderness. But above all, the beautiful Provençal, Lucinde, was among the rescued; she still suffered wretchedly from seasickness and almost vomited to death. I had not felt the least touch of it; and it delights me through and through that I still endure this element and its vigorous motion as well as when I was a boy.

Toward evening we put into the harbor of Villafranca, after we had cruised around in vain all day, to tend to the wounded, to bury our dead (we threw the fallen enemies overboard right away), and to let the aggrieved ladies enjoy some rest; only a couple of married ones among them had been smashed to bits by cannonballs, all the rest remained unscathed. We led them up the mountain into the small town, which lay at the end of the valley, like a hermitage, among olive trees, under a steep cliff, with only a few houses. I escorted Lucinde, who came to as soon as she was on dry land again, and encouraged her now that the danger had passed. "Ah," she answered with a sigh, "why do I still live, if only to be unhappy forever? No one knows my suffering. O, were I only up there with the chosen among the saints and angels!" And then she cast a languishing look toward heaven with her big black eyes and thus completely melted my heart. "So much beauty," I replied, "was not made to torment itself here on earth; cast all grief aside; and be as blissful yourself as you make others." She was silent and bowed her head like a withered flower and walked on with me, without paying attention to my speeches; her sad mien and pale color, her entangled hair and loosened garment completed the picture of a charming saint. We quartered them together in a house, and they were well looked after and attended to. I myself stayed in the small town and rested that night; my superficial wound was of no consequence.

After Mass the next morning I discussed the abduction a couple more times for a few moments alone with Lucinde, who had now regained her strength, and learned that the ringleader of the pirate galleys, whom I had struck down, had been one of Fulvia's admirers, a Genovese who had renounced his faith while in captivity and then served under the famous Ulazal, the greatest sea hero of our times. Enflamed for her, without his passion ever reaching its goal, he undertook the exploit after gathering sufficient intelligence about all details of the marriage, and would soon have carried it out successfully. He was a bastard by an Adorno, and in Genoa one called him Biondello. She chastely assured me that the bride had preserved her honor until now with fervent pleas and entreaties that he might at least spare her, given her ill health, until he went ashore; and that she was pure except for several kisses, which she had been forced to give the accursed man. Most of the others had been stricken with seasickness far worse still than the bride, so that even the barbarians had felt pity and mercy for them, without tormenting them even further. Besides, the need to reach safety had spurred the pirates on to extreme industry, and their large numbers had kept a tight rein on the desires of each individual; and thus the women had luckily been saved from shame after all, and one could vouch for the other.

In despair, Biondello had then wanted to cut down Fulvia out of jealousy, when I had rescued her. "Unholy gift of beauty," she exclaimed, "into how many hardships you plunge us! And if we make others happy with you, we ourselves thereby fall into the most extreme misery. Like kings, who can do anything, except that our rule lasts a short time, we have no friend through you; and the most excellent men, endowed with all perfections, as you are, for example, set ugly snares for us."

This apostrophe struck me like a bullet to the head, and I fell down in the dust before that holy woman.

In the afternoon the wind shifted, and we departed again, using our oars and sails. The young hero who had fought so bravely on the second conquered galley that we therefore lost our third vessel had been brought onto our ship with several other prisoners. I later heard him talking with one of his companions in modern Greek; and he still stamped his foot in anger because the two other galleys had left them in the lurch; yet wrongly, for these had been very badly mauled by our artillery right at the beginning of the battle. Meanwhile he spoke so freely and without fear in captivity, and his figure was so slim and noble with its wild color of sea and sunburn, that my heart welled with affection for him. I resolved to do everything possible to free him from slavery and was successful; even before we put into port at Genoa, Doria presented him to me in reward. I took him aside as we disembarked, declared to him that he was free, at which he flew to my breast, and let him leave for Constantinople a few days later on a Venetian ship. He asked me beforehand for my letter to you, which I then gave to him.

"You will not be disappointed with me," he said to me on parting; "people like us must help each other their whole lives long."

The men who got back their beautiful young wives were at least glad that they had not lost all their property; and mothers and fathers hoped for the best in the case of their daughters. Regarding the bride, various persons were separately questioned in secret by the family of the groom, who still lay wounded; and when their statements agreed and confirmed her innocence, everyone gave themselves completely up to joy again.

May heaven always grant me such a life from now on and never let me languish in inaction; but to be separated from you and Cecilia pains my heart. When will the time for reunion come once again! Ah, if only she is well! This is now all that I ask of her.

Ardinghello

Translated by Ellis Shookman

Glossary

Adorno. Ruling family in Genoa from the fourteenth to the sixteenth century; enemies of the Fregosi.

Anapestic rhythm. Greek meter consisting of three syllables, two stressed (or long) followed by one unstressed (or short).

Antistrophe. In Greek drama, the returning movement of the chorus, answering a previous strophe, was called an antistrophe.

Apollo. Among other roles, Greek god of the arts and sciences. Singers and poets sometimes regarded themselves as his "priests."

Apollo Belvedere. Roman copy of a Greek statue of Apollo. Beginning in the mid–eighteenth century, it was considered the highest ideal of ancient art.

Apostrophe. The addressing of a person usually not present, or of a thing usually personified, for rhetorical purposes.

Aspasia (fifth century B.C.). Greek courtesan, mistress of Pericles, renowned for her learning, wit, and beauty.

Beau monde. The world of high society and fashion.

Biondello. In Italian, "the blond one."

Boccadoro. In Italian, "mouth of gold."

Bochette. Alpine pass north of Genoa.

Caesar (102? B.C.–44 B.C.). Roman statesman and general considered one of the greatest military commanders of all time. In 48 B.C., he defeated Pompey in the Roman civil war.

Cecilia. The first of Ardinghello's many loves that Heinse lists. She eventually marries his narrator, the addressee of Ardinghello's letter.

Columbus (1415–1506). Came from Genoa but discovered America in the service of Portugal and Spain.

Damascus sword. A sword made of Damascus steel, which is ornamented with wavy patterns and noted for its hardness and elasticity.

Doria, Andrea (1468–1560). Genoese admiral and statesman.

Doria, Johann Andreas (Giovanni Andrea) (1539–1606). Descendant of Andrea Doria; navy commander who defeated the Turkish fleet in 1571.

Elysium. According to the Greeks and Romans, the dwelling place of happy souls after death.

Epithalamium. Greek or Roman poem written to celebrate a marriage.

Extempore. Instantaneously, on the spur of the moment.

Fregosi. One of the ruling families in Genoa from the fourteenth to the sixteenth century.

Golden Age. A period of great happiness, prosperity, and achievement; an idyllic state of nature held to have existed in the past; a time of ideal perfection regarded as attainable in the future.

Hannibal (247–182?b.c.). Carthaginian general who invaded Rome by crossing the Alps, one of the most remarkable military feats in history.

Hesperia. The occident, west; here, Italy, Latium, the countryside around Rome.

Homer (before 700 b.c.). Author of the *Iliad* and the *Odyssey*, traditionally thought to have come from Ionia in Asia Minor and to have been blind, as he was often depicted in ancient portraits.

Improvasitori. Plural of improvisatore, one who composes and recites verse extempore.

Maenad. A woman participating in the orgiastic Dionysian rites of ancient Greece; a frenzied female dancer; an unnaturally excited or distraught woman.

Olympus. Mountain in Thessaly that was considered the abode of the chief gods of ancient Greece.

Phalaris (570–554 b.c.). Tyrant who cruelly ruled over Sicily, "the golden island of the three capes."

Phryne (fourth century b.c.). Greek hetaera—a highly cultivated courtesan in ancient Greece. Accused of impiety, she was defended by one of her lovers, who won her acquittal by exhibiting her in the nude.

Pindar (518?–438 b.c.). Generally regarded as greatest Greek lyric poet, known for his odes celebrating victories in athletic contests. Pindar's syntax and meter were intricate and complex, and he wrote in an elevated tone appropriate to his lofty conception of the poet's vocation. "Golden Lyre of Apollo" are the opening words of his first Pythian ode.

Pulci, Luigi (1432–84). Italian Renaissance poet who wrote his best-known work in stanzas, a metric form and rhyme scheme likewise used by Heinse in German.

Saturn. Titan god, father of Zeus. When expelled from Olympus by his sons, he was said to have civilized the savage inhabitants of Latium, the region around Rome, and ruled them in a time of peace and plenty remembered as a golden age.

Scipio. Name of wealthy ancient Roman family known for its love of Greek culture and learning in the second and third century B.C. It produced two highly successful generals and statesmen, Scipio the Elder (237/6?–183 B.C.), who conquered Hannibal in the Punic Wars, and Scipio the Younger (185–129 B.C.), who destroyed Carthage.

Scirocco. Warm, moist, oppressive southeasterly wind blowing on the northern Mediterranean coast.

Stesichorus (c. 600 B.C.). Greek lyric poet said to have invented the choral "heroic hymn."

Themistocles (c. 525–c. 460 B.C.). Athenian statesman, naval commander, and hero of the Persian Wars.

Thetis. Greek water nymph mentioned in Homer's *Iliad*. All the gods except Eris, the goddess of discord, were invited to her wedding with the mortal Peleus. Heinse apparently makes light of her son Achilles and his feats in the Trojan War ("withered, eloped wife," "cuckold," "dreadful fuss").

Trireme. Ancient galley having three banks of oars.

Ulazal. Corsican renegade and pirate in Turkish service.

Villafranca. Villefranche-sur-Mer.

Ulrich Bräker

From
THE LIFE STORY
AND REAL ADVENTURES
OF THE POOR MAN
OF TOGGENBURG

Journey to Berlin

We finally left Rothweil on 15 March 1756,—sergeants Hevel, Krüger, Labrot, I, and Kaminsky, plus bag and baggage and, with the exception of the latter, all bearing small and side arms. Dear Mariane stitched the favor onto my cap and sobbed; I pressed a crownpiece into her hand, and could scarcely manage even that, so upset I was. For however resolutely I might undertake this journey and however little harm I suspected, it still weighed heavily on my breast, without my actually knowing why. Was it Rothweil or dear Mariane or the fact that I was to travel with my master, or my going further and further away from my homeland and Annie—I'd written my last farewell to all at home—or maybe a bit of everything?

Markoni gave me twenty florins for the journey; if I needed any more, he said, Hevel would advance it me. Then he clapped me on the shoulder: "God keep you, son, my dear, dear Ollrich! wherever you may go. It won't be long before we meet again in Berlin." He said this very sadly too; really he did have a soft heart.

Our first day's journey lasted seven hours, and took us as far as the small town of Ebingen, mostly along bad roads through mud and snow. The second nine hours to Obermarkt. At the former stopping place we lodged at "The Roe"; as regards the second I've long since forgotten what species of animal it was. At both places there was only a cold collation and some nameless pigswill to be had. The third evening to Ulm—again nine hours. It was then I began to feel the exertions of the journey; already I had blisters on my feet and altogether felt lousy. In the small town of Egna we hopped a lift on a peasant's cart for part of the way, when the tremendous jolting of this conveyance naturally *would* have its usual sickening effect, especially on me. When we got off not far from Ulm, I went all dizzy. I sank to the ground: "So help me God," I said, "I can't go on; you'll just have to leave me to lie in the gutter."

At last some good Samaritan came along and put me on his bareback jade, on which I got so jolted by the time we reached the next town that I could hardly stand up. At Ulm we stopped off at "The Eagle," and there we had our first day's rest. My comrades renewed old female acquaintanceships; I preferred to take it easy. I did however see a funeral procession there that quite took my fancy. The women walked along all dressed in white from top to toe. The fifth day we tramped seven hours to Gengen, the sixth to Nördlingen, another seven hours, and there had our second day's halt. Hevel was well in with some piece there at "The Wild Man." She was a good turn on the zither; he sang songs to it. Apart from this, honestly I can scarcely remember a thing about this, or any of the many other places we passed through. Usually it was nighttime before we arrived, knocked up and dead beat, and next morning we had to be off again. Under these conditions who could be expected to take in anything properly? Crimes! I'd often think, once I'm back home safe and sound, I'll never go on such a long journey again— and that's for certain!

Kaminsky was, as I've already hinted, a jolly Polack, a mountain of a man with a pair of legs like two great columns and the motion of an elephant. Labrot could also set up a pretty smart pace. Krüger, Hevel, and I, however, looked after our feet; even so we still had to have our boots stitched or soled every few days. On the eighth day we marched eight hours in the direction of Gonzenhausen. Getting on for noon we saw Hevel's bird come tripping towards us across a field: the poor girl had all the time been chasing after him along other paths, and wouldn't be dissuaded from accompanying him, at least as far as our next stopping place. The ninth day eight hours to Schwabach. The tenth nine hours via Nuremberg to Bayersdorf. The eleventh tenth hours to Tropach. The twelfth seven hours via Bareuth to Bernig. The thirteenth eight hours to Hof. The fourteenth seven hours to Schletz. Here we had a day's halt—and high time too. All the way from Gonzenhausen we'd not lain in a bed; all we'd managed, if we were lucky, was lousy straw. When you really thought about it, even though we did get through the ackers, it was a miserable form of existence—most of the time bad weather and often terrible paths.

Krüger and Labrot were damning and blasting the whole time; Hevel, on the other hand, was a fine upstanding fellow who never failed to instill patience and courage into us. On the sixteenth day we tramped twelve hours to Cistritz. Then came another halt. The eighteenth day seven hours to Weissenfeld. The nineteenth over the Elbe to Halle. Once we'd got across the wide river, the sergeants were dead pleased, for we were now on Brandenburg soil. At Halle we lodged with Hevel's brother, who, for all he was a clergyman, played cards and larked about the whole night with us, so much so I began to think his sergeant brother was the more godly man. In the meantime all my money had gone; Hevel had to lend me ten florins. From the twentieth to the twenty-fourth we marched forty-four hours via Zerbst, Dessau, Görz, Ustermark, Spandau, Charlottenburg, etc., to Berlin. These last three places especially were swarming with the military in all shapes and hues; I could hardly keep my eyes off them; we also got a view of the towers of Berlin, even before we reached Spandau. I thought we'd have reached it in an hour; you can imagine how astonished I was, when I was told we wouldn't get there until next morning. And how bucked I was to have reached that fine, great city at last.

We entered by the Spandau Gate, then along the pleasant, gloomy Lindenstrasse and a few more streets. Then I thought, mug that I was, no one'll shift you out of here! Here you'll make your fortune. And then you'll send a chap with letters to Toggenburg; he'll then bring your parents and Annie back with him; won't they gape! etc. I thereupon asked my guide to take me to my master. "Well now," answered Krüger, "I'm afraid we don't rightly know if he's arrived yet, much less where he's taking up quarters!" "Dash it!" I said, "has he no residence here?" At this question they laughed fit to bust. Go on, laugh!—I thought to myself—all the same I hope to God Markoni has that residence!

A Change in the Weather!

It was on that 8 April, when we marched into Berlin and I asked fruitlessly after my master, who, as I afterwards learned, had already arrived there a week before—that Labrot (for the others faded away one by one from me, without my knowing where they'd gone) took me along to the Krausenstrasse in Friedrichstadt, showed me my quarters and then left me abruptly saying: "You stop there, mate! till you get further orders!" Ooh Heck! I thought, what does this mean? Why, it's not even an inn!

While I was thus musing, a soldier named Christian Zittemann entered and took me to his room, where there were two other sons of Mars. Then they started bombarding me with questions: who was I, where did I come from? etc. I still couldn't make out their lingo. I answered briefly: I came from Switzerland and was his Excellency, my lord Lieutenant Markoni's footman; the sergeants had shown me here; I'd rather like to know whether my master had arrived in Berlin and where he lived. Thereupon the fellows burst out laughing so hard I felt like weeping; they reckoned they'd never even heard of such an Excellency. Meanwhile we were brought up a stodgy mess of pea soup. I ate some of it with little relish. We were scarcely finished when a skinny old cove entered the room, from whose bearing I could soon see he wasn't just a private. He was a sergeant. He had a soldier's uniform over his arm that he spread out on the table, putting down by it a six-groat piece, and said, "That's for you, son! I'll go and get your army bread right away." "What! for me!" I answered, "Who from? what for?" "Why! your uniform and pay, lad! Why all the questions? You're a recruit now." "Eh, what? Recruit?" I answered. "Not on your life! the thought never even crossed my mind. No! never! I'm Markoni's manservant. I'm engaged as that, and nothing else. That's the truth and no one can deny it!" "Well, I'm telling you, mate! you're in the army now! You can take my word for it. And that's it!" I: "Ah! if only my lord Markoni were here." HE: "You won't be seeing *him* again so soon. Surely you'd rather be a servant to our king than to his lieutenant."

With that he left. "For God's sake, Herr Zittemann!" I went on: "what does it all mean?" "Only," he replied, "that you're a soldier now—like me and the other blokes here; we're all in it together, and it's no use trying to resist—that is, unless you want to be put in the guardroom on bread and water, shut up behind bars and flogged till your ribs crack!" I: "Crikey! that'd be callous! Wicked!" HE: "You can take my word for it, mate, that's the way it is and that's the way it bleedin' well stands." I: "Then I'll complain to His Majesty the King."—At that they all fairly hooted. HE: "You'd never get near him, not in a month of Sundays." I: "Well, where else can I put my case?" HE: "To the major, if you like. But I'll tell you now, it won't get you anywhere." I: "All the same I'm going to try—just to see if . . . if!"—The lads were laughing again; but I definitely decided to go to the major next morning and enquire after my false master.

As soon as day broke, I asked to be shown to his quarters. Cor lummy! looked like a royal palace they did—and the major, the king himself, so majestic he was; a whopping great chap with the face of a hero and a pair of fiery eyes like stars. I trembled before him, stammered out: "Sir! I, I, I am Lieutenant Markoni's se-servant. Th-th-that's what I e-e-engaged as, and n-n-nothing else. A-a-ask him yu-yu-yourself. I don't know whe-whe-where he is. And now they're saying I'm a so-so-so-so-soldier and there's no-no two ways about it." "So!" he interrupted me, "so *you're* the fine fellow! That high-class master of yours—he's cost us a packet, I can tell you—and you'll probably have had your cut. Well, now you're serving His Majesty. The fun and games are over." I: "But, sir!"—HE: "Silence! scoundrel! or damme, I'll. . . !" I: "But I haven't enlisted nor received any bounty! Oh crumbs! If only I could have a word with my master." HE: "You won't be seeing him again so soon either; and as far as any bounty is concerned, you've already cost more than ten other men! Your lieutenant's run up a tidy bill, and you're at the head of it. As to enlisting, we'll see about that!"—I: "But . . ." HE: "Get out, you little squirt or I'll . . . !" I: "P-Please, sir, please . . ." HE: "Listen twerp! I've told you. Beat it!"

With that he drew his broadsword.—I shot out like greased lightning back to my quarters, which I could scarcely find, I was so petrified with fear. Then I bemoaned my fate to Zittemann, making an awful fuss. The kind fellow cheered me up: "Come on, son! Things'll soon pick up. You'll just have to put up with it for the time being; there's hundreds of fine lads from good homes in the same boat. Even assuming Markoni did have the power to keep you on, he'd have to hand you over to his regiment as soon as the order came through: 'Into battle! Quick march!' But for the time being he'd scarcely be in a position to keep a manservant; he's supposed to have gone through immense sums of money recruiting and sent in very few men for it, or so I've heard our colonel and major often complaining. I'm sure he won't be put on any more assignments like that for quite some time." So Zittemann consoled me; and I had to put up with that, seeing as there was no other consolation going. But I couldn't help thinking: "It's the rich what gets the gravy, but the poor what gets the blame."

What, Am I Really a Soldier?

In the afternoon the sergeant brought me my army bread together with side and small arms, etc., and asked: well, had I now thought it over? "Why not?" Zittemann answered on my behalf: "You've a good lad here." So they took me along to the quartermaster's stores and fitted me out with breeches, boots, and gaiters; handed me a hat, neckerchief, stockings, etc. Then along with twenty or so other recruits I had to report to Colonel Latorf. We were led into a great barn of a place, some tattered flags were brought in, and each of us was ordered to take hold of a corner. An adjutant, or whoever he was, read us out a whole string of army regulations and told us to repeat some words after him that were duly mumbled by most of those present; I didn't move my lips—I was thinking my own private thoughts—of Annie, I believe. Then he waved the flag over our heads and dismissed us.

After this I went to a cook shop and ordered a dinner with a mug of beer. I had to pay two groats for it. So out of the six there were only four left: I had to manage on these for four days—and there were only enough for two. Thus calculating, I burst out into loud lamentations to my comrades. But one of them, Cran by name, said with a laugh: "That'll teach you a lesson. But you needn't worry at the moment; you've still got all sorts of things you can sell. Take that whole livery of yours. Then you've even got two sets of arms; that can all be flogged. Then young lads like yourself often get an extra allowance—you can put in for it, but only direct from the colonel." "What! what! I'll never go near him again," said I. "Streuth!" answered Cran, "sooner or later you'll have to get used to being bawled at. And as regards managing on your pay, you just keep your eyes open and watch the others. Three, four, or five chaps'll muck in together and buy spelt, peas, spuds, and that, and do their own cooking. In the morning there'll be liquor for a threepenny joey and a cob of army bread: at dinnertime they'll go to the cook shop and get soup for another joey plus another cob of bread: in the evening swipes or small beer for tuppence, and more bread." "Blimey, that's no blinking life!" I replied. And he: "Well, I'm telling you: it's the only way. A soldier just has to get down to it; 'cos there's lots of other stuff he'll be needing—such as chalk, powder, shoe polish, oil, emery, soap, and God knows what else."—I: "And you mean to say a soldier has to pay for all that out of the six groats?" HE: "Aye! and a lot more besides, such as paying for his laundry, for instance, and having his weapons cleaned, etc., if he can't do such things himself."—With that we went to our billet, and I straightened up everything as best I could.

I was still on leave, however, that first week; went all over the town to all the parade grounds; saw the officers so bawling at and striking their men that the sweat dripped from my brow at the thought of what I had coming to me. I therefore asked Zittemann to give me some private tuition in musket drill. "Don't worry, you'll learn all right!" he said. "But the important thing is speed. Everything has to be done like lightning!" In the meantime he was good enough actually to show me the lot; how to keep my musket clean, press my uniform, do my hair military style, etc. On Cran's advice I sold my top boots and with the money bought a small wooden chest for my laundry. Back in my billet the whole time I practiced drilling, read the Halle Hymn Book, or prayed. Then I'd maybe stroll down to the Spree and there watch hundreds of soldier hands busy loading and unloading merchandise; or to the timber yards; there again everywhere was full of warriors hard at work. Or else to the various barracks, etc. Everywhere I found soldiers similarly employed on hundreds of different jobs—from creating works of art down to plying the distaff. If I called in on the main guard, there'd be men playing cards, drinking, and larking about; others comfortably puffing their old pipes and chatting; or perhaps there'd be one reading some edifying book and explaining it to his mates. It was the same in the cook shops and alehouses. In short, in Berlin—I imagine it's the same in all large states—they've got serving in the army, people from the four quarters of the globe, of all nationalities and religions, of all types and skilled in all those trades that enable a man to earn a little bit on the side. So I thought I, too, would make something extra—once I'd learned to drill properly.—Perhaps down by the Spree?—No! far too noisy there.—Maybe in a timber yard though, as I was pretty handy with an ax.

So there I was once again hard at it, hatching fresh projects regardless of the dismal failure of my first one. After all, even amongst the privates here—so I lulled myself into thinking—there are top people who have nice little incomes and go in for farming, commerce, etc. Of course I didn't consider the fact that men used to get quite different bounties from nowadays; that chaps like these had perhaps married into money, etc. But what was most important—they'd taken care of the pennies and only because of that the pounds had looked after themselves—while I couldn't even manage the pennies, never mind the pounds.—Finally, when all else failed, I still found some consolation, however meager, in the thought: if and when we do go into battle then the shot can carry off the lucky blighters just as easily as it can a poor sap like you! We're all in it together.

Now the Dance Begins

The second week I had to turn out every day on the parade ground, where I unexpectedly found three compatriots of mine, Schärer, Bachmann, and Gästli, who, as it happened, were all in the same regiment (Itzenblitz) with me, the first two actually in the same company (Lüderitz). There, first and foremost, I had to learn marching, from a grumpy corporal (Mengke by name), who had a bent nose. As it was, I couldn't stand the sight of the beggar, but when he started tapping me on the ankles, my blood was really up. Under him I'd never have learned a scrap, not in a month of Sundays. This happened to be noticed by Hevel, as he was maneuvering his men about the same square; he swapped me for another chap and took me into his platoon. I was dead pleased. I now picked up more in an hour than I'd otherwise have done in weeks. It wasn't long either before I also learned from the kind fellow where Markoni was living, but, he asked me, for goodness sake not to betray his name.

The next day, as soon as drill was over, I hurried to the quarters Hevel had indicated, murmuring the whole time to myself: "You wait, Markoni! you wait! I won't half rub your nose in the dirty trick you played me, and in your whole blinking hanky-panky. I'll show you! Now I know you're just a lieutenant and not 'my lord' at all!" On inquiring I soon found the house designated to me. In fact it was one of the worst in the whole of Berlin. I knocked; a little, thin, red-haired whippersnapper of a fellow opened the door to me and led me up a flight of stairs into my master's room.

As soon as he caught sight of me he rushed towards me, shook me by the hand, and addressed me with such a sweet angelic expression on his face that in a flash all my anger was assuaged and I found the tears starting from my eyes: "Ollrich! my Ollrich! No reproaches now. You were dear to me then, you still are and always will be. It was circumstances made me act as I did. Accept the situation. Remember, you and I now serve *one* master."—"Yes, my lord." "Not 'my lord!' " he said: "In the regiment it's plain 'sir!' " Then I bemoaned my present troubles to him at great length. He expressed entire sympathy. "But," he went on: "you know, you've still got all sorts of things you can flog; such as the musket I gave you, the traveling cap that Lieutenant Hofmann honored you with at Offenburg, etc. You just bring them along to me and I'll pay you the value of them. And you might try applying to the major for a raise like the other recruits." "Not blinking likely!" I interrupted. "Oh no! I've seen him once already. Never again!" Thereupon I told him how this particular "sir" had treated me. "Honestly!" he returned, "these buggers think, when you're out recruiting, you can live on air and simply lasso men in wholesale." "Yes," I said, "if only I'd known while I was in Rothweil, I'd have put a bit by for a rainy day." "There's a time for everything, Ollrich!" he replied: "Keep your pecker up, now! Once you've got your basic training behind you, I'm sure you'll be able to make something. And who knows?—perhaps we'll soon be going to the front, and then. . . ."—He didn't go on; but I knew full well what he was getting at, and went home as happy as if I'd been having a chat with my father.

After a few days I in fact took the musket, equipment, and the velvet cap along; he paid me rather a small sum for them, but in my eyes Markoni could do no wrong. Soon afterwards I also sold my laced hat, the green frock coat, etc., etc., going short of nothing so long as I had something to flog. Schärer was just as poor as I, but he got a few groats extra allowance and a double ration of bread; he was well in with the major, I wasn't. Still we were staunch comrades; so long as either of us had a bite to eat, the other got a share. But Bachmann, who shared billets with us was a mingy skinflint and never really fitted in; and yet whenever we weren't together the time seemed to drag. If we wanted to find G., we had only to search the brothels; he landed up in hospital soon after. Schärer and I were both fully agreed in finding the Berlin women disgusting and repulsive; you can bet your life neither of us ever went near one. No, as soon as drill was over, we'd make off together to Schottmann's Pub and there drink our mugs of Ruhin or Gottwitz beer, puff a pipe or two and warble a Swiss song. The Brandenburgers and Pomeranians there always loved to listen to us. Some gentlemen would even send for us to come over to a cook shop, specially to sing the *"ranz des vaches"* to them; usually payment consisted of nothing but a portion of fatty soup; but in such straits you're glad of even less.

Amongst Other Things, My Description of Berlin

Berlin is the biggest place I've ever seen in the whole world—I never got anywhere near covering all that's to be found there. We three Swiss often planned such a tour; but if we weren't short of time then it was money, or else we were so fagged out from our exertions that we preferred to lie flat out on our bunks.

The city of Berlin—many say, though, it consists of seven cities—but the likes of you and me only ever heard three named: Berlin, Neustadt, and Friedrichsstadt. All three differ in their style of building. In Berlin—or Cöl, as it's also called—the houses are high like in the imperial cities, but the streets are not as wide as in Neu- and Friedrichsstadt, where, however, the houses are built lower but more uniform; for there even the smallest, often inhabited by very poor people, at least look clean and tidy. In many places there are enormous great empty squares that are used partly for drill and parades, partly for nothing at all: further, plow lands, gardens, avenues, all within the city boundaries.

We'd make our way especially often to the long bridge, at the middle of which there stands a life-size statue cast in iron of an old Margrave of Brandenburg on horseback, and sitting in fetters at his feet a few of the curly-haired sons of Anak—then along the Spree to the Willow Causeway, where there's always plenty doing—and then on to the hospital to visit G. and B.—to witness the saddest spectacle under the sun, the mere sight of which would be enough to put anyone off debauchery for life, unless he was completely daft. In these great barns of wards stand row upon row of beds, in each of which some sad specimen of humanity lies awaiting death, each in his own way, and only a few with a chance of recovery—here a dozen who, at the hands of the army surgeons, utter fearful yells, there others writhing under their sheets like worms trodden underfoot, many with limbs beginning to rot or already rotted away, etc. Usually we could only stand it for a few minutes and would escape into the fresh air, go and sit by some green, and there our thoughts would nearly always transport us back involuntarily to our Switzerland, and soon we'd be recounting to each other life back home, how sweet it once was, how free we'd been, what a detested life it was here by contrast, etc. Then we made plans to get out. One moment we had high hopes that one of them would succeed, some day or other, the next we'd be overwhelmed by the insurmountable difficulties involved; but what terrified us most was the thought of the consequences of an attempt that didn't come off. For it wasn't long before we were hearing all the time fresh alarming stories of captured deserters, who, however cunningly they went about it, disguising themselves as bargees and other such craftsmen, or even as women, hiding in barrels and casks, etc., were none the less detected. Then we had to watch them run the gauntlet eight times up and down the long passage between ranks of two hundred men, until they sank to the ground gasping—and the next day had to go through it again, with the clothes ripped off their flayed backs, and once again they'd be flogged with renewed vigor, until shreds of congealed blood hung down over their breeches. Then Schärer and I would look at each other, trembling and deathly pale, and whisper: "The bloody barbarians!"

What followed on the drill square also provoked similar reflections on our part. Here too there was no end of cursing and whipping by sadistic, jumped-up junkers and the yelling of the flogged in return. We were always amongst the first to move, and really made it snappy. But we were still terribly cut up to see others so mercilessly treated on the slightest provocation and ourselves bullied like this time and time again, standing there stiff as a poker, often whole hours at a stretch, throttled by all our kit, having to march dead straight here, there and everywhere, uninterruptedly executing lightning maneuvers—and all on the command of some officer, facing us with a furious expression and raised stick and threatening to lay into us any minute, as if we were so much trash. With such treatment even the toughest couldn't help becoming half-crippled, even the most patient, fuming. And as soon as we'd got back, dead beat, to our billet, we had to race like mad to get our kit straight, removing every little spot, for, apart from the blue tunic, our whole uniform was white. Musket, cartridge pouch, belt, every single button on our uniforms—it all had to be got up immaculate. The slightest speck of dirt on any item of equipment or a hair out of place on a soldier when he appeared on the parade ground, and he'd be welcomed by a rain of lashes. This went on throughout the whole of May and June. We didn't even get Sunday off, for then we had to be all bulled up for church parade. And so we could only manage the odd hours to go on those walks of ours; in fact we had time for nothing—except to be cheesed off.—The truth of the matter is, our officers had just then received precise instructions to really get a grip on us; but we recruits were completely in the dark and merely thought, well that's soldiering! The old sweats suspected something of the sort but never let on.

Meanwhile Schärer and I were absolutely skint; everything that didn't actually grow on us, we'd flogged. Now we had to make do with bread and water (or small beer that is not much better). In the meantime I'd been moved from Zittemann and billeted with Wolfram and Meewis, the former a joiner, the latter a cobbler, and both doing nicely in the way of business. I messed with them to start with. They always saw to it they had good square meals: soup and meat with potatoes and peas. Each put in two threepenny bits towards the midday meal: as regards supper and breakfast it was every man for himself: I was especially partial to a neatsfoot, a herring, or a threepenny cheese. Soon, however, I couldn't keep up with them; I had nothing left to sell and most of my pay was going on laundry, powder, shoe polish, emery, oil, and rubbish like that. Now I began to be really in the dumps and there wasn't a soul to whom I could unburden myself. During the day I skulked about as miserable as sin; at night I'd lean on the windowsill, look up, weeping, at the moon, and tell her all my bitter misery: "You, who now also hang over Toggenburg, tell the folks at home the wretched state I'm in—tell my parents, my brother and sisters, my darling Annie—how I pine—how true I am to her—that they may all pray to God for me. But you're so silent, merely moving harmlessly on your way? Ah! if only I were a little bird and could fly off home to you! Poor, thoughtless creature that I am! God have mercy on me! I meant to make my fortune and all I've done is dig my own grave! What good is this wonderful place to me, if I'm to pine away in it! If I had my people here and as nice a house as that one opposite—and didn't have to be a soldier, oh yes! then it would be grand living here; then I'd work, trade, set up house and turn my back on my homeland forever!—But no! For even then I'd have the sight of so much misery thrust constantly before me! No, dear, beloved Toggenburg! You'll always have pride of place in my heart!—But, ah! Perhaps I'll never see you in my life again—lose even the consolation of occasionally writing to my loved ones who dwell in you! For everyone tells me it's impossible, once you're sent off to the front to have even a line posted—a line in which I could pour out my heart. But who knows? My kind father in heaven lives on; He knows full well I didn't choose this life of slavery from design or negligence, but evil men duped me. Ha! if all else should fail—But no! I won't desert. Rather die than run the gauntlet. And yet things may change. Even six years can be endured. But it's a long, long time; especially if it's true there's no hope of a discharge even at the end of it!—What's that? No discharge! I have one though; the enlistment forced on me?—Huh! They'd sooner shoot me! The king would have to listen to me! I'd run after his coach, hang on till he heeded what I said. Then I'd tell him everything, down to the last detail. The just Frederick must make an exception in my case," etc.—Such were my soliloquies then.

Soon Be Off Now

In these circumstances Schärer and I got into a huddle, whenever we could manage it; complained, made plans, decided, thought better. Schärer showed more persistence than I, but then he got more pay. Now, like so many others, I found myself spending my last penny on gin to drown my sorrows; so did a chap from Mecklenburg who was billeted by me and was in the same situation. But once the fumes had risen to his brain, he'd stand in the dusk outside the barracks, cursing and raging there all on his own, swearing at his officers and even at the king himself, calling down all the plagues he could think of on Berlin and all Brandenburgers, and finding in this crazy rampaging (as the poor devil would assert, as soon as he'd sobered up) his only consolation in misfortune. Wolfram and Meewis would often warn him about it, for, until shortly before, he'd been a really nice, pleasant bloke: "Listen, mate!" they'd say to him on such occasions, "if you're not careful, the way you're going, one day you'll find yourself in the madhouse." Actually it wasn't far away. I'd often see a soldier sitting there on a bench by the railings, and I once asked Meewis who he was, as I'd never seen him around in the company: "Just like the Mecklenburg chap," answered Meewis, "so he's been put away here; at first he bellowed like a stuck pig. But for some weeks now, they say he's been as quiet as a lamb."

This account made me keen on getting to know the man more closely. He was from Anspach. At first I only stole up to him now and again and with melancholy pleasure I'd watch him sitting there dolefully, his eyes raised to the sky or staring at the ground; sometimes, however, he'd smile gently to himself, apparently not noticing my presence. The physiognomy alone of a poor body in such straits was sacred to me. Finally I ventured to sit with him. He stared at me fixedly and at first came out with a stream of gibberish, which I, however, enjoyed listening to, as amongst it all he'd make the odd sensible observation. What troubled his mind most, so far as I could tell, was the thought that he'd come from a good family; it seemed he got into some scrape and landed up here, only to suffer pitifully from remorse and homesickness. I now hinted to him of my own state of mind, mainly in order to hear what he might have to say about a possible escape on my part, for the man seemed to me really to possess the gift of prophecy. "Listen, chum!" he said to me on such an occasion, "you bide your time, chum! It's obvious you're paying for your past sins, and hence what you suffer is punishment you've more or less brought on yourself. You'll only make it worse by thrashing about. There'll come a change, lots of changes. The king alone is king; the generals, colonels, majors are themselves only his servants—and we, ah! we—so many curs flung away and sold off—destined to be belted around in peacetime, and stabbed or shot dead in war. But keep your eyes open, chum! You'll maybe come to a door; if it opens—then do as you please. But bide your time, chum!—don't rush or force things—otherwise you'll ruin everything!" He often said such things to me and much more in the same vein. All the priests and levites in the world couldn't have preached to me nor consoled me as well as he did.

Meanwhile there was more and more talk of war. New regiments were arriving at intervals in Berlin; we recruits were put into one. Every day troops were marching through the city gates out onto maneuvers, advancing on the left and right, attacking, retreating, charging by platoon and division—and all the other things in Mars's repertoire. It ended up as a general review; what a to-do!—this whole book couldn't hope to take in that little lot, no matter how much I tried. First, on account of the great masses of all kinds of war junk that I saw here, most of it for the first time. Secondly, the whole time I had my head and ears so full of the appalling racket of banging muskets, of drums and martial music, of the shouts of commanders, etc., that I often nearly burst. Thirdly, for some time I'd had such a bellyfull of drill that I didn't feel like watching all the blinking cavortings the infantry and cavalry corps were getting up to. Mind you, later I was often very sorry I hadn't taken these things in better: if only all my friends and all the folk round here could see such a sight, just for one day; I'm telling you, it wouldn't half make them sit up! So just a brief account.

There were fields as far as the eye could see, covered with soldiers, and thousands of spectators on all sides. Here two great armies stand ranged in mock line of battle; already from the flanks the batteries of heavy artillery are roaring away at each other. They advance, open fire, kicking up such a tremendous din that you can't even hear the chap right next to you and can't see a thing for smoke; there some battalions try an enfilade; here they attack each other's flanks, there they cut off the batteries; there again they form a double cross. Here they march across a pontoon bridge, there cuirassiers and dragoons are lashing out and squadrons of hussars of all colors galloping head on at one another, sending clouds of dust over horse and man. Here they overrun a position; the advance guard in which I had the honor to maneuver, strikes camp and flees.—To repeat: I'd be a fool to think I've now described a Prussian general review. I therefore hope you'll put up with what little I've given. Either that, or—if you don't mind my saying so—you may as well stop listening to my twaddle right now.

So Long, Berlin!—It's Been Good to Know You

At last the moment arrived that everyone had been waiting for, when the order came through: "Into battle. Quick march!" Already in July regiments had been marching off from Berlin, while others were arriving from Prussia and Pomerania. All men on leave had now to report back for duty and the great city was swarming with soldiers. Even so no one knew yet what all the fuss was about. I kept my ears cocked like a pig at a fence. Some were saying, if war broke out, us new recruits wouldn't be sent to the front, but would be stuck in the depot. Just the thought of it put the wind up me, but I didn't believe it. Meanwhile in all the maneuvers I gave all I'd got to show I was hot stuff as regards soldiering (for some in my company who were older than I did in fact have to remain behind). And then on 21 August, late in the evening, came the eagerly awaited order for us to get ready to march off next morning. Crimes! you should have seen the bulling-up and packing that went on! Even if I hadn't been short of the money I'd still not have had the time to pay a certain baker for two loaves I'd got on the slate. Besides there were orders that no creditor could demand payment in a case like this; anyway I left my laundry chest behind, and if the baker hasn't taken it in payment I still have to this very day a creditor in Berlin—besides the odd debtor to the tune of a few coppers—so I suppose that makes it about quits.

On 22 August at 3 A.M. reville was sounded; and at dawn there stood our regiment (Isenblitz—splendid name!—otherwise known to the men jocularly as *Donner und Blitz* on account of our colonel's terrific strictness), on parade in the Krausenstrasse. Each of its twelve companies was 150 men strong. The regiments quartered nearest to us in Berlin were, as far as I can remember, Vokat, Winterfeld, Meyring, and Kalkstein; the four Prince's Own Regiments, viz: The Prince of Prussia's Own, the Prince Ferdinand, Prince Carl, and Prince of Württemberg's Own, all of which marched off either before or after us, but subsequently in the field were usually put alongside us. Then the drums struck up; tears from civilians, tarts, pros, etc., were flowing in torrents. Those warriors, too, who were natives of the place and leaving behind wives and children, were really cut up, brokenhearted they were; whereas the strangers amongst us were dead pleased on the quiet, saying: "Thank God, salvation's here at last!"

Each man was loaded up like an ass; first girded with a swordbelt, then the cartridge pouch slung over his shoulder on a five-inch strap; over the other shoulder the large pack crammed with laundry, etc., similarly small pack stuffed with bread and other forage. Next to this everyone had to carry some item of field equipment; a flask, kettle, pick, or some such thing, each on a strap; then on top of that a musket, also attached to one. So trussed up we all were—five times crosswise, with one strap on top of another—that each soldier at first thought he'd be throttled by the load. Then came the tight, constricting uniform and such scorchers of days that I often felt I was walking on live coals; if I opened my battledress tunic for a breather, steam came out like from a boiling kettle. Often I hadn't a dry stitch on my whole body and almost perished of thirst.

Line of March to Pirna

So off we marched the *first* day (22 August) out through the Köpenick Gate, taking as many as four hours to reach the town of Köpenick, where we were quartered in groups of thirty to fifty with civilians who had to put us up for a groat. Crimes! what carryings-on! Phew! did we scoff! Well, you imagine so many hulking great hungry brutes! Men all over the place, roaring: "Out with it, you buggers!—what you're hiding there in the corner!" At night the parlor was filled with straw: there we all lay in rows, in line with the walls. An odd assortment, I can tell you! In each house there was an officer to see to discipline: they were often the worst.

The *second* day (23) we marched ten hours as far as Fürstenwald; men were already going sick and having to be bundled onto carts, which wasn't at all surprising, seeing as we'd halted only once during the whole day to eat our packed lunches. It was the same at the last-mentioned place as at the first, only that here most of the men preferred to drink rather than eat, in fact many lay down half-cut. On the *third* day (24) we marched six hours to Jakobsdorf where we now had three days' halt (25, 26, and 27), but we carried on even worse there and the poor peasants were cleaned right out. On the *seventh* day (28) we marched four hours to Mühlrosen. On the *eighth* (29) to Guben—fourteen hours. On the *ninth* (30) we rested there. On the *tenth* (31) six hours to Forste. On the *eleventh* (1 September) six hours to Spremberg. On the *twelfth* (2) six hours to Hayerswerde and there another day's halt. On the *fourteenth* (4) to Camenz, the last place we were quartered at. For from then on we camped out in the open, marching and countermarching until I hadn't the foggiest notion what places we passed through, as it often happened in the dead of night. All I remember now is that we marched four hours on the *fifteenth* (5) and pitched camp by Bilzen, where we had two days' halt (6 and 7); then on the *eighteenth* day (8) did a further six hours, camped by Stolp, and spent a day there (9); finally on the *twentieth* day (10) we took four hours to reach Pirna, where several regiments joined up with us, and now a vast camp, almost as far as the eye could see, was pitched and the castles of Königstein overlooking Pirna on this side of the Elbe, and on the other side, Lilienstein, were occupied. For the Saxon army was in the vicinity of the latter. We could see straight across the valley into their camp, and below us in the valley of the Elbe lay Pirna, which was now similarly occupied by our men.

Spunk and Funk

Up to now the Lord has helped! These words were our padre's first text at Pirna. You're telling me He has! I thought; well let's hope He keeps it up—and sees me safely back home—'cos I couldn't care less about your wars!

Meanwhile—as is customary with an army on the march—everything was such an absolute shambles that I couldn't hope to describe it all; still I doubt if it would be worth the trouble anyway. Our major Lüderitz (for the officers were keeping a very sharp watch on every man) seemed to have gathered I was peeved from the expression on my face. Then he'd point his finger threateningly at me: "You watch your step, my lad!" whereas on similar occasions he'd be clapping Schärer on the shoulder and smilingly telling him what a grand chap he was; the latter was always bright and cheerful, singing away his bricklayer's songs or the *"ranz des vaches,"* although in his heart of hearts he felt just like me, only he knew better how to hide it. Other times though I'd perk up, thinking: God will turn everything for the best! If I happened to catch sight of Markoni—who after all was not a little to blame for my misfortune—on the march or in camp, I always felt I was seeing my father or my best pal, especially when, sitting up there on his horse, he offered me his hand, shook mine warmly and with tender wistfulness peered as it were, into my very soul: "How are you, Ollrich! how *are* you? Don't worry, it'll soon be all right!" and not expecting an answer, tried to read one in my eyes glistening with tears. Oh! to this day I wish the man, wherever he may be, dead or alive, all the very best; for after Pirna I never clapped eyes on him again.

In the meantime we'd been receiving clear instructions every morning to load our muskets live; this always started the old soldiers talking: "There's a flap on. We're in for a packet, you mark my words!" Then us youngsters would be sweating cobs, whenever we happened to march past bushes or a copse and had to keep ourselves at the ready. Then silently each man pricked up his ears, expecting a fiery hail and with it his death, and as soon as we came out into the open again, everyone would be looking left and right which way he could make off most conveniently; for the whole time we had hostile cuirassiers, dragoons, and infantrymen on both sides. Once when we marched half through the night, Bachmann tried to do a bunk and wandered around for several hours in the woods, but in the morning he was back in our midst, and just about managed to get away with it on the pretext: he'd got lost in the dark when he'd gone off for a piss. From then on we others realized more and more clearly the difficulty of making off—even so we were absolutely determined, whatever the consequences, not to be around for any battle that might be coming up.

The Camp at Pirna

You won't be expecting from me a detailed description of our camp between Königstein and Pirna as well as of the Saxon one facing us at Lilienstein. You might try that *Heroical, Political, and Biographical Volume of Frederick the Great's.* I write only about what I've seen, what went on immediately around me and particularly affected me. As regards the most important things, ordinary blighters like us were most ignorant, and not really bothered either. The only thing that interested me and so many others like me was—how to get to hell out of it and back home!

From 11–22 September we sat tight in camp; and any soldier worth his salt must have really been in his element then. For it was exactly like being in a town. There were canteen-women and army-butchers by the score. The whole day long, the whole length of the streets nothing but boiling and roasting. You could get anything you wanted, or rather could pay for: meat, butter, cheese, bread, all kinds of fruit and vegetables, the lot. Apart from guard duties, you could do just what you liked: play skittles, cards, go for walks inside and outside camp, etc. Only a few stuck idly in their tents: one chap might be occupied with cleaning his musket, another washing; a third was cooking, a fourth patching breeches, a fifth mending shoes; a sixth might be carving something out of wood ot sell to the local peasants. Each tent had its six men plus an extra one. Of these seven, one was always a lance corporal; he had to see to discipline. Of the six remaining one would be on guard, another had to cook, another draw rations, another went after wood, another straw, and one looked after the kitty; but together they made up *one* household, *one* table and *one* bed.

On the march every man thrust into his pack—it goes without saying, on enemy territory!—whatever he could lay his hands on: flour, turnips, spuds, poultry, ducks, etc., and whoever didn't contrive to pick up something was treated to abuse by the others, as indeed was often my lot. What a heck of a din there was, whenever we passed through a village—from women, children, geese, sucking pigs, etc.! Anything we could nab, went. Whoops! a twist to its neck and into the pack! We broke into all the stables and gardens, belted all the trees about and tore the fruit off, branches and all. It was "Every man for himself"; if *you* don't, somebody else will! No use protesting, as long as the officers let it go on, or at least connived at it. So every man jack of us did his duty with a vengeance.

We three Swiss, Schärer, Bachmann, and I (there were more of our fellow countrymen in the regiment, but we didn't know them), actually never entered each other's tents, nor were we ever put on guard together. We did, however, often stroll out of camp with one another to the outlying picket, to a certain hill in particular, where we had a lovely wide view of the Saxon camp and all of ours, and down the valley as far as Dresden. There we'd hold our council of war: what should we do, which way should we take, where should we meet up? But as regards the main problem, the way out, there we found every bolt hole stopped. Schärer and I, though, would have preferred to sneak off alone one fine night without Bachmann, for we never entirely trusted him; what's more we could see hussars bringing in deserters all the time, and heard the drums roll, as the culprits ran the gauntlet—and other such inducements. And still all the time we were waiting for battle to commence.

Taking of the Saxon Camp, Etc.

At last on 22 September the alarm was sounded and we received orders to decamp. Immediately everything was astir; a camp stretching for miles—like the largest city in the world—and in a few moments, destroyed, packed up, and quick march! Scram! Then we went down into the valley, threw a pontoon bridge across by Pirna, formed a passage, as for running the gauntlet,* above the town, facing the Saxon camp, with one end of the passage abutting on the Pirna gate, through which the whole Saxon army had to pass four abreast, having laid down their arms—and as you can well imagine—had to put up with streams of abuse and taunts the whole way along. Some went sadly, their heads bowed, others defiantly and fiercely, others again with a smile meant to answer the Prussian mockers in their own coin. And that's about all I and so many thousand others knew, as to the actual details of the surrender of this great army.

That same day we marched out some distance and then encamped by Lilienstein. On the twenty-third our regiment had to cover the supply wagons. On the twenty-fourth we executed a countermarch, and under cover of darkness landed up God knows where. On the morning of the twenty-fifth we again set out early, twenty miles to Aussig. Here we pitched camp, remaining until the twenty-ninth, and had to go out foraging every day. On such occasions we were often attacked by the imperial pandours, or out from a clump of bushes might come a hail of carbine fire straight at us, many being killed on the spot and still more wounded. Our artillerymen, how-

*Honestly the things you see when you're scared!

ever, only needed to direct a few cannons at the bushes for the enemy to pelt off out of it, as fast as their legs would carry them. This sort of nonsense never upset me; I'd have soon got used to it, often thinking: Pooh! if that's all there is to it! It could be a lot worse.

On the thirtieth we again marched all day, and it was dark by the time we came to some mountain that again had me and my mates completely fogged. Meanwhile we received orders not to pitch any tent, nor to set down any arms, but to keep ourselves at the ready, guns loaded with live ammunition, as the enemy was near at hand. At last, as day was breaking, we saw and heard a tremendous flashing and firing down in the valley.—During that fearful night many deserted; amongst others friend Bachmann. As regards myself, the time didn't seem ripe yet, however much I felt like it.

The Battle of Lowositz, 1 October 1756

Early in the morning we had to form up and march down through a narrow gully running into the main valley. We couldn't see far for the mist, so thick it was. When, however, we'd got right down to the plain and joined the main army, we advanced in three lines of battle, glimpsing through the mist away in the distance, as through gauze, enemy troops on the plain above the Bohemian town of Lowositz. It was the imperial cavalry; we never sighted the infantry, as they'd dug in outside the aforementioned town. At 6 o'clock the thunder of artillery fire, not only from our front line but also from the imperial batteries, became so terrific, that the cannonballs even came humming through into our regiment which was in the center. Till then I'd still had hopes of escaping before battle was engaged; now I could see no way out, whether in front or behind, to right or to left. Meanwhile we were advancing all the time.

Then all my courage sank into my breeches; my only wish was to creep into the bowels of the earth, and a similar fear, indeed deathly pallor, could soon be seen on all faces, even of those who'd always made out how tough they were. Emptied brandy flasks (every soldier has one) were flying through the air amidst the general rain of bullets; most of the men had drained their meager supply down to the last drop, on the principle of "Today we need our courage:

tomorrow we may be gone!" Now we advanced under the shells to where we had to relieve the front line. Crimes! how those iron cobs whizzed over our heads!—one minute driving into the earth before us, the next behind, sending stones and sods high into the air—now in amongst us, cracking men down right, left, and center like straws. All we saw was enemy cavalry on top of us, executing all sorts of movements, now stretching out in line, now forming a crescent, now contracting into a triangle or square. Then up came our cavalry; we opened a gap and let them through to gallop straight at the enemy cavalry. And what a clash! what a rattling and glinting, as they laid into them! It scarcely lasted a quarter of an hour, however, before our horsemen returned, beaten back by the Austrian cavalry, harried almost under the muzzles of our cannon. You never saw such a spectacle!—horses with riders hanging from the stirrups, others trailing their guts along the ground. Meanwhile we were still exposed to enemy cannon fire until close on 11 o'clock, without our left flank engaging with small arms, even though there was already fierce fighting on the right. Many thought we're bound to storm the imperial fieldworks. By now I wasn't so frightened as at the beginning, although the culverins were carrying off men on both sides of me and the battlefield was already strewn with dead and wounded—when all of a sudden about 12 o'clock the order came, our regiment was to retire, together with two others (Bevern and Kalkstein, I believe). Now we thought, we're returning to camp, we'll be well out of it. So we bounded up the steep vineyards, filling our caps with lovely red grapes as we went, eating all before us to our hearts' content; and I and those alongside me, never considered the danger, even though from high up there we could see our mates still standing in a welter of fire and smoke, could hear a dreadful thundering din and still not make out who was gaining the field.

Meanwhile our commanders were driving us higher and higher up the mountain, at the top of which a narrow, rocky path led down again on the other side. As soon as our vanguard had reached the said peak a terrific volley of musket fire started up; and only now did we catch on to what it was all about. Thousands of imperial pandours had been ordered up the other side of the mountain to take our army in the rear; this must have been betrayed to our commanders and we were there to forestall them: another couple of minutes and they'd have gained the heights from us and we wouldn't half have copped it! It now meant indescribable slaughter, dislodging the pandours from that wood. Our forward troops suffered heavily; but the rearguard followed up and got stuck in as well, until in the end we'd all gained the heights. We found ourselves stumbling over mounds of dead and wounded.

Then, yoiks, tallyho, helter-skelter down the vineyards after the pandours, leaping over one wall after another down to the plain. Our true-blue Prussians and Brandenburgers pounced on the pandours like the furies. I slewed about all over the place like a mad thing, and immune to the slightest fear, in *one* burst I shot off well-nigh all sixty of my rounds till my musket was pretty well red-hot and I had to drag it behind me by its strap; I don't believe I hit a living soul though—it all went into the air. The pandours reformed in the plain by the river close to the town of Lowositz and fired away briskly up into the vineyards, causing many comrades in front and alongside me to bite the dust. Everywhere Prussians and pandours lay higgledy-piggledy, and should one of the latter still stir, then he got a musket butt bashed into his face or a bayonet pushed through his body.

And now battle recommenced on the plain. But who shall attempt to describe it?—the smoke and fumes that now went up from Lowositz, the crashing and thundering as if heaven and earth were about to melt away, the incessant rattle of many hundreds of drums, the clangor of martial music of all kinds, rending and uplifting the heart, the shouts of so many commanders and roars of their adjutants, the moans and groans from so many thousands of wretched, mangled, half-dead victims of this day: it dazed all the senses! At that time—it was probably round 3 p.m.—as Lowositz already lay in flames and many hundreds of pandours, which our vanguard were pouncing upon again like savage lions, were jumping into the water, and battle was moving towards the town;—at that time I'm afraid I can't say I was right at the front; I kept a little way up in the vineyards amongst the rear guard, many of whom, as I've said, were leaping far more nimbly than I over one wall after another to hasten to the rescue of their brothers. As I stood there a little way up the slope, staring at the plain as into a murky thunder- and hailstorm—that very moment it occurred to me, or rather it was my guardian angel prompting me, that it was high time I fled for safety. So I looked about me on all sides. In front of me, all was fire, smoke, and fumes; behind me many more troops coming on, rushing towards the enemy, to the right two main armies in full battle array. Finally to the left I saw vineyards, bushes, copses, just the odd Prussian, pandour, or hussar dotted about, and of these more dead and wounded than living. There! there! that direction, I thought; otherwise you haven't a hope in hell!

Well—If Not Fought with Honor—at Least Successfully Absconded

So I first slunk in slow-march time a little toward this left side, through the vines. A few Prussians were still rushing past me. "Come on, brother! Come on!" they were saying: "To victory!" I never let on, but made as if I was slightly wounded and continued to make gradual progress; I was scared stiff, I must admit. But as soon as I'd got so far no one could see me any more, I doubled, trebled, quadrupled, quintupled, sextupled my steps, looked to left and right like a huntsman, still saw away in the distance—for the last time in my life—wholesale murder; then in full gallop I skirted a small wood that lay full of dead hussars, pandours, and horses, ran full tilt down towards the river and now found myself in a dell. Just then on the other side of it a few imperial soldiers came belting up, who'd also made off from the battle and when they saw me rushing along like that, they leveled their rifles at me a third time, in spite of my laying down my musket and giving them the customary sign with my cap. But they never fired. So I made up my mind to run straight towards them. Had I taken any other direction, they'd have fired at me without fail, so I gathered later. "You b——rs!" I thought, "you should have shown your courage at Lowositz!"

After I'd joined them and declared myself a deserter they took my musket from me with the promise they'd be sure to return it later. But the chap who purloined it disappeared soon after, taking the fusil with him. Well, good riddance! Then they took me to the nearest village, Scheniseck (probably a good hour's journey down from Lowositz). This meant crossing the river, with only one boat available. Then what a hullabaloo from men, women, and children! Each pushed his way to the front to get on board, for fear of the Prussians; they all thought they were right on top of them. I wasn't backward in coming forward either and jumped right into a crowd of women. If the ferryman hadn't thrown out some of them, we'd all have been surely drowned. On the other side of the river stood a main guard of pandours. My escorts took me to them and these red old mustaches received me in the friendliest manner; gave me, even though we didn't understand a blind word of what each other was saying, tobacco, brandy, and a safe conduct to Leutmeritz, I believe, where I spent the night amongst a proper gang of gypsies, not knowing if it was safe for me to put my head down—just as well, my brain was still reeling from all that had happened that day, otherwise I might have got worried. The next morning (2 October) I left with a transport detachment bound for the imperial main camp at Budin.

Here I met getting on for two hundred other Prussian deserters, all of whom had gone about the business carefully, so to speak, each in his own way and in his own time; and amongst others who else but friend Bachmann? How we leaped into the air to see each other set free so unexpectedly! Then we began laughing and talking about our experiences, as if we were already sitting at home by our stoves. But from time to time we'd come out with: "Ah, if only old Schärer from Weil was with us! Where on earth can he have landed up?" We had permission to take a look at everything in the camp. Officers and men would then crowd round us, plying us with questions the whole time about every little thing. Some of the men didn't half shoot a line, concocting hundreds of lies to the disparagement of the Prussians, all to flatter their present hosts. Then of course, there was many a big mouth among the imperial forces; even the most insignificant little squirt prided himself on having put to flight God knows how many long-shanked Brandenburgers—he himself being in full flight at the time!

After that we were taken to see a body of about fifty prisoners from the Prussian cavalry; a pitiful sight! Scarcely one who'd got off without wounds or bruises, some slashed all over the face, others in the neck, others across the ears, across the shoulders, the thighs, etc. Nothing but moaning and groaning from all sides. Didn't these poor wretches call us fortunate to have so luckily escaped a like fate, and didn't we ourselves thank the Lord we had! We had to stay overnight in the camp and each was given his ducat traveling allowance.

Then we were sent with a cavalry transport, about two hundred of us, to a Bohemian village, from which, after a short sleep, we set out on the following day for Prague. There we split up and received passes for groups of six, ten, or twelve, according as to who were using the same route, for we were the oddest assortment—Swiss, Swabians, Saxons, Bavarians, Tyroleans, Italians, French, Polacks, and Turks. Our six togther got one such pass for as far as Ratisbon. In the meantime everyone in Prague was shivering and shaking in their shoes at the prospect of the arrival of the Prussians. The outcome of the battle of Lowositz had reached there by then and people expected the victor to be already at their gates. There too whole crowds of soldiers and citizens swarmed round us, urging us to tell them what the Prussians were up to. Some of us set these nosey parkers' minds at rest: others had a grand time, however, putting the wind up them, telling them: the enemy will be on top of you in four days' time at the very latest, breathing fire and destruction! At this many threw up their hands; women and children even rolled about howling in the mud.

Home! Home! Must Get home!

On 5 October we began our real journey home. It was already evening when we tramped out of Prague. Soon we were going over a rise, from which we had an incomparable view of the whole of fine regal Prague. The kind sun was enchantingly gilding its countless metallic spires. We stood there for a while to enjoy this magnificent sight, indulging, as we did so, in all kinds of talk and a variety of feelings. Some pitied the splendid place, seeing it was likely to be bombarded; others wished they could be there, at least for the looting. I could hardly see enough of it; but, apart from this, all I wanted was to get home to my family, to dear Annie.

We managed to get to Schibrack, and on the sixth, Pilsen. There the landlord had a daughter, the most beautiful girl I've even seen in my life. Friend Bachmann tried to make up to her, and it was almost entirely on her account that we had a day's halt there. But the landlord made it clear to him: his child was not one of those Berlin women! From the eighth to the twelfth our journey continued via Stab, Lensch, Kätz, Kien, etc., to Ratisbon where we had our second halt. Up till then we'd only done short spurts of from eight to twelve miles a day, with correspondingly long rests. My allowance of ducats for the journey was already worn to a shadow; apart from this I hadn't a penny to bless myself with and was therefore obliged to go cadging round the villages. There I often got both pockets full of bread, but never a farthing in cash. Bachmann, however, still had some of his bounty money left, went into inns and sat down to good solid meals; only perhaps on calls at posh houses, vicarages, and monasteries did he deign to come with us. There we were frequently kept standing for ages, giving the fine gentlemen the whole story; Bachmann, in particular, would tend to get cheesed off, especially when a few coppers was all they'd fork out for the account of a whole battle—which he hadn't been around for anyway. He always made out he'd been at Lowositz as well and of course I had to back him up; in return he made sure he never stood me a single mug of beer during the whole journey. Still you could get soup at the monasteries, and often even meat.

In Ratisbon, or rather in "The Bavarian Arms," we split up again. Bachmann and I received a pass for Switzerland. The others, a Bavarian, two Swabians, and a Frenchman, of whom I have nothing more to say except that they were, all four, hefty blokes and far superior to us ninnies, went each his own way. Ours took us from the 14th to the 24th October, leaving out the smaller places, via Ingolstadt, Donauwerth, Dillingen, Buxheim, Wangen, Hohentwiel, Bregenz, Rheineck, Roschach (170 miles). Above Rheineck I had a nasty experience.

Up till then we'd traveled along in quite a matey fashion, chatting the whole time cheerily about our lucky escape, our earlier and more recent adventures and prospects for the future. Bachmann, who kept on returning to his favorite old subject of dogs and hares, had bought himself a fowling piece as soon as we were out of Prague and carried it with him. I'd long since got fed up with his endless burblings about coursing and beating, when, about Rheineck, as I say, we heard some dogs chasing in the vineyards. Hereupon the blighter actually started dancing for joy, declaring, by Christ! those were his old chums; he recognized them by their barks! I laughed in his face. He got mad at this, ordered me to halt and listen to the fine music. I didn't half make fun of him! I admit I shouldn't have gone so far. He was furious, planted himself before me, foaming at the mouth, with his shotgun raised and, grinding his teeth, stuck it at my head as if he was about to shoot me dead on the spot. I was terrified; *he* was armed, I wasn't; and leaving this and his fury aside, I doubt if I'd have been a match for such a tough customer, furious in the bargain and on top of that, almost two inches taller than me. However, I don't know whether out of courage or fear, I didn't budge, meanwhile glancing round on all sides to see if I couldn't call for help to someone. But—it was a lonely spot on a common—there wasn't a soul in sight. "Don't be a fool!" I said to him: "Can't you take a joke?"

With that his temper cooled off considerably. We went on in silence for a while, and I was glad when, almost before realizing it, we entered the town of Rheineck. Then he started pestering me again for a half-crown I'd borrowed from him *en route;* I often think it was this measly sum of money that saved my life. But from that moment all trust was gone between us. Yet I've never got my own back on him even though they were plenty of opportunities; and my father promptly paid him the half-crown, when he called at our house a few days after my return. We got as far as Roschach and on the following day (25 October) reached Herisau, for Master Bachmann didn't like rushing, and I couldn't help noticing he didn't fancy going home, without first inquiring which way the wind lay regarding his former misdemeanors.

O Beloved Sweet Fatherland!

I couldn't keep slow time with the fellow any longer; so near home, I was consumed with longing finally to reach it. And so early on the morning of 26 October. I set off for the last time, running along like a deer over bush and brake, spurred on by the thought of seeing parents, brothers, and sisters, and my darling once again. As I was now approaching my beloved Wattweil in this frame of mind, getting nearer and nearer and at last mounting the lovely rise from which I could see its church tower quite close beneath me, my whole being was moved and great tears coursed in streams down my cheeks. O you long sought, blessed place! now I have you once again and no one shall ever take me from you—I was thinking, most likely hundreds of times, as I toddled down; the whole time I was rendering thanks to God's providence, which had rescued me from so many perils, if not miraculously, then with the greatest of kindness. An old acquaintance, Gämperle, spoke to me on the bridge at Wattweil; he'd known before I left about my love affair and his first words were: "Eh, listen! Your Anne's gone off with somebody else; your cousin Michael's been the lucky one, and she's already got a child."—It cut me to the quick, but I didn't betray anything to the nasty talebearer. "Ah well," I said, "No use crying!" And in fact, to my great astonishment, I composed myself again very soon, actually thinking: "I will admit I didn't expect it of her. But since that's the way it has to be, fair enough. Let her have her Michael!"

Then I hurried to our house. It was a beautiful autumn evening. As I entered the parlor (Father and Mother were not at home) I soon noticed that not a single one of my own brothers and sisters recognized me, and that they were pretty scared at the unusual spectacle of a Prussian soldier addressing them there in full kit, with large pack on back, hat pulled down low, and a luxuriant mustache. The little ones trembled; the eldest boy reached for a hayfork, and—made off. Nevertheless I was determined not to reveal myself until my parents were there. At last my mother came. I asked her for lodgings for the night. She had her doubts; her husband was not at home, etc. I couldn't restrain myself any longer, seized her hand, saying: "Mother! Mother! Don't you know me anymore?" Oh, first there were tumultuous cries of joy from large and small, from time to time mingled with tears, then such a welcoming, a touching and staring, asking and answering, it was enough to gladden anyone's heart. Each one was telling me about everything he or she had tried to get me back in their midst. My eldest sister, for instance, had been prepared to sell her Sunday dress and fetch me home with the proceeds.

In the meantime my father had got back; he'd had to be summoned from quite a distance. Teardrops were also running down the good man's cheeks: "Ah! Welcome, welcome, my son! God be praised you're back home safe and sound and I've now all my ten under one roof again. Though we're poor, there'll always be work and bread." Now my heart blazed up high, and I felt such joy deep within me at delighting so many people—and my own flesh and blood—all at once. Then that evening and on several successive ones

I related my whole story to them, down to the last detail. Oh! I felt such gladness as I'd not known for ages!

After a few days along came Bachmann, picked up, as I've said, his half-crown, and confirmed my whole account. On Sunday morning I tidied up my uniform, as in Berlin, for church parade. All my friends welcomed me back; others gaped at me as if I were a Turk. And so did my—but not *my* any more, rather cousin Michael's Anne—rather pertly in fact, without turning a hair. I, for my part, thanked her drily, with a sardonic smile. All the same I went to see her some time later, after she'd let me know she wanted to have a word alone with me: whereupon she actually made all kinds of hollow excuses: viz., she thought she'd lost me forever, that Michael had duped her into it, etc. Then she was even still willing to oblige. But I thanked her, told her not to bother, and left.

Translated by Derek Bowman

Glossary

Acker. A ripple or a patch of ruffled water. Here, "get through the ackers" is like "cover a lot of ground." Bräker's German literally means "go through a lot of money."

Annie. Ulrich's sweetheart back home.

Bargee. Bargeman, master or deckhand of a barge.

Bird. Facetious term for a girl or young woman.

Blighter. A worthless or contemptible person; fellow, guy.

Blimey. Gorblimey, a euphemism for "God blind me," used to express amazement, surprise, or perplexity.

Blinking. Damned, blasted; complete, utter.

Brake. Rough, broken, or marshy land.

Brandenburg. Prussian province in northeastern Germany (around Berlin) ruled since the early fifteenth century by the Hohenzollerns, under whom it emerged from the Thirty Years' War as a military power. Its leaders became electors of the Holy Roman Empire, kings of Prussia, and German emperors.

Bucked (up). Vigorous, cheerful; encouraged, elated.

Bulled-up. Subjected to unnecessary routine tasks or nonsensical discipline.

Bunk. A hurried departure, usually in escaping something—used in the phrase "do a bunk." Leave, scram.

Cadge. Get by begging, especially habitually or as a means of livelihood. Sponge.

Cheesed off. Bored, exasperated.

Cob. A lump or piece (as of coal or stone) or a rounded heap or mass (as a small loaf of bread).

Cöl. Kölln, a Wendish village along the river Spree that merged with neighboring Berlin in 1307.

Cop. Catch, capture.

Copper. A minor coin made of copper.

Cor lummy. "Lord love me!"—an exclamation used to express surprise, interest, or approval.

'Cos. "Cause," short for "because."

Cove. Man, chap, fellow, bloke.

Crikey. Euphemism for "Christ." A mild oath, often in the phrase "by crikey."

Crimes. An interjection that is probably another euphemism for "Christ."

Cuirassier. A mounted soldier wearing a cuirass (piece of armor originally made of leather and covering the body from neck to girdle); a soldier of a certain type of heavy cavalry in the French and other European armies.

Culverin. A firearm, originally a rude musket; in the sixteenth and seventeenth centuries, a long cannon (as an eighteen-pounder) with serpent-shaped handles.

Distaff. A staff for holding the bunch of flax, tow, or wool from which thread is drawn in spinning by hand or with the spinning wheel.

Donner und Blitz. Thunder and lightning.

Dot about. Scatter (all over) like dots.

Dragoon. A mounted infantryman of the seventeenth and eighteenth centuries, especially one armed with a carbine; cavalryman.

Ducat. A gold coin in Europe copied from models bearing a portrait of the doge (chief magistrate in the former republics of Venice and Genoa).

Enfilade. A condition permitting the delivery of fire at an objective (as a trench or a line of troops) from a point on or near the prolongation of its longest axis; to rake with gunfire in a lengthwise direction.

Farthing. A coin, originally of silver, later of copper and of bronze, equal to one-fourth of a penny.

Flog. Take (as government property) for purposes of resale.

Flogged. Worn out, exhausted.

Florin. A gold coin in Europe, patterned after one first struck in Florence.

Frederick the Great. Frederich II (1712–86), king of Prussia (1740–86). With his victory over Austria and Saxony in the Seven Years' War (1756–63), he made Prussia the foremost military power in Europe. He wrote extensively on politics, history, military science, and philosophy—mostly in French.

Getting on for. Approaching (an age, time, etc.).

Groat. One of several onetime European coins of varying, chiefly small, value; a British coin worth four-pence.

Half-cut. Half-dead.

Halle Hymn Book. Halle is a city in the German province of Saxony where Pietism and the first Bible Society flourished in the eighteenth century.

Hussar. A horseman of the Hungarian light cavalry organized in the fifteenth century; a member of the light cavalry of various European armies, usually distinguished by a brilliant, much-decorated uniform.

Imperial cities. Cities directly subject to the Holy Roman Empire rather than to any other ruler or state.

Joey. A British coin, a threepenny or fourpenny piece.

Joiner. Craftsman who works in wood and specializes in fine details of building interiors.

Jumped-up. Newly or recently sprung up or arisen.

Junker. A German noble; a Prussian landed aristocrat characterized by extreme militarism, nationalism, and antidemocratic views.

Knocked up. Knocked out, exhausted.

Lark. Frolic, behave sportively or mischievously.

Mariane. Young woman with whom Ulrich flirts in Rothweil.

Markoni. Prussian recruiting officer whom Ulrich is tricked into meeting but whom he enjoys serving as long as he is not forced to become a soldier.

Margrave of Brandenburg. Friedrich Wilhelm, the "Great Elector" (1620–88), who as elector of Brandenburg (1640–88) consolidated the Hohenzollern's scattered lands after the Thirty Years' War (1618–48) and thus laid the foundation of the modern Prussian state.

Mingy. Stingy, mean.

Muck in (with). Go in with another person, share tasks equally.

Mug. Foolish or guillible person, blockhead.

Neatsfoot. Foot of common domestic bovine or cattle like it.

Nosey parker. A meddlesome, prying busybody.

Packet. Severe mental or physical distress, especially as the result of a beating.

Pandour. Member of a Croatian regiment in the Austrian army of the eighteenth century, originally organized as a local militia and having a reputation for cruelty and plundering.

Pecker. Courage, spirits.

Pros. Prostitutes.

Put the wind up. Frighten.

Ranz des vaches. Strophic song of Swiss cowherds.

Rothweil. City in southwestern Germany.

Shoot a line. Talk pretentiously.

Sit up. Show interest or alertness or surprise, as in "sit up and take notice."

Skint. Having no money.

Skittles. English ninepins played by pitching or sliding a wooden disk or rolling a wooden ball to knock down pins.

Sons of Anak. Giants. See Numbers 13:33: "And there we saw the giants, the sons of Anak."

Sons of Mars. Soldiers. Mars was the Roman god of war.

Spelt. A wheat grown in Germany and Switzerland.

Spree. River in eastern Germany that runs through Berlin.

Streuth (or Struth). Short for "God's truth," an interjection used as a mild oath.

Swipes. Poor, thin, or spoiled beer; small beer.

Tallyho. Cry sounded by hunters upon sighting the fox as it breaks from cover.

Tart. A wanton or loose woman; prostitute.

Toggenburg. Poor, remote mountain valley in Switzerland where Braker lived.

Tuppence. Twopence, a coin worth two British pennies.

Wattweil. Bräker's home town.

Yoiks (or Yoicks). Cry of encouragement to foxhounds; expression of excitement or exultation.

Bibliography

Listed below are books, essays, and articles in English on the authors and works included in this volume. Dissertations are not cited. Entries are arranged alphabetically for each author. Separate lists of complete translations, where available, and of readily available German editions follow.

1. General

Blackall, Eric. *The Emergence of German as a Literary Language, 1700–1775*, 2d ed. Ithaca, NY: Cornell University Press, 1978.

Bruford, W. H. *Germany in the Eighteenth Century: The Social Background of the Literary Revolution*. 7th ed. Cambridge: Cambridge University Press, 1968.

Garland, Henry and Mary, ed. *The Oxford Companion to German Literature*. 2d ed. Oxford and New York: Oxford University Press, 1986.

Hardin, James, and Christoph E. Schweitzer, ed. *Dictionary of Literary Biography*. Vol. 94, *German Writers in the Age of Goethe: Sturm und Drang to Classicism*. Vol. 97, *German Writers from the Enlightenment to Sturm und Drang*. Detroit: Gale Research, 1990.

Lange, Victor. *The Classical Age of German Literature 1740–1815*. New York: Holmes & Meier, 1982.

McCarthy, John. "The Art of Reading and the Goals of the German Enlightnment." *Lessing Yearbook* 16 (1984): 79–94.

Ward, Albert. *Book Production, Fiction, and the German Reading Public 1740–1800*. Oxford: Clarendon Press, 1974.

Zantop, Susanne, and Jeannine Blackwell. *Bitter Healing: German Women Writers from 1700 to 1848. An Anthology in English*. Lincoln, NE: University of Nebraska Press, 1990.

II. Ulrich Bräker

Bowman, Derek. Introduction to *The Life Story and Real Adventures of the Poor Man of Toggenburg*, by Ulrich Bräker. Tr. Derek Bowman. Edinburgh: University Press, 1970.

Hardin, James. "Ulrich Bräker." *Dictionary of Literary Biography* 94: 16–21.

III. Georg Forster

Bohm, Arnd. "Georg Forster's *A Voyage round the World* as a Source for *The Rime of the Ancient Mariner:* A Reconsideration." *ELH* 50 (1983): 363–77.
Kahn, Robert L. "The History of the Work." Afterword to *A Voyage round the World,* by Georg Forster. Ed. Robert L. Kahn. Vol. 1 of *Georg Forsters Werke: Sämtliche Schriften, Tagebücher, Briefe.* Berlin: Akademie Verlag, 1968.
Saine, Thomas P. *Georg Forster.* New York: Twayne, 1972.
———. "Georg Foster." *Dictionary of Literary Biography* 94: 36–45.
West, Hugh. "The Limits of Enlightenment Anthropology: Georg Forster and the Tahitians." *History of European Ideas* 10, no. 2 (1989): 147–60.

IV. Wilhelm Heinse

Brandon, Wallace R. "Wilhelm Heinse and Italian Literature." *Comparative Literature Studies* 5 (1968): 249–58.
Hatfield, Henry. *Aesthetic Paganism in German Literature: From Winckelmann to the Death of Goethe.* Cambridge, MA: Harvard University Press, 1964.
Klinger, Uwe. "Wilhelm Heinse's *Ardinghello:* A Re-Appraisal." *Lessing Yearbook* 7 (1975): 28–54.
Reed, Eugene E. "The Transitional Significance of Heinse's *Ardinghello.*" *Modern Language Quarterly* 16 (1955): 268–73.
Terras, Rita. "Wilhelm Heinse." *Dictionary of Literary Biography* 94: 67–71.
Wallach, Martha Kaarsberg. "The Female Dilemma in Heinse's *Ardinghello.*" *Lessing Yearbook* 16 (1984): 193–203.

V. Sophie von La Roche

Blackwell, Jeannine. "Sophie von La Roche." *Dictionary of Literary Biography* 94: 154–61.
Britt, Christa Baguss. Introduction to *The History of Lady Sophia Sternheim.* Tr. Christa Baguss Britt. Albany: SUNY Press, 1991.
Craig, Charlotte. "Sophie von La Roche's Enlightened Anglophilia." *Germanic Notes* 8 (1977): 34–40.

Mielke, Andreas. "Sophie La Roche: A Pioneering Novelist." *Modern Language Studies* 18, no. 1 (Winter 1988): 112–19.

Petschauer, Peter. "Sophie von LaRoche, Novelist between Reason and Emotion." *Germanic Review* 57, no. 2 (Spring 1982): 70–77.

Winkle, Sally. "Innovation and Convention in Sophie La Roche's *The Story of Miss von Sternheim* and *Rosalia's Letters*." In *Writing in the Female Voice: Essays on Epistolary Literature*, ed. Elizabeth Goldsmith, 77–94. Boston: Northeastern University Press, 1989.

———. *Woman as Bourgeois Ideal: A Study of Sophie von La Roche's "Geschichte des Fräuleins von Sternheim" and Goethe's "Werther."* New York: Peter Lang, 1988.

VI. Karl Philipp Moritz

Allentuck, Marcia. "Karl Philipp Moritz's *Anton Reiser:* Its Relations to the Picaresque and the *Bildungsroman*." *Humanities Association Review/La Revue de l'Association des Humanites* 28 (1977): 328–32.

Boulby, Mark. "*Anton Reiser* and the Concept of the Novel." *Lessing Yearbook* 4 (1972): 183–96.

———. "The Gates of Brunswick: Some Aspects of Symbol, Structure, and Theme in Karl Philipp Moritz's *Anton Reiser*." *Modern Language Review* 68 (1973): 105–14.

———. *Karl Philipp Moritz: At the Fringe of Genius.* Toronto: University of Toronto Press, 1979.

Davies, Martin L. "The Theme of Communication in *Anton Reiser:* A Reflection of the Feasibility of the Enlightenment." *Oxford German Studies* 12 (1981): 18–38.

Durden, William G. "Parallel Designs: Space, Time, and Being and Karl Philipp Moritz's *Anton Reiser*." *Germanic Review* 54 (1979): 67–71.

Garlick, D. Stevens. "Moritz's *Anton Reiser:* The Dissonant Voice of Psycho-Autobiography." *Studi Germanici* 21–22 (59–64) (1983–84): 41–60.

Saine, Thomas P. "Karl Philipp Moritz." *Dictionary of Literary Biography* 94: 190–98.

VII. Christoph Martin Wieland

Abbé, Derek Maurice van. *Christoph Martin Wieland (1733–1813): A Literary Biography.* London: Harrap, 1961.

Bohm, Arnd. "Ancients and Moderns in Wieland's *Process um des Esels Schatten*." *Modern Language Notes* 103, no. 3 (Spring 1988): 652–61.

McCarthy, John. *Christoph Martin Wieland.* Boston: Twayne, 1979.

Starnes, Thomas C. "Christoph Martin Wieland." *Dictionary of Literary Biography* 97: 256–90.

Whiton, John. "Sacrifice and Society in Wieland's *Abderiten.*" *Lessing Yearbook* 2 (1970): 213–34.

Yuill, W. E. "Abderitis and Adberitism: Some Reflections on a Novel by Wieland." In *Essays in German Literature,* ed. F. Norman, vol. 1, 72–95. London: Institute of Germanic Studies, 1965.

VIII. Complete Translations

Bräker, Ulrich. *The Life Story and Real Adventures of the Poor Man of Toggenburg.* Tr. Derek Bowman. Edinburgh: University Press, 1970.

La Roche, Sophie von. *The History of Lady Sophia Sternheim: Attempted from the German of Mr. Wieland* [sic]. Tr. Joseph Collyer. 2 vols. London: Collyer, 1776.

———. *The Adventures of Miss Sophia Sternheim.* Tr. E. Harwood. 2 vols. London: Becket, 1776.

———. *The History of Lady Sophia Sternheim: Extracted by a Woman Friend of the Same from Original Documents and Other Reliable Sources.* Tr. Christa Baguss Britt. Albany: SUNY Press, 1991.

Moritz, Karl Philipp. *Anton Reiser: A Psychological Novel.* Tr. P. E. Matheson. London: Oxford University Press, 1926. Reprint. Westport, CT: Hyperion Press, 1978.

Wieland, Christoph Martin. *The Republic of Fools: Being the History of the State and People of Abdera in Thrace.* Tr. Henry Christmas. 2 vols. London: W. H. Allen, 1861.

IX. German Editions

Bräker, Ulrich. *Lebensgeschichte und natürliche Ebenteuer des Armen Mannes im Tockenburg.* Ed. Werner Günther. Stuttgart: Reclam, 1975.

Forster, Georg. *A Voyage round the World.* Ed. Robert L. Kahn. Vol. 1 of *Georg Forsters Werke: Sämtliche Schriften, Tagebücher, Briefe.* Berlin: Akademie Verlag, 1968.

Heinse, Wilhelm. *Ardinghello und die glückseligen Inseln.* Kritische Studienausgabe. Ed. Max L. Baeumer. Stuttgart: Reclam, 1985.

La Roche, Sophie von. *Geschichte des Fräuleins von Sternheim.* Ed. Barbara Becker-Cantarino. Stuttgart: Reclam, 1983.

Moritz, Karl Philipp. *Anton Reiser: Ein phychologischer Roman.* Ed. Wolfgang Martens. Stuttgart: Reclam, 1979.

Wieland, Christoph Martin. *Geschichte der Abderiten.* Ed. Karl Hans Bühner. Stuttgart: Reclam, 1975.

ACKNOWLEDGMENTS

Every reasonable effort has been made to locate the owners of rights to previously published works and the translations printed here. We gratefully acknowledge permission to reprint the following material:

From *Anton Reiser: A Psychological Novel* by Karl Moritz translated by P. E. Matheson (1926) by permission of Oxford University Press.

The Poor Man of Toggenburg by Ulrich Bräker, translated, with an introduction by Derek Bowman, by permission of Edinburgh University Press.

"A Voyage round the World" (chapter VIII, pp. 155–92) from *Georg Forsters Werke*, Sämtliche Schriften, Tagebücher, Briefe, bearbeitet von Robert L. Kahn, Berlin: Akademie-Verlag, 1968.

THE GERMAN LIBRARY
in 100 Volumes
Select List of Titles

Wolfram von Eschenbach
Parzival
Edited by André Lefevere

Gottfried von Strassburg
Tristan and Isolde
Edited and Revised by Francis G.
  Gentry
Foreword by C. Stephen Jaeger

German Medieval Tales
Edited by Francis G. Gentry
Foreword by Thomas Berger

German Mystical Writings
Edited by Karen J. Campbell
Foreword by Carol Zaleski

*German Humanism and
  Reformation*
Edited by Reinhard P. Becker
Foreword by Roland Bainton

*German Poetry from the
  Beginnings to 1750*
Edited by Ingrid Walsøe-Engel
Foreword by George C.
  Schoolfield

Gotthold Ephraim Lessing
*Nathan the Wise, Minna von
  Barnhelm, and other Plays and
  Writings*
Edited by Peter Demetz
Foreword by Hannah Arendt

Immanuel Kant
Philosophical Writings
Edited by Ernst Behler
Foreword by René Wellek

Friedrich Schiller
*Plays: Intrigue and Love and
  Don Carlos*
Edited by Walter Hinderer
Foreword by Gordon Craig

Friedrich Schiller
Wallenstein and Mary Stuart.
Edited by Walter Hinderer

Johann Wolfgang von Goethe
The Sufferings of Young Werther
and *Elective Affinities*
Edited by Victor Lange
Forewords by Thomas Mann

German Romantic Criticism
Edited by A. Leslie Willson
Foreword by Ernst Behler

Friedrich Hölderlin
Hyperion and Selected Poems
Edited by Eric L. Santner

Philosophy of German Idealism
Edited by Ernst Behler

G. W. F. Hegel
*Encyclopedia of the
Philosophical Sciences in
Outline and Critical Writings*
Edited by Ernst Behler

*German Poetry from 1750 to
1900*
Edited by Robert M. Browning
Foreword by Michael Hamburger

Karl Marx, Friedrich Engels,
August Bebel, and others
*German Essays on Socialism in
the Nineteenth Century*
Edited by Frank Mecklenburg
and Manfred Stassen

German Lieder
Edited by Philip Lieson Miller
Foreword by Hermann Hesse

Arthur Schnitzler
Plays and Stories
Edited by Egon Schwarz
Foreword by Stanley Elkin

Rainer Maria Rilke
Prose and Poetry
Edited by Egon Schwarz
Foreword by Howard Nemerov

Robert Musil
Selected Writings
Edited by Burton Pike
Foreword by Joel Agee

Essays on German Theater
Edited by Margaret Herzfeld-
Sander
Foreword by Martin Esslin

Friedrich Dürrenmatt
Plays and Essays
Edited by Volkmar Sander
Foreword by Martin Esslin

Max Frisch
Novels, Plays, Essays
Edited by Rolf Kieser
Foreword by Peter Demetz

Gottfried Benn
Prose, Essays, Poems
Edited by Volkmar Sander
Foreword by E. B. Ashton
Introduction by Reinhard Paul
Becker

German Essays on Art History
Edited by Gert Schiff

German Radio Plays
Edited by Everett Frost and
Margaret Herzfeld-Sander
Foreword by Klaus Schöning

Hans Magnus Enzensberger
Critical Essays
Edited by Reinhold Grimm and
Bruce Armstrong
Foreword by John Simon

All volumes available in hardcover and paperback editions at your book-
store or from the publisher. For more information on The German Library
write to: The Continuum Publishing Company, 370 Lexington Avenue,
New York, NY 10017.